Modernizing the Public Sector

T0383071

As policymakers and scholars evaluate possible ways forward in the reform and renewal of public services by governments caught up in a recessionary environment, this book aims to offer something different – a comprehensive analysis of the development of the 'Scandinavian' way of modernizing public-sector management. No book has yet provided an inside view of the development and character of New Public Management (NPM) in Scandinavia. Although there is a general perception that there is a clear-cut 'Scandinavian' model of public policy and management, this book offers a more nuanced interpretation, illuminating subtle distinctions in political, social and economic context which are significant in identifying receptive contexts for the adoption of modernization policies.

Organized into three main themes in the modernization of the welfare state – management, governance and marketization – the contents revolve around unique empirical accounts, revealing distinctive Scandinavian characteristics of reform initiatives. The received wisdom may be that of Scandinavia as a hesitant follower of the UK and the USA, but this book offers an alternative interpretation, revealing an edginess in certain Scandinavian settings, particularly in Sweden, which is largely unrecognized. Without compromising the welfare state, it may be a bold frontrunner in the development of New Public Management.

Irvine Lapsley is director of the Institute of Public Sector Accounting Research at the University of Edinburgh Business School, UK.

Hans Knutsson is a senior lecturer at the School of Economics and Management at Lund University, Sweden.

Routledge Critical Studies in Public Management
Edited by Stephen Osborne

The study and practice of public management has undergone profound changes across the world. Over the last quarter century, we have seen

- increasing criticism of public administration as the overarching framework for the provision of public services,
- the rise (and critical appraisal) of the 'New Public Management' as an emergent paradigm for the provision of public services,
- the transformation of the 'public sector' into the cross-sectoral provision of public services, and
- the growth of the governance of inter-organizational relationships as an essential element in the provision of public services.

In reality these trends have not so much replaced each other as elided or coexisted together – the public policy process has not gone away as a legitimate topic of study and intra-organizational management continues to be essential to the efficient provision of public services, while the governance of inter-organizational and inter-sectoral relationships is now essential to the effective provision of these services.

Further, while the study of public management has been enriched by contribution of a range of insights from the 'mainstream' management literature it has also contributed to this literature in such areas as networks and inter-organizational collaboration, innovation and stakeholder theory.

This series is dedicated to presenting and critiquing this important body of theory and empirical study. It will publish books that both explore and evaluate the emergent and developing nature of public administration, management and governance (in theory and practice) and examine the relationship with and contribution to the overarching disciplines of management and organizational sociology.

Books in the series will be of interest to academics and researchers in this field, students undertaking advanced studies of it as part of their undergraduate or postgraduate degree and reflective policymakers and practitioners.

It is a common mistake to equate 'New Public Management' with the ideas and practices of the Anglo-American world. This book provides a valuable corrective to that view by analysing the development of New Public Management from a Scandinavian perspective. It brings out the Scandinavian historical roots of some important ideas about modern pubic service management, traces their dynamics and brings out the special social context that shapes their outcomes. Anyone interested in how to make public services work effectively should read this book.

Professor Christopher Hood, *Emeritus Fellow, All Souls College, University of Oxford, UK*

Modernizing the Public Sector

Scandinavian perspectives

**Edited by Irvine Lapsley
and Hans Knutsson**

Routledge
Taylor & Francis Group

LONDON AND NEW YORK

First published 2017 by Routledge

2 Park SQuare, Milton Park, Abingdon, Oxfordshire OX14 4RN
52 Vanderbilt AVenue, New York, NY 10017

Routledge is an imprint of the Taylor &Francis Group, an informa business

First issued in paperback 2019

British Library Cataloguing in Publication Data
A catalogue record for this book is available from the British Library

Library of Congress Cataloging in Publication Data
Names: Lapsley, Irvine, editor. | Knutsson, Hans, 1965- editor.
Title: Modernizing the public sector : Scandinavian perspectives /
edited by Irvine Lapsley and Hans Knutsson.
Description: Abingdon, Oxon ; New York, NY : Routledge, [2017] |
Series: Routledge critical studies in public management | Includes
bibliographical references and index.
Identifiers: LCCN 2016029090 | ISBN 9781138675940 (hardback :
alk. paper) | ISBN 9781315560328 (ebook)
Subjects: LCSH: Public administration–Scandinavia. | Administrative
agencies–Scandinavia–Management. | Welfare state–Scandinavia. |
Organizational change–Scandinavia.
Classification: LCC JN7011.M625 2017 | DDC 352.3/67–dc23
LC record available at https://lccn.loc.gov/2016029090

ISBN: 978-1-138-67594-0 (hbk)
ISBN: 978-0-367-87853-5 (pbk)

Typeset in Bembo
by Wearset Ltd, Boldon, Tyne and Wear

Contents

Figures

Tables

Contributors

Fredrik Andersson is professor of economics and dean of the Lund University School of Economics and Management. His recent research has mainly been focused on the application of contract theory to questions of public organization and privatization. He has also worked on organizational and competitive issues in the school sector, as well as with questions relating to international labour mobility and tax competition.

Anders Anell is a professor at the Lund University School of Economics and Management. He has published several books, reports and articles within the area of governance and management control in health care services. Current research areas include incentives and resource allocation, performance measurement and organization of primary care. He has worked as a consultant and adviser for a number of Swedish and international organizations.

Christine Blomqvist is a senior lecturer at the Lund University School of Economics and Management. She has published within the field of public administration, leadership, change and decision processes. Her current empirical research focus is academic leadership and how to organize, manage and lead research organizations as well as higher education. In addition to her role as senior lecturer, Christine also has an assignment, on behalf of the vice chancellor, to facilitate the development of management teams at Lund University.

Louise Bringselius is an associate professor and senior lecturer at the Lund University School of Economics and Management. Her primary research interest is issues of autonomy and accountability in central government. Bringselius's publications include articles in *Financial Accountability and Management*, *European Political Science Review* and *International Journal of Public Administration*, and also books and book chapters.

Thomas Carrington is a senior lecturer at Stockholm Business School, Stockholm University. His research interests primarily cover auditing in various forms. Empirically this interest has been addressed by attending to a broad spectrum of actors from private-sector financial auditors, their supervisory body (the Swedish Supervisory Board of Public Accountants) and the Swedish National Audit Office, as well as auditees in both the private and public sectors.

Anna Häger Glenngård is a senior lecturer at the Lund University School of Economics and Management. She has published in peer-reviewed journals, book chapters and reports at Swedish and international public agencies and research organizations in the area of health policy, health economics and health management and administration. Current areas of research include studies of different aspects of quality of care and studies on management, governance and accountability in health care, with a particular interest in primary care.

Åge Johnsen is professor of public policy at Oslo and Akershus University College of Applied Sciences. His current research interests are strategic planning, performance management, performance audit and evaluation in the public sector. He has published articles in many journals, including *Administration and Society, European Accounting Review, Evaluation, Financial Accountability and Management, Journal of Public Administration Theory, Public Management Review* and *Scandinavian Political Studies.*

Tom S. Karlsson is a senior lecturer at the School of Business and Economics, Linnaeus University. His research concerns management and accounting control within the public sector, focusing on historical and contemporary central government reforms in Sweden and how such reforms have come to cause institutional change among actors within the public sector.

Kim Klarskov Jeppesen is professor of auditing at Copenhagen Business School. His research interest is in auditing in broad terms, covering topics in private-sector auditing, public-sector auditing and internal auditing. His research is published in leading journals such as *European Accounting Review, Accounting, Auditing and Accountability Journal, Financial Accountability and Management* and *International Journal of Auditing.*

Hans Knutsson is a senior lecturer at the Lund University School of Economics and Management. He has published articles on strategic management, benchmarking and competitive tendering, all relating to the public sector. Empirical issues of interest span social welfare reforms and public procurement, with a special focus on local government and municipalities.

Nikolaj Kure is an associate professor at the School of Business and Social Sciences, Aarhus University. His work, mainly drawing on systems theory and pragmatic constructivism, focuses on organizational change, the shaping of new identity images in organizations and management accounting.

Irvine Lapsley is director of IPSAR, University of Edinburgh Business School. His main research interests are in public-sector reforms. He is editor of *Financial Accountability and Management* and chair of the EIASM Public Sector Conference. He has held appointments at the Universities of Edinburgh, Stirling and Warwick. He is KEFU guest professor at Lund University. He is a visiting professor at Trondheim University Business School and at Politecnico di Milano. He is honorary professor at Queen's University Belfast.

Margit Malmmose is an assistant professor at the Department of Economics, Aarhus University. Her publications and research focus are mainly within management accounting in health care but also include other areas of management accounting. She has been a visiting PhD at Auckland University in New Zealand and is currently a visiting scholar at the University of Maryland, School of Public Health.

Ola Mattisson is senior lecturer in strategy and public management at the Lund University School of Economics and Management. Ola received a PhD in Business Administration in 2000 and he is now a researcher at Public Management Research in Lund (PUMAR). The research interest is directed towards strategy and management control in both public and private contexts, with a special focus on competition and cooperation. Another interest is service management and service organizations. Ola is the author of a number of books and articles on strategy and public management.

Salme Näsi is professor (emerita) at the University of Tampere with an expertise in accounting and management control systems in both private- and public-sector contexts, accounting research, research design and methodology in the field of business economics. After 40 years' experience as a university teacher and researcher she is still active in research and postgraduate education in Finland and in some neighbouring countries.

Kari Nyland is professor in management accounting at NTNU Trondheim Business School. She has published articles and book chapters on management accounting and control in public-sector organizations. Her empirical focus has mainly been on the hospital sector.

Alexander Paulsson is a researcher at the Pufendorf Institute, Lund University, and is currently a postdoc at the Swedish National Knowledge Center for Public Transportation. His publications include a book on the bureaucracy and the gift economy of an entrepreneurial city and articles and book chapters on organizational resistance and multinational corporations. His research is centred on economic processes, such as marketization, commodification and bureaucratization, with a specific empirical focus on public administration.

Gert Paulsson is an associate professor at the Lund University School of Economics and Management. He has published articles and book chapters on management accounting and control in public-sector organizations. His empirical focus has been on central government and the health care sector.

Ulf Ramberg is associate professor of management control and public management at the Lund University School of Economics and Management. He is also the director of the Council for Local Government Research and Education (KEFU). Ulf received his PhD in business administration in 1997. He is a researcher at Public Management Research in Lund (PUMAR) and the author of several books and articles on management control and public management.

Kristin Reichborn-Kjennerud is a senior research fellow at Oslo and Akershus University College of Applied Sciences. Her research interests are performance audit in the public sector, organizational control and learning, and innovation and urban studies. Her research has been published in *Administration and Society, Evaluation, International Journal of Gender and Entrepreneurship, International Journal of Public Administration, Public Administration* and *Public Organization Review*.

Peter Skærbæk is professor of accounting at Copenhagen Business School and professor II at Trondheim Business School. He has published several articles about the implementation of New Public Management reforms in Denmark. His work is based on substantive field work in the Royal Theatre, the Danish Defence Forces, the Danish Police, Scandlines, etc. He has a particular interest in highlighting the importance of economic theory and expertise in the implementation of the reforms and the implications for public-sector professionals.

Anna Thomasson is an associate professor at the Lund University School of Economics and Management. She has published articles and one book on hybrid organizations and issues concerning accountability and governance in hybrid solutions. Besides this she has conducted research on public procurement and published an article on innovation in the public procurement process.

Robert Wenglén is a senior lecturer at the Lund University School of Economics and Management. Robert divides his time between research, teaching, executive education, consulting and local politics. His research is focused on leadership, managerial work, learning and professionalism – mainly in the empirical field of elementary education. He has recently published a book on leadership (together with Professor Mats Alvesson) and a number of academic articles on skilled incompetence and leadership.

1 Making sense of public-sector reforms

Scandinavian perspectives

Irvine Lapsley

Summary

This chapter examines the emergence of New Public Management (NPM) as the dominant paradigm in government attempts at the modernization of the state over recent decades. This discussion proceeds by considering both past and current practices in the organization and coordination of public services. Despite the preoccupation of contemporary scholars and practitioners with an NPM agenda, this study presents the case for examining the landscape of the public sector as a site for layers of ideas and policies on public administration and management. This perspective argues that the durability of bureaucratic ideas in contemporary society is evidence of this. Policy analysts and scholars should not regard practices and initiatives as straightforward sequential reforms over time. While this book offers insights into NPM-type ideas, such as marketization, in practice it also reveals the deep-seated nature of reform processes and cautious attempts to pigeonhole the nature and dissemination of reform ideas in public services. This phenomenon of the fusion of ideas over time is evident in Scandinavian public administration, notably in Sweden. This chapter also offers a glimpse of what the future holds for public administration in a dynamic, changing world where the Scandinavian practices can resonate with the challenges facing governments internationally.

Public-sector reforms

This chapter discusses the past, present and future of public management. It takes a longitudinal perspective, which is necessary to understand the nature of public-sector reforms and contemporary challenges in making public services efficient and effective. This book examines Scandinavian experiences of public-sector reform. This study reveals the distinctive nature of Scandinavian-style interpretations and implementations of public service reforms, which will be of interest to other mature economies but also to developing countries as an alternative vision of how to deliver public services from the dominant Anglo-Saxon model. These reforms are discussed as management processes, governance systems and marketization. The major results presented in this book are Scandinavian, particularly Swedish, given the willingness of Sweden to embrace public-sector reform. Indeed, Hood (1995) placed Sweden alongside the UK, New Zealand, Australia and Canada as having a high emphasis on NPM, but it was the only country with a political tradition from the left. This view of Sweden as a long-standing, leading-edge reformer of public services was confirmed by Pollitt and Bouckaert (2000). They described Sweden (along with Finland, Canada, the Netherlands and France) as an 'adventurous moderniser', a country which saw the need for a significant role for the state in contemporary society, but which also saw the need for fairly fundamental changes in public administration (Pollitt and Bouckaert, 2000, p. 93).

This chapter also uses UK experiences as a reference point in its discussion of public management reforms. There are three reasons for this. First, the UK is widely regarded as a leading-edge country in public-sector reform. Second, there is a closeness between the UK and the northern European countries of Scandinavia, which is partly historical, partly cultural and partly from trading links. Third, the UK is part of the countries which form the dominant Anglo-Saxon nexus of public-sector reformers. This makes the UK a useful reference point in the discussion of the distinctive interpretations of Scandinavian public-sector reforms and practices.

This chapter is organized into four sections: a reflection on reform processes in public management; an overview of public management as administration and its past; an examination of present practices in public management (including New Public Management and New Public Sector Governance) and concludes with comments on the future of public management. A major focus of this chapter is the manifestation of different aspects of the different schools of thought (public administration, New Public Management and New Public Sector Governance) and whether they are distinct and mutually exclusive phenomena or whether they can all coexist simultaneously within the public sector. It is suggested here that the latter circumstance more accurately depicts public-sector reforms, particularly in the Scandinavian context.

Reform processes

This chapter adopts the literature on reform processes as its theoretical lens for the study of modernization initiatives in Scandinavian countries. The discussion of reform processes is examined in three parts. First, there is an examination of the importance of political context. Second, the key characteristics of reform processes are considered. Finally, trajectories of reform are examined.

1 Political context

In his seminal paper of 1991, Hood stated that NPM was a policy which was politically neutral. In his view these policies could not be attributed simply to neo-liberal governments. By politically neutral, Hood meant that governments of different political persuasions were content to adopt NPM-type reforms. At that time, his reference points were Australia and New Zealand, both of which had centre-left governments and both of which were enthusiastic adopters of NPM ideas. However, the political context is very important in setting the conditions for the adoption of NPM. An interesting example is provided by Italy (Arnaboldi *et al.*, 2016). Italy has had a variety of governments which have made moves to adopt NPM policies but which have never secured the political legitimacy to fully adopt them. The Italian government context is shaped by highly politicized processes which may be attributed to pre-modern practices and deep historical roots in the Italian state (Putnam *et al.*, 1993). The above reference point underlines how significant the political context is to secure an active NPM agenda. Within the Scandinavian countries, Sweden offers a fascinating example of a reforming country. Karlsson (2017) reveals the long-standing importance of the Social Democrats, a centre-left party, in the adoption of NPM ideas in Sweden before the expression NPM was coined. This circumstance is taken up further below.

2 Key characteristics of reform processes

Table 1.1 shows the key characteristics of reform processes (adapted from Arnaboldi *et al.*, 2016). It can be seen that this literature is preoccupied by both the simplicity of design and the complexity of implementation. There are both negative and positive influences at work. The motivating factors are positive influences which are most likely to lead to effective implementation. The negative influences identify problematic and perverse outcomes for modernizing reformers.

Motivating factors in public services policy design

1 Private-sector mimicry

The mimicry of private-sector practices is a central feature of the NPM phenomenon (Hood, 1991, 1995). The NPM movement is encapsulated in the public sector embracing ideas of the rational organization (which is perceived to be the case in the private sector) and by the adoption of private-sector practices to improve the efficiency of public administration (Cheung, 2005;

Table 1.1 Key characteristics of reform processes

Motivating factors in public services design	*Perverse outcomes in policy formation*
1 Private-sector mimicry	1 Failure
2 Rationality	2 Forgetfulness
3 Strong beliefs	3 Deception and hypocrisy

Cole and Jones, 2005; Lodge and Gill, 2011; Cristofoli *et al.*, 2011). One feature of this is likely to be mimicry of the private-sector organization as a means of obtaining legitimacy. Brunsson and Sahlin-Andersson (2000) portray this as a desire by modernizers to be considered part of a 'complete organization', in which public-sector organizations have all the trappings of the modern private-sector corporation (boards of directors, CEOs and private-sector management techniques and practices).

2 Rationality

As noted above, this reform process is fused with ideas of *rationality*. The NPM policy development was influenced by ideas of public choice theory (Buchanan, 1986; Hayek, 1960), which are themselves imbued with a strong sense of rationality. This literature criticized public bureaucracies. It favoured markets for the expression of individual preferences. In particular, these reformers and modernizers are receptive to the idea of rationality and the rational organization (Brunsson, 2006, p. 229). This affords opportunities for symbolic phenomena, rituals and ceremonies to assume greater significance in the political context than more instrumental or functional explanations of political acts (March and Olsen, 1983).

3 Strong beliefs

These enactments of reform are influenced by strong beliefs. Policymakers and their advisers are susceptible to the presentation of ideas as being new and novel, where prior experience lacks validity (Brunsson, 2006, p. 229). Where reforms are seen as impractical, in practice advocates can continue to 'talk' their ideas rather than to practise reform. These phenomena can then recur, with reforms generating new reforms and even demands for further reforms aimed at the same problem and propagating the same solutions (Brunsson and Olsen, 1993, p. 42). In this way, Brunsson and Olsen regard policymakers as 'relentless modernizers'.

Perverse outcomes in policy formation

1 Failure

The antecedents of policy formation are important. While there is a general lack of understanding of policy formation, changes in policies and the conditions which constrain or facilitate policy implementation (Capano and Howlett, 2009; Mele and Ongaro, 2014), the context of politicized organizations offers a distinct set of reform experiences. In highly politicized organizations, reform processes exhibit distinct characteristics. In particular, they often fail (Lapsley, 2009), generating a 'long history of disappointment' (March and Olsen, 1983, p. 289). There are a number of dimensions to these processes of reform failure. A noticeable feature of this human endeavour is persistence (March and Olsen, 1983, pp. 288–289; Brunsson, 2009, p. 98) – the repetition of similar ideas and relatively similar arguments over long time periods. This persistence may continue in the face of apparent failure, particularly in the domains of 'strong beliefs and ambiguous experience' (March and Olsen, 1983, p. 289).

2 Forgetfulness

A further, distinct feature of policy formation is the importance of organizational memory and forgetfulness in the acceptance of reforms (Brunsson and Olsen, 1993). This phenomenon cuts across the entire process of policymaking, with issues for government policymakers, who devise policy and for the public service organizations which are subject to policy change. It has been suggested that our understanding of organizational memory (how and where it works within organizations and in interactions between organizations and public agencies) is a major neglected area of research within public services (Pollitt, 2009). Indeed, Pollitt (2009) argues that hierarchical organizations have greater retention of organizational memory. This may confound the reform of public agencies but it also points to the durability of bureaucracies.

3 Deception and hypocrisy

Reforms may also involve deception and hypocrisy (Brunsson, 1989; Ongaro, 2011). Thus, Brunsson (2009, p. 96) suggests that reforms have to be presented as 'better' than the solutions currently in use, whether this can be substantiated or not. Indeed, Brunsson (2009, p. 114) suggests that reforms are described as simple, general, very sensible, as 'beautiful principles' but which then change on implementation. Specific adaptions will need greater detail and they may become 'less beautiful' and more like the old ones that they are replacing. This phenomenon may occur as modernizers or political reformers articulate visions of reforms which emerge from relatively macro theories of broad political and social trends to translate into a vision of confusion at the micro level (March and Olsen, 1983, p. 292). As part of this process of deception, modernizers or reformers may present 'reorganizations' as a tactic for the illusion of progress where none exists (March and Olsen, 1983, p. 290).

The above discussion identifies ambiguity (of purpose and outcomes), complexity (particularly of implementation) and uncertainty (of practical and policy outcomes) alongside a conviction on the part of the modernizers of how public-sector reforms can and should be devised. This certainty in the mind of modernizing reformers reveals a particular mind-set in the design of public-sector reforms. As Figure 1.1 shows, this is the case of reformers starting with *a blank sheet of paper*. An empty space to fill in their ideas of how public-sector organizations should look and behave. But the reality of the social, economic and organizational space is already occupied by actors,

Figure 1.1 Public management reforms as a blank sheet of paper.

procedures, processes and all manner of administrative machinery. This takes to the actual, possible or widely regarded trajectory for public-sector reforms.

3 The reform trajectory

The literature on processes of reform suggests that repetitive patterns of behaviour may occur in the formulation and implementation of reforms. Therefore, this theoretical perspective benefits from a research approach which examines reforms over time.

The NPM had early adopters, notably New Zealand, Australia and the UK. The NPM has met sticking points in countries with legalistic contexts such as those in continental Europe (see for example Arnaboldi *et al.*, 2016). Developing countries are trying NPM with varying degrees of success. There is, and always has been, variation of diffusion and capacity for local interpretation. A phenomenon, a movement without a prescriptive model, which is still active.

A major preoccupation of many writers has been a focus on the demise of NPM. Such commentators point to the importance of alternative facets of the delivery of public services. This can be depicted as a trajectory in which shifting practices move from bureaucracy to NPM and from NPM to the New Public Sector Governance, emerging in a post-NPM world. This can be depicted as set out in Figure 1.2.

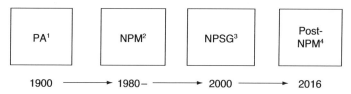

Figure 1.2 Trajectories of public management reforms: the general linear model.

Notes
1 Public Administration.
2 New Public Management.
3 New Public Sector Governance.
4 Post-New Public Management Era.

While this depiction of the trajectory of public management reforms has considerable attraction within the extant literature, it is questionable on several grounds. In the first instance, it can be seen as an oversimplification of complex processes. Second, the idea of a linear trajectory of substantive change may have immediate appeal but cannot capture the realities of public management. The model set out above may be seen as overly precise in start and end dates for these new initiatives, but there are authors who have felt confident enough to offer this degree of precision. Third, this simple model presumes all contexts – international, national and subnational – are progressing along the same path, at the same speed and with the same intensity. There is a distinct body of knowledge which suggests that this is simply not the case (see, for example, Pollitt and Bouckaert, 2011). Finally, this depiction of a parade of alternative models in logical sequence is over-specified. In particular, there are phenomena at work within these different strands of public management practice which may lead to a coexistence or melding of these different models. This issue is taken up further below. But first we explore these key dimensions of public management change, indicating, where appropriate, Scandinavian translations and interpretations of reform movements.

The past: public management as administration

In the public-sector landscape of the nineteenth and early twentieth centuries, the government dominated large organizations. This included large government departments but also activities such as the Post Office and the armed forces. The major commercial undertakings of the nineteenth century were railway companies. Many managers of large corporations such as railway companies may have had a military or civil service background. The late nineteenth and early twentieth centuries saw the emergence of large industrial organizations with a need for managers, too.

This was the era of classic administrative theory, often characterized as bureaucracy. An interesting example of classical administrative theory is the work of the nineteenth-century French industrialist Henri Fayol (1949), who had a military background. His ideas included thoughts on authority, discipline, chain of command, hierarchy, order, subordination and *esprit de corps*. This was an example of the bureaucratic model, the formal organization in action. A more recent example is Herbert Simon's (1957) work on administrative behaviour, in which he acknowledged that individual behaviour may be irrational but within organized entities there was scope for rational behaviour, especially with clear goals for efficiency. This contribution to the literature supports the idea of the organization as a bureaucracy underpinned by ideas of rationality and the pursuit of efficiency.

The idea of the bureaucratic organization is most closely associated with the classic work of Weber (1958). Weberian bureaucracy was based on the rational–legal model. It was rational because the means achieved specified goals and legal because the exercise of authority was defined by the specific office held by a given administrator. There is a written definition of each officer's authority which ensures orders are obeyed. He argued that, technically, bureaucracy is the most efficient form of organization. Weber likened bureaucracy to a modern machine. In this machine, precision, speed, unambiguity, knowledge of files, continuity, discretion, unity, strict subordination and the reduction of friction and of material and personnel costs are all raised to the optimum in the strictly bureaucratic organization.

The era in which bureaucracy flourished was one in which the government or its agencies provided public services to recipients. The role of those engaged in the running of the bureaucracies was one of a top-down implementation of policies which emerged from democratic processes. In this regard, the politicians held sway and the bureaucrats were accountable to them, with little voice for citizens except the ballot box.

However, the rosy view of the benefits of bureaucracy espoused by its arch-proponent, Weber, has been under sustained attack from the managerialists. In the view of modernizing managers, bureaucracy has become synonymous with public administration. The assault on bureaucracy has become a critique of public administration. This typifies the bureaucratic approach as (see, for example, Dunleavy and Hood, 1994) slow, inefficient, resistant to change, impersonal, unresponsive 'red tape' with organizational rigidity, poor internal communication and a preoccupation with the concerns of those delivering services, rather than the people receiving them…

However, despite this powerful critique of bureaucracy, there remain more recent proponents who write of the durability of bureaucracy and its ability to act as intermediary between political ideal and managerial action (Schofield, 2001), and of the capacity of bureaucracies to diffuse environmental uncertainties and perform well (Stazyk and Goerdel, 2011). These latter observations suggest that there is a continuing role for the bureaucratic model in contemporary public services. We return to this issue later.

Given these potential attractions of bureaucracies, we should not be surprised to see such entities survive in the twenty-first century. Indeed, this book has an exceptional example of such a phenomenon. Paulsson (2017) writes on the example of the unique ID number assigned to all Swedish citizens at birth. This number – the person number – is known by all Swedish citizens. This is unlike the UK National Insurance number, which is assigned to citizens at age 16 and is related to employment status. The person number has been part of the Swedish welfare system since 1947 – a bureaucratic device which endures to the present day. It is a remarkable story of a bureaucratic procedure which survives more recent public-sector reforms. This is a story about a reform climate which is pragmatic rather than occupied by relentless modernizers.

The present: the melding of models

In studying a phenomenon which has lasted over a century, a discussion of the present cannot be about this particular day or year. Indeed, it is suggested here that any sensible analysis of what the present means requires a period of time. In this discussion we take 'the present' as being *c*.1980 to the present day. This focus allows us to see antecedents of change and position current practices more carefully. It offers a more compelling perspective on the existence, emergence and melding of different models of administering and managing public services.

Just as public administration evokes images of procedures, form filling, due process, regulatory compliance and the discharge of responsibilities for the execution of prescribed programmes, as set out above, there is a sharp contrast with what public *management* means. Public management evokes images of action, of proactive intervention, of a problem-solving mentality which may extend to risk-taking. The question remains whether these are contrasting species which necessitate the elimination of one or other. There is also the possibility of some kind of melding or even fusion of these different approaches.

It is suggested here that the reality of organizational life for public services in Scandinavian countries can be depicted as a set of layers embracing key models concurrently (see Figure 1.3). This represents a coalescence or melding of ideas – produced by a middle way of pragmatism, in the continuation with things which work, in the moderate manner in which new models are implemented and in the openness and willingness to discuss, review and change practice. The pragmatism of the Scandinavian reformers is crucial to the adoption and adaption of ideas of bureaucracy, of NPM and of NPSG. In the following sections these models are examined more closely from a Scandinavian perspective, first considering NPM, then NPSG.

New Public Management

The emergence of NPM is often depicted as a neo-liberal policy (Lipsky, 2010). In this interpretation, NPM is an ideologically driven reform in which the private sector is always better than the public sector. This perspective

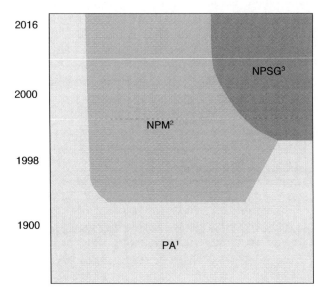

Figure 1.3 A stylized, layered depiction of public management reforms.

Notes
1 Public Administration.
2 New Public Management.
3 New Public Sector Governance.

maintains that there is nothing distinctive about the public sector and that 'management is management', regardless of locus. The trappings of NPM presume that there is a need for the elimination of public-sector inefficiency – the elimination of public-sector waste and inefficiency can be achieved by following the NPM recipe: the introduction of markets and performance management, with citizens recast as customers. However, as noted above, when Hood (1991) initially mooted the idea of an NPM he described it as politically neutral. This stance was influenced by the actions of centre-left governments in Australia and New Zealand. However, he was writing in 1991. The centre-left government of New Labour in the UK (1997–2010) was also a proponent of NPM.

However, intriguingly, the Swedish Social Democrats endorsed and practised NPM-type principles from the early twentieth century (Karlsson, 2017). The characteristics of NPM can be depicted as the adoption of private-sector management styles. These include decentralization, or pushing management responsibility down the line. The Swedish government was open to these new ideas. It was prepared to adopt private-sector practices to enhance the efficiency of the public sector. The post-World War II decades can be seen as particularly influential in laying the basis for all ensuing NPM developments in Sweden. The embedded nature of this blending of the importance of the state, the need for the state to be efficient and the political leadership and willingness to regard government as business were crucial factors in the Swedish public-sector reforms.

However, perhaps the single most important dimension of NPM is its pre-occupation with measurement and quantification and in a belief that all things can be measured and that the subsequent measures are the most important way of examining, understanding and managing public service delivery. In this quantification focus, the *person number* was embraced as a logical quanti-fication. This presumption of rigorous and accurate measurement facilitated the emergence of a results-driven approach to the management of public services.

A central feature of the old public administration has been the pre-eminence of the professions. The arrival of NPM was to challenge entrenched professions, create (in)security of employment conditions and establish a new cadre of influential agents – the managers. Wenglén (2017) demonstrates how the teaching profession has been affected by the new managerialism in priva-tized schools. Interestingly, all the major political parties are agreed that this policy should not be reversed. It is important to note that all management initiatives are regarded in the same way in different settings. The Danish health care reforms exhibit a top-down managerial approach to performance management, despite a slow burn reform process which appears to advocate local democracy (Kure and Malmmose, 2017). Despite the contradictory results on Danish health care, there are examples of innovative practice in Swedish hospitals as they align process control of activities within vertical hierarchies (Paulsson, 2017). This is indicative of a lack of coherence around a distinctively Scandinavian model of reforms. Nevertheless, there are exam-ples of classic NPM reforms which focus on structural change (Lapsley, 2008). Bringselius (2017) recounts the story of the creation and direction of the Swedish Social Insurance Agency. The establishment of this entity fits funda-mental NPM ideas of decentralization. But the changes in direction and style over its life indicate high levels of discretion, which suggests a pragmatic approach to reform. Similarly, Blomqvist (2017) identifies the way in which managerialism has spread to universities, but in a manner which is shrouded in ambiguity and in which the Swedish tradition of pragmatism in reforms is making sense of managerial imperatives.

However, while the *first wave* of NPM practices in Sweden was ushered in by the Social Democrats, they hesitated to go for full-blown NPM with mar-ketization. This model of public management embraced markets for public services and private-sector finance, whether as the complete privatization of entities or as the use of private finance as a means of acquiring public assets through the Private Finance Initiative or public–private partnerships. The *second wave* of NPM reforms – the introduction of markets or internal (quasi-) markets in the provision of public services – was down to the centre-right government in Sweden from 1991–1994 (Andersson, 2017). This approach was not without difficulties. The implementation of the quasi-market in primary health care has proved extremely difficult to evaluate (Glenngård and Anell, 2017). The actual model chosen was heavily influenced by the traditional primary care model in Sweden (Glenngård and Anell, 2017), which supports the view of Swedish modernizers as pragmatic reformers. In the search for market solutions to welfare, reformers' attentions turned to a groundbreaking reform for so-called 'functionally impaired' people (Knutsson, 2017). This development is attributed to relentless modernizers. However, Knutsson (2017) observes that there has been ambiguity of policy choice and implementation, with ideas of 'the market' becoming confused with ideas of 'individual choice'.

While the above depiction of NPM appears to offer a picture of a dominant species, its emergence has not gone without criticism. In his 1991 paper, Hood observed that one key claim of NPM proponents was for the universality of NPM. It is interesting that proponents of NPM are not found within academia but rather within the ranks of special advisers, management consultants, major world oversight bodies and networks of such people. The ideas of NPM were considered so appropriate that they could be applied in any situation. This 'one size fits all' idea of NPM does not capture public-sector subtleties, but the existence of a state which operates with bureaucracies, NPM and NPSG may.

New Public Sector Governance

Proponents of New Public Sector Governance (NPSG) as the dominant mode of public management stress the proliferation of networks, partnerships and hybrid organizations (Osborne, 2010). This proliferation of networks has been advanced as a significant factor in the development of a post-NPM world, in which 'organizational silos' are replaced by networks. This has been depicted as the twentieth century being the time of organizations, with the twenty-first century being the era of networks (Osborne, 2010).

However, there are long-standing observations on the networks phenomenon. In their seminal paper, Meyer and Rowan (1977) commented on the emergence of complex networks. At the same time, the emergence of networks was attributed to resource dependency by Pfeffer and Salancik (1978). The proliferation of complex inter-organizational networks gathered pace in the 1980s with this feature of mutual resource dependency by key actors in networks (Rhodes, 1988). The emergence of what has been labelled the New Public Sector Governance and NPM ideas occurred at much the same time (Peters and Pierre, 1998). This raises issues of whether these paradigms can coexist or whether they are mutually exclusive. Recent research by Hyndman and Liguori (2016) reveals that UK policymaking used ideas and terminology of both NPM and New Public Sector Governance throughout the late twentieth and early twenty-first century, although the ideas of NPM dominated policy documents. This indicates that a melding of ideas of networks and NPM is both feasible and likely. There are good reasons why this should be the case. The networks may be short-lived or informal arrangements. The constituent organizations cannot ignore the need to deliver results for their organizations as well as the network. In this way, networks add a further layer of complexity to the everyday existence of public organizations. Nevertheless, public organizations have to focus on their own performance management and may be open to new ideas from the private sector in delivering their services.

In the Swedish context, Mattisson (2017) observes that organizational networks are highly visible. He observes that the idea of cooperation is a Swedish imperative ('a word of honour'). Mattisson (2017) identifies scarce resources and expertise as major motivations for the establishment of network arrangements. The concern that municipalities may not be able to provide a statutory service is a driving force for many arrangements, which historically have been soft, informal agreements. However, within the contemporary scene in Sweden there have been networks which take the form of joint boards or joint authorities, which are regulated by public law or networks formed as contracts and by the establishment of limited liability companies. This adds further layers of complexity to governance arrangements. There is also the uncertainty that the proliferation of these arrangements is not tracked, with there being no complete list of all the network arrangements in Swedish municipalities. While the impetus for these networks is well intentioned, Thomasson (2017) raises important matters of transparency and potential gender discrimination in senior appointments in these networks. These matters further complicate the effective governance of networks.

The future

One fundamental feature of public organizations, given their obligations to citizens and their disbursement of public monies, is the impact of these reforms on the democratic process. It has been suggested that the role of democratically elected representatives in the new managerial state is undermined both by NPM practices and by elaborate network arrangements. This is a present and future challenge for public services. It is an enduring issue for effective transparency and accountability in public services everywhere. However, within the Scandinavian countries there is the distinct advantage of having national auditors who embrace the latest auditing technologies and who operate in the interests of their citizens in a high-trust environment (Johnsen *et al.*, 2017). This particular feature of the Scandinavian scene reveals ambiguity, complexity and uncertainty. Fundamentally, the apparatus of NPM reforms is geared to low-trust environments and yet here we have examples of the progressive use of NPM practices. An interesting paradox.

In Scandinavia, there is a set of countries which, to varying degrees, accept the need for the state to have a dominant role in public services. The precise role of government bodies is not seen as static. There is dynamism in evidence, with management technologies, practices and operating contexts changing.

This is a picture of both complexity and uncertainty. There is also ambiguity present in both the design and the operation of activities. A picture of layers of practices and of thinking has built up over time of a strong state which both retains enduring ideas from bureaucracy and takes new ideas from NPM and NPSG.

The processes of reform evidenced in this book reveal an adherence to rational thinking, with strong beliefs mobilized to drive reforms through. But there is a contrary picture – of ambiguity and of pragmatism to make things work. Can these reforms be described as failures or acts of hypocrisy? Perhaps they can. But this articulation of what is happening in these countries may not capture the long-run aim of providing effective public services and the willingness to change all manner of facets of reforms as they proceed.

The result is a distinctive public sector, one which is both valued (by citizens and by their representatives) and challenged (by all) to perform better in the delivery of public services. The desire and need to deliver more service at high quality with fewer resources is evident, as is an extraordinary depth of willingness to adopt, adapt, improvise and make reforms which recognize those parts of services which work well and those which need change. This reform process is a continuous endeavour. It is challenging. Yet this setting and these reform processes exhibit a remarkable resilience, which makes them an exciting focus for politicians, policymakers, public services managers, researchers and commentators on affairs of the state.

References

Andersson, F. (2017) Market Solutions, in I. Lapsley and H. Knutsson (eds), *Modernizing the Public Sector: Scandinavian Perspectives* (London and New York: Routledge).

Arnaboldi M., M. dal Molin and I. Lapsley (2016) 'Modernizing public services: subtle interplays of politics and management'. *Journal of Accounting and Organizational Change*, Vol. 12, forthcoming.

Blomqvist, C. (2017) Leadership and Strategy in a Transforming Academic Field, in I. Lapsley and H. Knutsson (eds), *Modernizing the Public Sector: Scandinavian Perspectives* (London and New York: Routledge).

Bringselius, L. (2017) The Unfolding of Agency Autonomy Over Time: The Swedish Social Insurance Agency 2003–2015, in I. Lapsley and H. Knutsson (eds), *Modernizing the Public Sector: Scandinavian Perspectives* (London and New York: Routledge).

Brunsson, N. (1989) *The Organization of Hypocrisy: Talk, Decision and Actions in Organizations* (Chichester: John Wiley).

Brunsson, N. (2006) *Mechanisms of Hope: Maintaining the Dream of the Rational Organization* (Copenhagen: Copenhagen Business School Press).

Brunsson, N. (2009) *Reform as Routine: Organizational Change and Stability in the Modern World* (Oxford: Oxford University Press).

Brunsson, N. and J. Olsen (1993) *The Reforming Organization* (London: Routledge).

Brunsson, N. and K. Sahlin-Andersson (2000) 'Constructing organizations: the example of public sector reform'. *Organization Studies*, Vol. 21, No. 4, pp. 721–746.

Buchanan, J. M. (1986) *Liberty, Market and State – Political Economy in the 1980s* (Brighton: Harvester Press).

Capano, G. and M. Howlett. (2009) 'The determinants of policy change: advancing the debate'. *Journal of Comparative Policy Analysis: Research and Practice*, Vol. 11, No. 1, pp. 1–5.

Cheung, A. B. L. (2005) 'The politics of administrative reforms in asia: paradigms and legacies, paths and diversities'. *Governance: An International Journal of Policy, Administration and Institutions*, Vol. 18, No. 2, pp. 257–282.

Cole, A. and G. Jones (2005) 'Reshaping the state: administrative reform and new public management in France'. *Governance: An International Journal of Policy, Administration and Institutions*, Vol. 18, No. 4, pp. 567–588.

Cristofoli, D., G. Nasi, A. Turrini, and G. Valotti (2011) 'Civil services reform in Italy: the importance of external endorsement in administrative leadership'. *Governance: An International Journal of Policy, Administration and Institutions*, Vol. 24, No. 2, pp. 261–283.

Dunleavy, P. and C. Hood (1994) 'From old public administration to new public management'. *Public Money and Management*, July–September, pp. 9–16.

Fayol, H. (1949) General Principles of Management, in D. S. Pugh (ed.), *Organization Theory: Selected Readings* (London: Penguin, second edition, 1984), pp. 135–156.

Glenngård, A. H and A. Anell (2017) Introducing Quasi-Markets in Primary Care: The Swedish Experience, in I. Lapsley and H. Knutsson (eds), *Modernizing the Public Sector: Scandinavian Perspectives* (London and New York: Routledge).

Hood, C. (1991) 'A public management for all seasons?'. *Public Administration*, Vol. 69, 1, pp. 3–19.

Hood, C. (1995) 'The "new public management" in the 1980s: variations on a theme'. *Accounting, Organizations and Society*, Vol. 20, Nos. 2/3, pp. 93–109.

Hyndman, N. and M. Liguori (2016) 'Public sector reforms: changing contours on an NPM landscape'. *Financial Accountability and Management*, Vol. 32, No. 1, pp. 5–32.

Johnsen, A., K. Reichborn-Kjennerud, T. Carrington and K. K. Jeppesen (2017) Audit in A Trusting Climate, in I. Lapsley and H. Knutsson (eds), *Modernizing the Public Sector: Scandinavian Perspectives* (London and New York: Routledge).

Karlsson, T. (2017) Shaping NPM: Social Democratic Values at Work, in I. Lapsley and H. Knutsson (eds), *Modernizing the Public Sector: Scandinavian Perspectives* (London and New York: Routledge).

Knutsson, H. (2017) Welfare Choices: A Story of Market Forces and Social Progress, in I. Lapsley and H. Knutsson (eds), *Modernizing the Public Sector: Scandinavian Perspectives* (London and New York: Routledge).

Kure, N. and M. Malmmose (2017) Challenging The Myth of NPM in Denmark – An Argument from the Health System, in I. Lapsley and H. Knutsson (eds), *Modernizing the Public Sector: Scandinavian Perspectives* (London and New York: Routledge).

Lapsley, I. (2008) 'The NPM agenda: back to the future'. *Financial Accountability and Management*, Vol. 24, No. 1, pp. 77–95.

Lapsley, I. (2009) 'New public management: cruellest invention of the human spirit?' *Abacus*, Vol. 45, No. 1, pp. 1–21.

Lipsky, M. (2010) *Street-Level Bureaucracy: Dilemmas of the Individual in Public Services* (New York: Russel Sage Foundation).

Lodge, M. and D. Gill (2011) 'Toward a new era of administrative reform? The myth of post-NPM in New Zealand'. *Governance: An International Journal of Policy, Administration and Institutions*, Vol. 24, No. 1, pp. 141–166.

March, J. G. and J. P. Olsen (1983) 'Organizing political life: what administrative reorganisation tells us about government'. *American Political Science Review*, Vol. 77, No. 2. pp. 281–296.

Mattisson, O. (2017) Local Government Cooperation: A Better Way to Respond to Conditions? in I. Lapsley and H. Knutsson (eds), *Modernizing the Public Sector: Scandinavian Perspectives* (London and New York: Routledge).

Mele, V. and E. Ongaro (2014) 'Public sector reform in a context of political instability: Italy 1992–2007'. *International Public Management Journal*, Vol. 17, No. 1, pp. 111–142.

Meyer, J. and B. Rowan (1977) 'Institutionalized organizations: formal structure as myth and ceremony'. *American Journal of Sociology*, Vol. 83, No. 2, September, pp. 340–363.

Ongaro, E. (2011) 'The role of politics and institutions in the Italian administrative reform trajectory'. *Public Administration*, Vol. 89, No. 3, pp. 738–755.

Osborne, S. P. (2010) 'Delivering public services: time for a new theory?'. *Public Management Review*, Vol. 12, No. 1 pp. 1–10.

Paulsson, A. (2017) The Welfare State that Wanted to Keep Track of its Citizens: Personal Identity Numbers as Administrative Technology, in I. Lapsley and H. Knutsson (eds), *Modernizing the Public Sector: Scandinavian Perspectives* (London and New York: Routledge).

Paulsson, G. (2017) Process Orientation and Management Control in Health Care Organizations, in I. Lapsley and H. Knutsson (eds), *Modernizing the Public Sector: Scandinavian Perspectives* (London and New York: Routledge).

Peters, B. G. and Pierre (1998) 'Governance without government? Rethinking public administration'. *Journal of Public Administration Research and Theory*, Vol. 8, No. 2, April, pp. 223–243.

Pfeffer, J. and Salancik, G. R. (1978) *The External Control of Organizations: A Resource Dependence Perspective* (New York: Harper and Row).

Pollitt, C. (2009) 'Bureacracies remember, post-bureaucratic organizations forget?'. *Public Administration*, Vol. 87, No. 2, pp. 198–218.

Pollitt, C. and G. Bouckaert (2000) *Public Management Reform: A Comparative Analysis*, 1st edition (Oxford: Oxford University Press).

Pollitt, C. and G. Bouckaert (2011) *Public Management Reform: A Comparative Analysis – New Public Management, Governance, and the Neo–Weberian State*, 3rd edition (Oxford: Oxford University Press).

Putnam, R. D., R. Leonardi and R. Y. Nanetti (1993) *Making Democracy Work: Civic Traditions in Modern Italy* (Princeton, NJ: Princeton University Press).

Rhodes, R. (1988) 'Interorganisational networks and the "problem" of control in the policy process: a critique of the "new institutionalism"'. *West European Politics*, Vol. 1, No. 2, pp. 119–130.

Schofield, J. (2001) 'The old ways are the best? The durability and usefulness of bureaucracy in public sector management'. *Organization*, Vol. 8, No. 1, pp. 77–96.

Simon, H. (1957) *Administrative Behavior: A Study of Decision-making Processes in Administrative Organization* (New York: Macmillan).

Stazyk, E. and H. Goerdel (2011) 'The benefits of bureaucracy: public managers' perceptions of political support, goal ambiguity, and organizational effectiveness'. *Journal of Public Administration Research and Theory*, Vol. 21, No. 4, pp. 645–672.

Thomasson, A. (2017) What About the Boards? Issues of Transparency and Accountability in Board Composition, in I. Lapsley and H. Knutsson (eds), *Modernizing the Public Sector: Scandinavian Perspectives* (London and New York: Routledge).

von Hayek, F. (1960) *The Constitution of Liberty* (Chicago: University of Chicago Press).

Weber, M. (1958) *From Max Weber: Essays in Sociology*. Translated by H. H. Gerth and C. Wright Mills (New York: Oxford University Press).

Wenglén, R. (2017) Managing Profits and Professionalism in the Swedish School System, in I. Lapsley and H. Knutsson (eds), *Modernizing the Public Sector: Scandinavian Perspectives* (London and New York: Routledge).

2 New Public Management in a Scandinavian context

Hans Knutsson, Ola Mattisson, Salme Näsi, Kari Nyland and Peter Skærbæk

Summary

This chapter gives an overview of the main NPM reforms and trends in the Nordic countries. The idea of a uniform Scandinavian model of NPM is discussed – the chapter presents the different countries as members of a shared public administration tradition, albeit with different traits and particular reforms. The Swedish constitution and the organization of the public sector in a centralized and a two-part local government structure are presented, both as a backdrop to the subsequent chapters and for a reflection about whether there is a uniqueness to be found in the Swedish NPM initiatives. The long history of decentralized public decision-making and its ramifications on the structure of the Swedish public-sector organization is given special attention. From a Scandinavian perspective, the public-sector structures and characteristics in Norway, Denmark and Finland are presented, by which the idea of a single Scandinavian model for all is discussed and contested.

Modernizing government: public-sector reform in Scandinavia[1]

> The 'Nordic model' is a distinct way of organising society, managing institutions and conducting politics. It is characterised by a large public sector financed with high taxes, redistributive welfare services and extensive collaboration between unions, trade organisations and the state.
>
> (Johnsen and Vakkuri, 2006, p. 291)

Sweden, Denmark, Norway and Finland not only share a long history but are also seen as representing one distinct Scandinavian (natives call it Nordic) model of public administration. From a political science angle, Robert Cox (2004) has reflected on the Scandinavian welfare state model. It is, he argues, a matter of universality, solidarity and market independence. Universal solutions, where all are included in the welfare state, solidarity is expressed in progressive and redistributive tax systems, and no citizen is left to finance and buy from private firms its own share of welfare services, are at the core of the Scandinavian welfare states.

In Table 2.1 below, an overall presentation of how each country has adhered to the basic NPM toolbox is made. The presentation suggests that Sweden and Finland have been more ready to apply NPM-like reforms than Denmark and Norway, and have done so more intensely. The intensity is indicated by stars; more stars represent higher intensity.

Sweden had already initiated reforms akin to the Hood (1991) NPM doctrines in the mid-1980s, so Swedish adoption was early but still a few years after Finland's (Yliaska, 2015). Sweden is often mentioned as a special case, but Finland's NPM trajectory resembles the Swedish one. Agencification in government, a strong municipal autonomy, results–orientation and quantification, as well as privatization and marketization reforms, unite the two countries. Likewise, the hesitant accommodation of payment by results and turning citizens into customers also place the two countries close to each other when it comes to NPM inclinations.

Denmark displays a somewhat mixed pattern. As Kure and Malmmose point out in Chapter 4, Denmark is by many commentators seen as a 'tortoise' or careful 'modernizer' rather than a 'marketizer'. The OECD (2000) remarks that regulatory reform had been hesitant in Denmark and slowed by consensus-driven policy processes. In a direct comparison with Sweden, Green-Pedersen (2002) noted that market-type reforms have been greater in Sweden than in Denmark, not least in the health care sector. Greve (2003, 2006) also draws the picture of a rather flat NPM trajectory. However, as Skærbæk points out in the section on Denmark below, Denmark was engaged early on in NPM-like reforms, mainly taking place at the administrative levels in the Danish public sector.

Norway is often described as a 'reluctant reformer' of NPM concepts (Christensen, 2003). In the last decades, the pressure on Norway to engage in public reforms has been comparatively low due to a healthy economic situation and a well-functioning supply of public services. However, there have been different waves of reform over the decades, usually with a pragmatic approach focusing on managerial tools (Laegreid *et al.*, 2013). Christensen *et al.* (2008) characterize the Norwegian reform work as a gradual move, but

Table 2.1 NPM trajectories for Sweden, Finland, Denmark and Norway

NPM trajectory	Sweden	Finland	Denmark	Norway
Government agencification	★★	★★	★	★
Municipality autonomy	★★★	★★★	★	★★
Results-orientation and quantification	★★	★★	★★	★
Incentives and payment by results	★	★	★	★
Citizens as customers	★★	★★	★	★
Marketization	★★★	★★★	★★	★
Audit society	★★	★	★★	★

one that is still lagging behind typical NPM countries. Still, the hospital sector went through a restructuring in 2002 characterized by NPM ideas, calling for a number of successive management reforms. Further, the municipalities have shown a great willingness to experiment with internal structures since the 1990s. However, over the last decade there has also been a focus on structural issues such as interactions with central government agencies or with other municipalities (Bezes *et al.*, 2013).

In the following discussion on the nations, major reforms in each respective nation are presented. The section on Sweden begins with an overview of the institutional settings found in the Swedish public sector, in order to give the reader necessary points of reference when reading the Swedish chapters in the book.

Sweden

Institutional settings

The public sector in Sweden is organized into two main administrative levels: central government and local government. Furthermore, the local level is divided into county councils/regions (*landsting/regioner*) and municipalities (*kommuner*).

The central government consists of the parliament (Riksdag) and the government (Regeringen). The executive comprises the government offices (*regeringskansliet*) and the central government agencies (*myndigheter*). Enactment of laws and decisions about central government expenditures and revenues are the main responsibilities of the Riksdag.

In 2015, the cabinet consisted of a prime minister and 23 ministers. The government offices were organized in the prime minister's office (Statsrådsberedningen) and 10 separate ministries. Each ministry is headed by a minister, who is supported by a small staff. Decision-making in the government is collective. Hence, a minister is not individually responsible to the Riksdag either for the activities within that ministry or for the activities of the agencies. The number of government agencies has shrunk gradually over the last 15 years, from more than 600 (in 2000) to 349 today (SCB, 2016). In an international comparison, Sweden has a long tradition of the organization of independent agencies. The agencies are by law relatively independent from the government in the accomplishment of the ongoing tasks to which they are assigned.

At the local level there are two different administrative systems in Sweden. One is the 290 municipalities, which are responsible for the public and local issues close to the citizens, such as preschool activity, primary and secondary schools, care of the elderly, and roads, water and sewerage. There is a great variation in size of these municipalities. The other local government system consists of 20 county councils/regions.[2] They operate at a regional level and are primarily responsible for handling health care. They are also involved in other across-the-board tasks that would be too costly or difficult for a single municipality to deal with, such as public transport, tourism and cultural development. County councils and regions vary widely in size.

For both municipalities and county councils, the same basic legislative framework is applicable. The Municipality Act (Kommunallagen) regulates the autonomy of the local governments in dealing with issues concerning competence, organization structure, budgeting and accounting. With respect to the direction of activities, county councils and municipalities are relatively autonomous. Both are run by elected bodies that are made up of politicians who are directly elected by citizens every fourth year. The locally elected bodies are in general free to organize their activities according to what is needed locally, with a low degree of interference from central government.

Despite high formal independence, central government has influence over the local governments through the transfer system. Local governments receive either dedicated or general grants from central government. In 2014, these transfers amounted to almost 20 per cent of the total revenues of the municipalities. Hence, a large proportion of the activities in local governments actually has to do with implementation of policies that are decided upon by the Riksdag. In order to treat citizens in an equal manner, there is a financial equalization system. Local governments with high revenues from taxation and/or low costs from good of social, geographical and demographic conditions have to share, by way of an elaborate algorithm, their surpluses with local governments with less fortunate conditions. Overall, the ambition is to make sure that, no matter where in the country people live, government policies are carried out to the same standard. Accordingly, there is a continuous tension between, on the one hand, the principle of giving local government autonomy, and, on the other, the central government giving directives for policy implementation. This is an issue that comes back constantly in the public policy debate.

Major reforms

From an NPM point of view, Sweden has seen major administrative changes at all levels of government. The general direction may be seen as a top-down movement, as the central government in the 1970s suffered from too much detailed control over the allocation of means and too little control over the resulting consequences of public spending. The resource allocation was too centralized and became more and more inefficient (Statskontoret, 2012). In 1985, the real reform work began (Regeringen, 1984/1985). It saw two major themes: performance management (central government) and the deregulation and privatization of a wide range of operations. From a situation where agencies were measured by the extent to which allocated funds were used or not, more attention was given to what each agency could perform with the available funds. Detailed allocations for various cost items, down to stationery and individual positions to be maintained, agencies were allocated 'frames', whereby they received an aggregated budget in relation to perform-ance targets. Since the beginning of the 1990s, gradual adjustments have been made to the public spending rules and there are now both legislation and tra-dition to, first, define total central government spending, then allocate it to separate spending areas. In a similar vein, local governments are bound by law to have a 2 per cent surplus in their annual income statement budgets.

Organizationally, the direction for the different agencies was previously set in a model of corporatism, where incumbent interest groups held positions in the different agency boards, thereby creating legitimacy for policy formation and implementation. This regime ended at the beginning of the 1990s. Gradually, government agencies have become more influential in policymak-ing (Lindvall and Rothstein, 2006). In recent years, agencies have been, on the one hand, geographically consolidated and, on the other, institutionally split into two parts, representing executive and oversight functions. Legality and the equal treatment of citizens are advanced as the main reasons for this development.

Deregulation, privatization and marketization have been widely applied but have not had extensive impact on Swedish welfare provision. In most areas, deregulation is a necessary first legal step to allow private companies to offer welfare services. Many sectors have been deregulated and the first public procurement legislation was introduced in 1992. In 2009, the Act on System of Choice in the Public Sector (LOV), opened up the opportunity for local governments to arrange customer choice solutions. Some areas remain a strict public-sector responsibility (e.g. water).

In search for the 'typical Swedish', Statskontoret found that the inde-pendent agencies model gave central government officials a sense of high autonomy concerning issues of internal management and organization but lower autonomy on issues like policy design and policy implementation. Another observation was that the ideas of governance structures and division of tasks between politicians and officials are well established. The concepts of performance management and performance measurement are now regarded as central in the Swedish central government management model (Statskon-toret, 2015).

In the local government sector, the overall structure has regularly been questioned. At the same time, local government autonomy is considered crucial. Over time, municipalities have been given more responsibility for welfare activities and policy implementation. More obligations and provisions are also more demanding for the organization, requiring more extensive capa-cities. The main answer to this challenge has been size and two structural reforms of merging municipalities have been completed (SOU 2007:10). For a long time the internal structures were seen as homogenous, with only minor differences between organizations. But, after the introduction of the new and more flexible Municipality Act (in 1991), an intense experimentation started where organizational forms were adapted to local conditions and needs. The management and organization of Swedish health care underwent profound

changes between 1960 and 1992, when several central government responsibilities were transferred to the county councils. Escalating challenges such as
demographics and regional differences in welfare services, however, currently
raise questions about the need for new ways to control and organize health
services.

Finland

Structure of the Finnish public administration

The Finnish public sector consists of two administrative levels: the state
(central government) sector and the municipal (local government) sector. In
addition to the parliament, ministries and central state agencies and offices,
the state administration in Finland today also consists of six Regional State
Administrative Agencies (AVI-agencies) and 15 Centres for Economic Development, Transport and the Environment (ELY-keskus).

Local authorities in Finland (in 2016) consist of 313 municipalities and 184
joint municipal authorities. Municipal services are provided by the core
municipalities and/or by joint municipal authorities. The most important
joint authorities include hospital districts (which are responsible for specialist
medical care), districts for the care of the disabled and joint authorities set up
to perform functions related to public health and education. Joint authorities
are independent legal public entities governed by municipal legislation (the
latest Municipal Act 410/2015).

At the beginning of 2019, a radical governmental reform is going to take
place in Finland. The plan is to transfer the organization of health care and
social services and other regional services (such as emergency services and
environmental and regional development duties) to counties on 1 January
2019. The aim is to coordinate and simplify the regional state administration
(alueuudistus.fi). There will be 18 autonomous regions or counties in the
country, of which 15 will organize health care and social services in their area
themselves. Under the new regional system, the remaining three regions will
provide the services with the support of one of the other autonomous
regions. The legislation to establish regional reform is under development
and, as at 5 April 2016, only the reform guidelines have been decided by the
Finnish government.

Major reforms

Finland was a forerunning country in adopting the NPM ideas, having already
started in the 1980s and continuing very actively in the first half and middle
of the 1990s. One of the first concrete reforms, in both the state sector (1998)
and municipal sector (1997), was the transfer from the traditional cameralistic
accounting to accrual-based accounting. In the municipal sector, the same
accrual-based model is applied in both budgeting and accounting. In the state

sector, budgeting still is based on modified cash. Expectations concerning the 'betterness' of accrual accounting compared to the traditional modified cash accounting were high but – if you look at the problems of the Finnish public-sector economies today – the accrual accounting models really couldn't help to keep the public finances in balance. In the last decades, the public sector – the welfare state service provision – has grown too big to be financed with tax and other public-sector income.

As to the IPSAS standardization, the state sector (i.e. Valtion kirjanpitolau-takunta, the Finnish State Accounting Board) investigated the similarities and differences of the Finnish accrual accounting model and the IPSAS standards during the 2000s, coming to the conclusion that there is no reason to adopt IPSAS, at least not entirely (Dnro 545/58/2006; see also Oulasvirta, 2014). There are currently some people from the Finnish state administration act-ively involved in developing the EPSAS. The municipal sector has expended hardly any effort on the international standardization issue, but the Finnish municipal accrual accounting model has needed several amendments in order to block creative accounting behaviour of municipalities in balancing their economy (see Vinnari and Näsi, 2008).

As to the adoption of the performance-based management and steering system, the Finnish state sector has been very active since the turn of the 1990s. The terms *tulosjohtaminen* (management by results) and *tulosohjaus* (steering by results) are used in Finland. The former refers to the management inside a state agency, and the latter to the steering of agencies by the minis-tries and other higher authorities. Results-based steering started with some pilot projects at the turn of the 1990s and became obligatory in all state agen-cies by the middle of the 1990s.

Often the cost accounting systems of the agencies have been stumbling blocks in applying the results-based management and steering systems in the Finnish state government. Services of agencies are many, calculations of unit costs are ambiguous and therefore funding decisions are in practice often made at least partly on a historical basis – the results-based management and steering being only the terms used as part of doing politics (see Treuthardt and Näsi, 2010). Several development projects have been carried out in dif-ferent governmental sectors during the last two decades (e.g. in the Finnish Defence Forces and in universities) in order to improve the cost accounting systems and to sharpen the results-based steering. It is difficult to say anything in general about how well the results-based systems work in practice. It cer-tainly depends very much on the context. In any case, the Finnish central governmental agencies have now been steered and managed based on their results/output/performance for some 20 years. Adoption and adaption of the BSC was a fad some 15 years ago in different sectors.

Adoption of performance-based management and steering means that, e.g. all the Finnish universities have got their funding from the government based on the results-based negotiations between the Ministry of Education and Culture and the university leaders in question (the rector and his/her staff).

The structure, extent and quality of the higher education, the number of universities, university funding and education and research performances have been handled very often in the Finnish media – and not with soft hands at all.

Historically, all the Finnish universities were state agencies (part of the state) but since the beginning of 2010 they have all been private entities and more independent from the state, at least in theory. Still, most university funding comes from the state budget. Annual results-based negotiations have been replaced by 'agreement negotiations' for the next four years. Students' fees (at least from foreign students coming from countries outside the EU and EEA) have been a regularly discussed issue at least since the 2000s, but so far only some piloting has been possible according to Finnish legislation. The current government, however, has decided to start collecting fees from foreign students in the coming years. Students are of course strongly against this. They fear that soon all students will have to pay an annual fee.

Several structural reforms have happened in the Finnish university sector. During the 1960s several new universities were established. During the 1970s all the private universities were taken over by the state. In the 1990s, the number of universities was 20; today this number is 14. This has meant mergers of the universities, with the first aim being to decrease universities' administrative costs. The number of universities, the scale of higher education and the number of degrees are very obviously going to decrease; the most current and radical thought (presented by the Federation of Finnish Techno-logy Industries) being that half of the universities could still be closed.

The new University Act (558/2009) brought external members to the boards of directors of the universities. At least 40 per cent of the board members must be from outside the university's own staff and broadly represent the surrounding society. The chair and vice-chair of the board must be external board members; it is therefore perhaps easier today to initiate radical structural changes both inside the universities and between the universities and other higher education institutions.

In addition to the universities, Finnish higher education also includes 26 polytechnics or universities of applied sciences around the country. These institutions function as limited companies, most owned by the municipalities. The aim in the years to come is also to decrease the number of polytechnics. Currently there are several projects to merge universities and polytechnics – i.e. to give up the 'dual system' of higher education. All the reforms that have happened during the 20 last years have added managerialism, competition and marketization in the sector of higher education.

As to the Finnish health care sector, the municipalities are still responsible for providing services, either by themselves, by the municipal joint authorities or using external service providers. Outsourcing has been a trend since the 2000s and the role of private-sector companies has increased steadily. There are at least 20 sizeable health care companies currently acting in Finland (e.g. Attendo Finland, Mehiläinen, Terveystalo, Pihlajalinna, Plusterveys and Diacor). The Finnish governments (both previous and current) have been preparing fundamental reforms in the social and health care service provision. There have been several points of political disagreements. Now, finally (in 2016), a principal decision has been made: the responsibility for providing social and health care services in the new model is to be given to 15 SOTE-regions. This reform, which will be established in 2019, means that the Finnish public sector will get a new third level – 18 autonomous counties – obviously with the right to levy taxes. In the meantime, it seems that the municipal sector is unwilling to develop the health care services and the private-sector companies are capturing the market.

The health care, social welfare and regional government reform package is going to be one of the biggest ever administrative and operational overhauls in Finland. The reform impacts the jobs of hundreds of thousands of people and affects the services of every citizen in the country. It also has an effect on the financial resources, steering and taxation of health care and social welfare services (www.alueuudistus.fi).

Denmark

Denmark has for long been implementing what Hood (1991) called New Public Management. Hood describes seven NPM doctrines, and Denmark has engaged with all of them. Ever since its formal initiation in 1983 in Denmark, NPM has been the object of public debate among public-sector employees and professionals. The Ministry of Finance (MoF) and the National Audit Office of Denmark (NAOD) have been involved with paving the way for the reforms as kind of instigators (Skærbæk and Christensen, 2015). Within the parliament, any attempts at intervention in the reforms from the angle of the political parties have been rejected and there has over the years been a broad consensus (Henrichsen, 2013) that the parliament should not interfere with the 'administration policies' and reforms of the MoF and more broadly the administration, despite the fact that the parliament has to approve most of the reforms. NPM, despite its investing nature, is not much an object of parliamentary discussions that can lead to much more than a few modifications. However, over the last five years or so, NPM has in Denmark become even more controversial, with the implementation, among others, of a major school reform, a municipality merger reform, a police merger reform and new performance measurement reforms, all blended with attempts of achieving savings on operating budgets. In contrast to the last 25–30 years of NPM reforms in Denmark, these later reforms seem to generate a much more impactful criticism, and opponents, particularly those from professional groupings, like school teachers' unions, are seeking to identify the forces behind the reforms and much debate centres around the role of civil servants. The current debate centres around civil servants trained in political science and a few economists dominating within MoF, NAOD and elsewhere, in ministries (equipped with staff recruited frequently from MoF) supported by prominent consultancy houses like McKinsey & Co (frequently with political science backgrounds) and several influential political science professors at universities, and with significant inputs from economic theory, such as economies of scale, spans of control (Skærbæk and Christensen, 2015) and principal agency theory.

Here, the more enduring reforms are presented in order to demonstrate how, in more overall terms, Denmark has been seeking to comply with the seven doctrines of NPM, showing that many of the reforms are basically accounting reforms.

As Hood (1995) describes it, NPM is first and foremost a matter of establishing decentralization among public-sector agencies and institutions and then to equip them with appropriate budgeting and management accounting and control systems in order to accommodate for accountability and disciplined resource consumption. As part of this development, many institutions have been split into several independent units, each with its own management, budget and accounting and control systems. Examples are the State Bus division of Danish Rail (later sold to the British company Arriva for DKK 99 (GBP 10)), the Scandlines Ferry division of Danish Rail (later sold to private investors), Postal Services etc.

In a major accountability reform from 1995, the annual report was introduced to the public sector and wherever the disclosure of unit cost information was central as a way to demonstrate increased efficiency (Skærbæk, 2005, Skærbæk and Thisted, 2004), but at the same time this also implied a weakened trust in professionals and a perceived need to strengthen management. How such reforms have inflicted on professionals' identities is written about: on artists by Christiansen and Skærbæk (1997), on military officers by Skærbæk and Thorbjørnsen (2007) and on police officers by Christensen and Skærbæk (2010). That reform was later (from 2003) supplanted with the introduction of accrual accounting to be applied to both budget and costs (Finansministeriet, 2003). In both state and municipalities, from kindergartens to universities, institutions were requested to make annual reports based on accruals, opening the way for private audit firms to audit those reports. Both of these related reforms have implied massive investments in accounting systems and the crafting of accounting reports. An example of that, within the Danish Defence Forces, is reported by Skærbæk (2009).

Closely linked up with these reforms, and especially the attempts of calculating unit costs, are the attempts to reform the funding of institutions. Within the national health services, a Diagnostic Related Groupings (DRG) allocation system has been implemented to hospitals to allocate funding based on outputs and calculated unit prices. Such a system has also been implemented into universities' teaching funding and increasingly on research. In this way, attempts have been made to make the allocation of funding a technical bureaucratic exercise rather than something that politicians decide on. Within the Danish Police, a comprehensive number of unit costs have been sought to be calculated, but these are still not used as a basis for the allocation of funding (Skærbæk and Thisted, 2004). Instead, they have implemented contracts for police senior management, with a wide range of targets on specific outputs, like that of speed measurements and detained prisoners. In this way, based on principal agent theory and its (somewhat problematic) assumptions about agents' opportunistic behaviour, senior management salaries are made dependent on meeting set targets. Contracts have also been made with a lot of other institutions, among them not least universities. For instance, targets have been defined at universities for the relative proportion of female professors to that of male professors. The contracts are reported within the annual report.

In terms of adopting private-sector styles of management practice, the public sector has also equipped a lot of institutions like theatres, universities, kindergartens and public schools with boards of directors as in private companies. In particular, CEOs of private and public corporations prominently appear on universities' boards. Another trend is the wide application of management concepts like activity-based costing and the balanced scorecard (Justesen and Skærbæk, 2010). Along with performance contracts we also witness a tendency towards outsourcing, with pressure from the EU and the OECD. Within municipalities, we have particularly seen such a development, whereas within the state and hospitals it has mostly been cleaning and canteen services that have been outsourced. The Danish Defence Forces decided in 2009 to outsource their larger facilities management on all barracks in Denmark to two private companies. Further outsourcing is considered.

Norway

Norway is usually described as a 'late reformer' where NPM-oriented organizational changes are less frequent (Bezes *et al.*, 2013). In this section, we seek to describe how the Norwegian public sector has been influenced by administrative reforms (performance management, decentralization trends and changes in structures) and how post-NPM reforms through mergers have become increasingly important during the early 2000s.

Norway has, like Sweden, a long tradition of agencies. The principle of local self-government has a strong position, creating tensions with the principle of sectoral specialization following ministerial responsibility. The dual principle of ministerial responsibility and local self-government solves some coordination problems and produces others (Fimreite and Lægreid, 2005). Besides increasing efficiency, reforms in various sectors have sought to influence this relation.

The Norwegian approach to NPM reforms has been characterized as pragmatic, focusing mainly on the managerial tools of NPM, management by objectives and increased management autonomy to agencies and state-owned companies. The most comprehensive reform in that sense was the reform package which constituted the Hospital Enterprise Reform in 2002. The objectives of these reforms are expressed as ways of increasing efficiency by creating autonomous, state-owned enterprises with distinct accountability relations. Transferring ownership of the hospitals from 19 counties to the state and organizing hospitals into four regional health enterprises (RHEs) have been viewed as examples of administrative decentralization and political centralization (Lægreid *et al.*, 2005).

Structuring hospitals into larger health enterprises was supposed to create entities that are more autonomous. On the other hand, the state imposed a number of detailed objectives, regulated service delivery through patient rights and strictly limited the level of investments by regulating the supply of loans (Pettersen and Nyland, 2011). The role of management by objectives and performance management is observed in the contracts between the state as owner and the RHEs as providers of services. These contracts (The Ministry of Health and Social Affairs, 2015) include about 80–100 different indicators (objectives) to monitor performance and quality of care. Hospital managers are supposed to document performance compared with these indicators on economic and clinical activities. The DRG system has been a powerful tool in measuring performance in hospitals. This system was introduced in 1997 as a tool for activity-based funding, and from 2002 about 50 per cent of the total funding from the state to the RHEs has been set according to activity, measured by DRG points.

Another part of the hospital reform was the introduction of professional hospital boards (by law) from 2002, with the intention to remove politicians from the boardroom and to pave the way for the boards to take strategic roles. This part of the reform was reversed in 2005 when the centre-left government changed the law to bring back politicians onto the boards (Nyland and Pettersen, 2015).

Another trend in Norwegian reforms has focused on horizontal coordination issues. Within the health care sector, the Norwegian coordination reform has many similarities to what has been termed 'joined-up government', 'whole-of-government' or 'holistic government' and is part of the so-called post-NPM reforms (Christensen *et al.*, 2014). This reform was implemented in 2012 to improve cooperation and coordination between state and municipal service providers. The reform introduced a set of juridical and financial instruments. A common law for municipal health services provides a duty for local authorities and hospitals to cooperate. Various forms of payment per patient between the municipality and the hospital were introduced. However, after a short trial period, the state chose to reverse significant parts of the financial incentives. The only element left is that municipalities have to pay a fixed day rate for patients who have been fully processed at the hospital but still have to remain in the hospital due to a lack of municipal health services.

A similar coordination reform implying municipals and the state working together to supply services to citizens has been the reform in the Norwegian welfare administration from 2005. Through a merger between the employment administration and the national insurance administration, a single new 'labour and welfare agency' was created (NAV). A new local frontline – a 'one stop shop' – was organized, comprising a partnership between the NAV and the municipal social services. NAV manages about one-third of the state budget through schemes such as unemployment benefits, rehabilitation, pensions and social assistance. The holistic aspect of this reform was central and, although controversial, the reform has been considered successfully implemented (Christensen *et al.*, 2007).

The ongoing municipal reform may also be seen as a coordination reform calling for new solutions to ensure that municipalities continue to serve as service providers, community developers, exercisers of authority and democratic fora. Over the last decades, various forms of cooperation have developed between municipalities, between state and municipal enterprises and between private and public organizations. In the recent report of the Expert Committee (Ministry of Local Government and Modernisation, 2014), inter-municipal cooperation is also referred to as a challenge, as the municipalities' ability to *control* high-quality collaborative relationships is claimed to be essential. The municipal reform entails structural changes towards larger municipal entities and fewer inter-municipal collaborations. The principle of local freedom for municipalities to choose their solutions and possible mergers has a strong position. The instruments of the reform are governmental reports and recommendations as well as economic incentives. The same way of thinking, 'concentration for quality' (White Paper, 2014–2015), applies to structural reform in the university and higher education sector. Hence, these reforms follow the Norwegian policymaking style '*made of peaceful coexistence and "revolution in slow motion" based on common interests and consensus*' (Bezes *et al.*, 2013, p. 53).

The way forward – the chapters ahead

The country overview indicates that a single Scandinavian model of public management is not directly obvious. First, it is seen that Sweden and Finland have been adopting NPM ideas since early in the 1980s, whereas Denmark and Norway – although also starting early – suggest a somewhat flatter trajectory. The most obvious common denominator for all four countries, though, is how all struggle with finding the right size and scope in municipalities, regions and state sectors.

In the following chapters, the book will focus on Swedish experiences of NPM-related reform. First, in Chapter 3, we will take a closer look at the development of NPM-style reforms in Sweden, dating as far back as the early 1900s. In Chapter 4, it is discussed to what extent one Danish NPM-related health care reform is to be considered a myth. In Chapter 5, we look into two Swedish NPM experiments in the health care sector, where process-based management control is presented and discussed. Last in the management section, in Chapter 6 we are introduced to a unique trait of Swedish NPM, which also bears witness to the Swedish progressive approach to modernization. In Sweden, there is a long-established system of recording citizens, a true precursor and facilitator of universal welfare services.

In the second part, on governance, we can read about the changing relations between central government and the single largest agency, the Swedish Social Insurance Agency (SIA), illustrating how personal relations may actually influence the balancing of control and autonomy between central government and agencies. Chapter 8 presents a multi-country survey of Supreme Audit Institutions in Scandinavia, and is as such an illustration of similarities and differences among the incumbent nations' NPM applications. In Chapter 9 there is a comprehensive account of how far municipal cooperation may provide solutions to the current challenges of governing welfare provision in Sweden. A rather different governance aspect is covered in Chapter 10, where an illustration of how municipalities appoint board members in publicly owned companies indicates that the issues of transparency and corruption are not completely off the table in the Swedish public sector. Chapter 11 illustrates the strategy development process in Lund University and elaborates on the tension between professional and administrative control in Sweden.

The third part, on marketization, begins with an overview of the general market solutions present in Sweden (Chapter 12), of which quasi-markets in the primary health care sector are one prominent example of how Sweden has experimented with marketization (Chapter 13). In Chapter 14, another example of marketization, this time in the Swedish primary school sector, is presented, though from a political angle. This shows how the polarization and resolve in politics may influence the actual implementation, in this case torn between professional teaching and learning how to manage. Chapter 15 contains a contentious case of an NPM-related policy implementation, where a unique but costly welfare reform rests on choice and privatization. In Chapter 16, we return to the modernization of the Scandinavian public sector and reflect upon the contents of the book.

Notes

1 Scandinavia comprises the mainland of Sweden and Norway. The Nordic countries include also Denmark (including Greenland and the Faroe Islands), Iceland and Finland. Outside the region, the Nordic countries are referred to as Scandinavia (Hirsch *et al.*, 2002).
2 Sometimes the number of counties in Sweden is said to be 21. Gotland, an island in the Baltic Sea, is a municipality with added responsibility for health care and therefore effectively also works as a county.

References

Bezes, P., A. L. Fimreite, P. Le Lidec and P. Lægreid (2013) 'Understanding organizational reforms in the modern state: specialization and integration in Norway and France'. *Governance*, Vol. 26, No. 1, pp. 147–175.
Christensen, M. and P. Skærbæk (2010) 'Consultancy outputs and the purification of accounting technologies'. *Accounting, Organizations and Society*, Vol. 35, No. 5, pp. 524–545.

Christensen, T. (2003) 'Narrative of Norwegian governance: elaborating the strong state'. *Public Administration*, Vol. 81, No. 1, pp. 163–190.

Christensen, T., A. L. Fimreite and P. Lægreid (2007) 'Reform of the employment and welfare administrations – the challenges of co-coordinating diverse public organizations'. *International Review of Administrative Sciences*, Vol. 73, No. 3, pp. 389–408.

Christensen, T., A. L. Fimreite and P. Lægreid (2014) 'Joined-up government for welfare administration reform in Norway'. *Public Organization Review*, Vol. 14, No. 4, pp. 439–456.

Christensen, T., A. Lie and P. Lægreid (2008) 'Beyond new public management: agencification and regulatory reform in Norway'. *Financial Accountability and Management*, Vol. 24, No. 1, pp. 15–30.

Christiansen, J. K. and P. Skærbæk (1997) 'Implementing budgetary control in the performing arts: games in the organizational theatre'. *Management Accounting Research*, Vol. 8, No. 4, pp. 405–438.

Cox, R. (2004) 'The path-dependency of an idea: why Scandinavian welfare states remain distinct'. *Social Policy & Administration*, Vol. 38, No. 2, pp. 204–219.

Dnro 545/58/2006 (2006) 'Valtion kirjanpitolautakunnan selvitys ipsas-standardien soveltamisesta valtion kirjanpidossa. 30.11.2006'.

Fimreite, A. L. and P. Lægreid (2005) Specialization and Coordination. Implications for Integration and Control in a Multilevel System, in U. R. Centre (ed.), *Working Paper* (Bergen).

Finansministeriet (2003) 'Omkostninger og effektivitet i staten – rapport fra udvalget om omkostningsbaserede budget-og regnskabsprincipper' (White Paper).

Green-Pedersen, C. (2002) 'New public management reforms of the Danish and Swedish welfare states: the role of different social democratic responses'. *Governance: An International Journal of Policy, Administration, and Institutions*, Vol. 15, No. 2, pp. 271–294.

Greve, C. (2003) 'Public sector reform in Denmark: organizational transformation and evaluation'. *Public Organization Review*, Vol. 3, pp. 269–280.

Greve, C. (2006) 'Public management reform in Denmark'. *Public Management Review*, Vol. 8, No. 1, pp. 161–169.

Henrichsen, C. (2013) Forord: 30 år med npm. Et kritisk review af new public management, in *Futuriblerna* (Selskabet for Fremtidsforskning).

Hirsch, E. D., Jr, J. F. Kett and J. S. Trefil (2002) *Scandinavia. The New Dictionary of Cultural Literacy* (Boston: Houghton Mifflin Company).

Hood, C. (1991) 'A public management for all seasons?'. *Public Administration*, Vol. 6, No. 3, pp. 3–19.

Hood, C. (1995) 'The "new public management" in the 1980s: variations on a theme'. *Accounting, Organizations and Society*, Vol. 20, No. 2–3, pp. 93–110.

Johnsen, Å. and J. Vakkuri (2006) 'Is there a Nordic perspective on public sector performance measurement?'. *Financial Accountability and Management*, Vol. 22, No. 3, pp. 291–308.

Justesen, L. and P. Skærbæk (2010) 'Performance auditing and the narrating of a new auditee identity'. *Financial Accountability & Management*, Vol. 26, No. 3, pp. 325–343.

Laegreid, P., Å. Dyrnes Nordö and L. H. Rykkja (2013) *Public Sector Reform in Norway: Views and Experiences from Senior Executives*.

Lægreid, P., S. Opedal and I. M. Stigen (2005) 'The Norwegian hospital reform – balancing political control and enterprise autonomy'. *Journal of Health Politics, Policy and Law*, Vol. 30, No. 6, pp. 1035–1072.

Lindvall, J. and B. Rothstein (2006) 'The fall of the strong state'. *Scandinavian Political Studies*, Vol. 29, No. 1, pp. 47–63.

Ministry of Local Government and Modernisation (2014) *Sluttrapport fra ekspertutvalg. Kriterier for god kommunestruktur* [Final report of the expert committee. Criteria for good local government structure].

Nyland, K. and I. J. Pettersen (2015) 'Hybrid controls and accountabilities in public sector management: three case studies in a reforming hospital sector'. *International Journal of Public Sector Management*, Vol. 28, No. 2, pp. 90–104.

OECD (2000) *OECD Reviews of Regulatory Reform: Regulatory Reform in Denmark 2000.*

Oulasvirta, L. (2014) 'The reluctance of a developed country to choose international public sector accounting standards of the IFAC. A critical case study'. *Critical Perspectives on Accounting*, Vol. 25, No. 3, pp. 272–285.

Pettersen, I. J. and K. Nyland (2011) 'Reforms and accounting system changes: a study on the implementation of accrual accounting in Norwegian hospitals'. *Journal of Accounting & Organizational Change*, Vol. 7, No. 3, pp. 237–258.

Regeringen (1984/1985) *Regeringens skrivelse (1984/85:202) om den offentliga sektorns förnyelse.*

SCB (2016) *Myndighetsregistret.* Available online at www.myndighetsregistret.scb.se.

Skærbæk, P. (2005) 'Annual reports as interaction devices – the hidden constructions of mediated communication'. *Financial Accountability and Management*, Vol. 21, No. 4, pp. 385–411.

Skærbæk, P. (2009) 'Public sector auditor identities in making efficiency auditable: the National Audit Office of Denmark as independent auditor and modernizer'. *Accounting, Organizations and Society*, Vol. 34, No. 8, pp. 971–987.

Skærbæk, P. and M. Christensen (2015) 'Auditing and the purification of blame'. *Contemporary Accounting Research*, Vol. 32, No. 3, pp. 1263–1284.

Skærbæk, P. and J. A. Thisted (2004) 'Unit costs in central Danish government – a critical appraisal of the practices developed'. *European Accounting Review*, Vol. 13, No. 1, pp. 7–38.

Skærbæk, P. and S. Thorbjørnsen (2007) 'The commodification of the Danish defence and the troubled identities of its officers'. *Financial Accountability and Management*, Vol. 23, No. 3, pp. 243–268.

SOU 2007:10 (2007) 'Hållbar samhällsorganisation med utvecklingskraft, SOU 2007:10'.

Statskontoret (2012) *Den effektiva staten. En antologi från statskontoret* (Stockholm).

Statskontoret (2015) *Förändringar i svensk statsförvaltning och framtida utmaningar.* Report for (Stockholm).

The Ministry of Health and Social Affairs (2015) *Bestillerdokument for helse midt-norge* [The steering document for a regional health enterprise].

Treuthardt, L. and S. Näsi (2010) The Performance-based Steering and Management System of the Finnish Universities Analysed through the Conceptual Framework of Politics, in J. Backhaus, R. Eamets and D. Eerma (eds), *In Economics of Education: Issues of Transition and Transformation* (Berlin: Lit Verlag).

Vinnari, E. M. and S. Näsi (2008) 'Creative accrual accounting in the public sector: milking water utilities to balance municipal budgets and accounts'. *Financial Accountability & Management*, Vol. 24, No. 2, pp. 97–116.

White Paper (2014–2015) Concentration for Quality, in M. O. E. A. Research (ed.).

Yliaska, V. (2015) 'New public management as a response to the crisis of the 1970s: the case of Finland, 1970–1990'. *Contemporary European History*, Vol. 24, pp. 435–459.

Part I

Modernization through management

> Management – which is the organ of society specifically charged with making resources productive, that is, with the responsibility for organized economic advance – therefore reflects the basic spirit of the modern age. It is, in fact, indispensable, and this explains why, once begotten, it grew so fast and with so little opposition.
>
> (Drucker, 1954)

'The basic spirit of the modern age', stated in 1954, still rings true, not least in the public sector. The standard view on New Public Management is that it is an adoption and adaption of neo-liberal thinking. However, (Hood, 1991) declared NPM as politically neutral, because both centre-left and centre-right governments adopted it. However, political neutrality does not capture the Swedish context. Its centre-left government adopted NPM wholeheartedly. In this part, the history of the Swedish Social Democratic Party is a history of the Swedish adoption and adaption of modern ideas of managing public sector organizations. It is a history of pragmatic deliberation and compromise, readily trying new ways to build a coherent system based on solidarity and universality. Remarkably, the fundamental critique of NPM as a project, which purports to be universal but, in practice, is not, proved ideal for the Scandinavian context, particularly in Sweden.

NPM practices privilege management over professionals, resulting in conflict with professional values. This could be seen as the underlying theme in the case study of the Danish health care sector. Power, Kure and Malmmose say in Chapter 4, is an invisible coercive force. Professionals in Danish health care, it is argued, chose to comply with an administrative economic discourse of productivity substituted for a professional humanistic one. The case illustrates how quality may be effectively neglected when focus is put on cost-efficiency, a potential side effect of some of the commonly used NPM techniques. This is also discussed from a Swedish perspective in the context of process orientation as a means to putting the end result in focus. However, in two separate cases it is shown how these initiatives evolved into efficiency-driven change efforts, where managers were unable to change a strong 'silo mentality' and professional values.

The NPM has a preoccupation with quantification. The Swedish management of its welfare rests on a specific personal identification number. But this is a product of an earlier era which continues into the present day. Thus the universal civic right to public services requires an identification of who owns such rights, and, not to be forgotten, the state's tax subjects. It may be that the Swedish person number is a grossly underrated condition for the Swedish welfare state. What we see at the end of this part is how Sweden moved towards a more secular society and public administration. The state relieved the clergies of the registration function it had had for ages. A single personal identity number was introduced and used throughout a person's life. Citizens agreed to be 'managed' as the individual registration system developed in tandem with the main Swedish social reforms during the first half of the twentieth century. Registration of quantities, be it production or citizens, is perhaps the key modernizing principle underpinning the modernization and public management of the welfare state.

References

Drucker, P. F. (1954) *The Practice of Management* (New York: Harper & Brothers).
Hood, C. (1991) 'A public management for all seasons?'. *Public Administration*, Vol. 6, No. 3, pp. 3–19.

3 Shaping NPM

Social democratic values at work

Tom S. Karlsson

Summary

In this chapter, New Public Management (NPM) reforms are discussed, with focus on the Swedish public sector. The purpose is to question assumptions concerning the emergence of NPM within a Swedish context. A historical review reveals that reforms within the Swedish public sector express a heavy influence from the private sector; the idea of letting business and commercial logics guide the rationales of public-sector reforms can be traced back to the early twentieth century. The findings presented in this chapter are of particular interest for policymakers and public managers within public organizations. One conclusion is that the pragmatism and reformism characterizing Swedish social democracy during the post-World War II era has enabled an adaption and adoption for emerging NPM policies; Scandinavian thinking has not focused on bad practices but rather on evolving reforms. This has resulted in responsiveness for reforms, ultimately leading to a distinctly Swedish form of NPM emerging from the need to satisfy both socialism and capitalism.

Introduction

The basis and origin of New Public Management (NPM, cf. Hood, 1991) have been widely discussed among scholars during the last 30 years. Some (Cheung, 1997; Pollitt, 1993), argue that NPM is primarily a neo-liberal construction instigated during the early 1980s. As such, the seemingly agreed-upon description for the emergence of NPM has become associated with the leaderships of Margaret Thatcher and Ronald Reagan. The increased use of market solutions and competition as a driving factor for administrative efficiency has through such explanations been transformed into an alleged neo-liberal agenda for the public sector in general. Although the reference to a neo-liberal emergence may certainly have its merits within Anglo-Saxon countries such as the UK or the USA, it fails to explain the dispersion of NPM in welfare states with a different political incumbency (cf. Hood, 1995).

Studies focusing on the receptiveness of the Swedish welfare state have concluded that there is a high implementation factor for tools associated with

NPM (Wockelberg and Ahlbäck Öberg, 2014) when compared to Europe at large. During the 1990s and 2000s, marketization through competitive tendering (Almqvist, 2001; Almqvist, 2004; Bryntse, 2000) or quasi-markets governed by citizen choice (Glenngård, 2013) became a common ingredient in organizing the public sector. In addition, the Swedish public sector implemented elaborate performance measurement systems (Modell and Wiesel, 2008), Lean production and accounting (Funck and Larsson, 2014), Total Quality Management (Modell, 2009), detailed business process management (Karlsson, 2012; Karlsson, 2014) and the growing extent to which citizens were reconceptualized as being customers (Byrman, 2007; Damm, 2014; Huzell, 2005; Modell, 2005). The story is aligned to that of other NPM countries. What is different in Sweden, as compared with, for example, the UK, is the dominance of the Swedish Social Democratic Party (SAP).

The emergence and responsive adoption of NPM in a seemingly left-wing – even socialist in some sense – welfare state such as Sweden needs an alternative explanation to that of countries dominated by neo-liberal traditions. In order to understand how and why governmental reforms have been successful, it is important to analyse party competition within the state (Green-Pedersen, 2001; Green-Pedersen, 2002). This chapter covers a review of historical government documents containing a number of key reforms within the Swedish public sector during the twentieth century. The purpose is to portray an emerging welfare state, which readily discussed and implemented reforms that – today – would be identified as NPM. It will serve as a basis for understanding Sweden's adaption to and adoption of NPM as well as form an answer to the posited question: can neo-liberalism really be used as an explanation for the Swedish responsiveness towards NPM?

Social democracy in Sweden

Social democracy has a long and well-rooted tradition in Swedish society. In many ways it has shaped the manner in which Swedish society has progressed during the twentieth century. In this section, a brief description of the history of social democracy in Sweden is given. This description will serve as a basis for understanding the historical review and analysis undertaken in the following sections.

Social democracy in Sweden stems back to the early nineteenth century and to the period in which the working class was made aware of the schism between them and the bourgeois class. This trend could be seen throughout Europe and Sweden was certainly no exception. It lasted until 1889, however, before the Social Democratic Party (SAP[1]) was founded. The first person from SAP to become a formal member of parliament – in 1896 – was Hjalmar Branting. He eventually went on to become the party leader in 1908 and is considered to be one of the most important figures in Swedish social democracy.

The turn between the nineteenth and twentieth centuries proved to be a turbulent period for the working class in Sweden. The formalization of SAP paved the way for continuing the confrontation with the bourgeoisie class, albeit from a parliamentary perspective. Outside parliament, and quite closely linked with SAP, the Swedish Trade Union Confederation (LO[2]) emerged as a formal power in 1898. One of the first items on their agenda was the demand for reducing the working hours from up to 16 hours a day to a standardization cap at 8 hours per day. In 1902 the foundation of LO was met with the foundation of the Swedish Employer Confederation (SAF[3]), taking a stance against the union and workers. Whereas LO argued for increased involvement in the workplace, SAF demanded that employers should be recognized as having a mandate to govern and control. The December Agreement of 1906 gave workers the right to organize into unions and form collective agreements regarding salary and working conditions, while employers were recognized as having the authority for leading and organizing work as well as hiring or firing personnel freely.

In 1917, SAP held an open congress in which a crucial matter was on the agenda. Within the party there was a rising left-wing revolutionary phalanx, arguing for revolutionary actions. The other group stood for cooperation and reformism. In what is referred to as the 'Breaking Time' (Ohlsson, 2014) by social democrats, the revolutionaries left SAP and formed the Socialist Left Party, which during the twentieth century changed into the Swedish Communist Party and today is known as the Left Party. The winning side in the 1917 congress voted for a reformist approach, wherein small steps of reforms should be used within the parliamentary system in order to shape the welfare state.

The late 1910s and early 1920s proved to be a rather pivotal period for Swedish politics. In 1918, universal suffrage was implemented; men and women alike were now allowed to partake in free and public elections (although the first such election was not held until 1921). In 1919 the Swedish parliament voted for the 8-hour work day argued for by LO since the late nineteenth century. The first Social Democratic government was elected in 1920, re-elected in 1921 and then again in 1924. In 1928, the Swedish parliament voted for a 'Work-Peace-Regulation' focusing at reducing the number of unsanctioned strikes by allowing LO to form collective agreements and further reinforcing SAF's mandate for organizing and controlling the work places. The agreement seriously hampered the more revolutionary forces located at the Swedish workplaces as they aimed for more unregulated strikes as a weapon against capital owners. The law in many ways fitted well with the reformist agenda begun within SAP.

In 1928, Per-Albin Hansson was elected as SAP party leader and in 1932 he led the party to a great victory with 41.1 per cent of the people's votes. This was the beginning of an uninterrupted place in power for SAP up until 1976, when the conservatives came into power. Hansson is perhaps most famous for his rhetoric of a 'People's Home' (connected to the German *Volksgemeinschaft*), wherein all citizens should be treated on the basis of equality and equity. The People's Home attacked the inequality that resided within the current capitalistic society but also established a distance from more orthodox class struggle. Rather than focusing purely on the socialist agenda of class inequality, Swedish social democracy took a middle ground and thereby affirmed the foundation for reformism and pragmatism.

1938 was a hallmark year in Swedish political history, as this was when LO and SAF made a formal agreement for how conflicts between unions and employers should be resolved. The Saltsjöbaden Agreement insisted that the parties themselves, without any interference of the government, should solve every conflict. This contract is still valid and has undergone only minor revisions since 1938.

Between 1932 and 1976, SAP governed Sweden through different political coalitions. Sweden experienced soaring economic growth, allowing the welfare state to develop quite rapidly. During the 1950s a mandatory general pension was implemented, securing a higher welfare for retired citizens. The 1960s and 1970s contained a number of pivotal reforms regarding the Swedish social insurance, giving, among others, the opportunity for fathers to receive financial reimbursement for taking a leave of absence in order to stay home with their children for a short period of time (this was previously solely available to mothers). Another important reform during the 1970s was SAP's victory in the legal restriction of a 40-hour work week (an advancement of the 8-hour work day progressed during the early twentieth century, but with this reform the week was reduced to five, not six, days).

During the 1980s, the ties between SAP and LO came to be rather strained. The loss of power in 1976 hurt SAP rather badly, and the party began to question how to regain the confidence of the voters. Although they regained power in the 1979 election, they were not as large as they once were. In 1982, the newly appointed minister of finance launched what he referred to as a third way policy (almost a decade before the concept was launched by Tony Blair in the UK and Bill Clinton in the US). The third way policy was a way in which SAP could reaffirm the pragmatic stance between socialism and capitalism, this time through modest market solutions. LO opposed the policies so forcefully that they nearly broke relations with SAP. It was a 'War of the Roses', in light of the fact that the red rose was symbolic of social democracy.

In 1991, SAP lost the election once again to the conservatives and Sweden was rapidly dealing with financial austerity measures. A long line of reforms was implemented during the conservative government of 1991–1994, but these were essentially a consequence of the politics progressed by SAP during the 1980s. Although the conservatives surely did bring in neo-liberal policymaking during this period, SAP carries responsibility through its tenure in Swedish politics.

Swedish reforms – antecedents to a New Public Management

The constitution from 1809 can in many ways be understood as a starting point for the contemporary Swedish government. The constitution broke with the Gustavian autocracy stemming from the 1772 constitution, which was adopted after the *coup d'état* by King Gustav III. The 1809 constitution is based upon the separation of powers, leaving the king with the power of execution but essentially being responsible to the elected parliament.

The role of the higher civil servant came to be highlighted in the 1809 constitution. Holding public office came to be protected by law in that the king had no formal authority to remove civil servants without proper examination and judgement. In this respect, civil servants became appointed for life (Nilsson, 1999). The practice, however, of protecting civil servants was stated as early as 1719, in the royal declaration by Queen Ulrika Eleonora (cf. Nilsson, 1999). The 1809 constitution – stemming from the 1634 constitution – further contained a separation of politics and administration, in that politicians had no (formal) right of directly affecting the work of civil servants. This separation is focal in contemporary NPM reforms but was institutionalized quite early in Swedish public administration.

During the aftermath of World War II, Sweden was coping with a growing public sector. The welfare state grew fast and the need to analyse the manner in which public organizations and governmental agencies were managed became evident. In 1949, a group of officials was assigned the task of investigating how the public sector could be made more efficient. Minister Gunnar Danielson (SAP) argued in a public statement on 22 April 1949 that:

> In a time of pronounced scarcity of labour it is highly urgent, that one within the public administration as well as within the individual business, strictly economises with the available human resources.
>
> (SOU, 1950:8)

The group gave themselves the name '1949 Years Rationalisation Investigation' (Swedish: 1949 års Rationaliseringsutredning). Their task was to investigate different alternatives for rationalizing the public sector. In the governmental report they explicate their fundamental understanding of why the public sector should strive for rationalization:

> It is obvious that within a corporation the size of the Swedish central government, there always exists a latent need for rationalisation.
>
> (SOU 1950:8, p. 12)

The choice of associating the central government with a corporation should not be exaggerated, but it does suggest that the investigation glanced at the private sector in order to find ways in which efficiency could be gained. The concurrent search for ways in which activities could be rationalized is in itself indicative of a manner of trying to implement a basis for continuous improvements. Something that at this point in time – during the late 1940s – was well ahead of its time.

The 1949 Years Rationalisation Investigation furthermore argued that, in order to find inspiration and ideas concerning how to change the public sector, one needs to understand how the industries and foreign countries went about rationalizing (SOU 1950:8 sections 3 and 4, respectively). The latter included rather detailed descriptions from previous work undertaken in the US, the UK and the Scandinavian countries. This indicates a distinct characteristic of the Swedish society, namely its open nature in seeking ideas from other countries and readiness to transform such ideas into contextual reforms.

Accounting at this time followed the outline stated in the budgetary reform of 1911. The Swedish encyclopaedia Nordisk Familjebok points out that:

> The accounts shall be made when the relevant amounts are received paid and thus always relate to actual received or paid amounts.
>
> (Nordisk Familjebok, 1926, p. 486)

The 1911 budgetary reform clearly marked a beginning of cash-based budgeting. But, with rapidly increasing costs for the public sector during the post-World War II period, new reforms were investigated in order to come to terms with rapidly increasing public spending. In 1967 a governmental report was released, arguing for the need for better control and basis for analysis. It was stated that:

> Likewise, the need for improved control that the funds utilized are most efficiently used has become increasingly apparent. A more detailed analysis of the relationship between cost and performance in the public sector has come to be seen as desirable.
>
> (SOU 1967:11, p. 9)

During the 1960s there is already evidence that the public sector experimented with different ways of introducing managerial ideologies in organizations. In a way, it can be related to more recent fixations about management and means as creating focus from a control perspective, and thereby indicates a public management in emergence. One of the key aspects of achieving increased control and the ability to assess how performance was linked to established costs was argued to concern a fundamental change concerning the manner in which budgeting was undertaken. It was argued that although cash-based accounting and budgeting had in many respects achieved increased cost control during the first half of the twentieth century, there was dire need to change towards cost-based accounting and budgeting.

This reform came to be known as the implementation of programme budgeting (this is dicussed in SOU 1967:11, SOU 1967:12 and SOU 1967:13). The inherent aim of the programme budgeting reform was to create integrated systems, which extended the accounting within central government. Different programmes were constructed so that incurred costs could be linked to performance. This is stated in the governmental report as:

The core of a program budgeting system is an arrangement of the budget where operations have been divided by program. These programs represent plans of performance and costs of an activity – and aims to achieve a specified goal. Programs should therefore ideally be linked to any form of performance reporting.

(SOU 1967:13, p. 12)

In order to assess performance, the programme budgeting reform discussed the importance of goals. A close reading of the government reports discussing the reform (SOU 1967:11; SOU 1967:12; SOU 1967:13) reveals the progression of goals as focus for efficient control of central government. The actual assessment of performance was supposedly achieved by establishing goals expressed in terms of productivity, ideas not far from the management by objectives perspectives emerging during the mid–twentieth century (cf. Drucker, 1954). The report reflects on this by stating that:

The productivity concept that is commonly used within corporations can also be used within central government. When measuring productivity agencies' performance can be expressed either in physical measurement such as number, volume, and weight or in monetary terms.

(SOU 1967:13, p. 9)

It was furthermore stated that 'the economic assessments should therefore be based on a comparison of inputs and achievement at various alternatives' (SOU 1967:13, p. 12). In achieving this, the public sector launched different charts of accounts labelled 'S-plan' and 'K-plan'. These charts were derivative of the chart of accounts used within the for-profit industry – the 'M-plan' – wherein standards and GAAP were used.

The programme budgeting reform led to a time of trial and error within the Swedish central government during the late 1960s and early 1970s, and led to the implementation – among other things – of a more modern view of controlling the public sector: the government's Financial Management System (SEA, cf. SOU 2007:75, pp. 74–75) in 1975.[4] A central part of the SEA was to come to terms with some of the deficiencies of the programme budgeting reform and to further the implementation of assessing performance in relations to set goals. It is claimed (cf. Nordiska Ministerrådet, 1995) that the programme budgeting reform and implementation of the SEA firmly planted the idea of performance management and management by results within a Swedish setting. In a way, the programme budgeting reform arranged a scene on which further reforms could be implemented within the Swedish context.

As part of extending substantive knowledge about how central government should be organized and governed, the government authorized an official investigation to produce new insights on the matter. The report was named the Management Investigation[5] and was published in 1979 (SOU 1979:61). What is most interesting, in the context of public reforms, is where the Management Investigation looked for inspiration. In terms of organizational structures, there was a clear impact from the private sector, in that, for instance, matrix organizations were suggested to increase the opportunity for efficiency. In terms of 'flexible administration', the Management Investigation argued that:

> The matrix organization increases its contact surfaces with the surrounding world in that it can be divided into product type as well as geographical area. This allows that the agency's different parts can have good contact with customers within an area, while production can be kept cohesive.
>
> (SOU 1979:61, p. 148)

By adopting an organizational structure previously only observed in a few private-sector organizations, it was argued that the government could meet the 'stated requirements for a strengthened focus on profitability' (SOU 1979:61, p. 148). Granted, this discussion mainly concerns the public enterprises at the time, but it indicates how the Swedish public sector was not unfamiliar with adopting techniques and gathering inspiration from the private sector. Performance and profitability in terms of working towards situations wherein customers are satisfied arguably demands certain choices in terms of organization and control mechanisms.

By the end of the 1980s and beginning of the 1990s, public administration was heavily reformed. From politicians there were discussions about reducing the amount of explicit control in favour of allowing individual agencies to define how organization and work were to be implemented. This is evident in the supplementary proposition from 1988:

> Agencies are given progressively greater responsibility to run the activity with their own decision-making competence. The terms include a reduction of detailed regulation concerning the utilization of appropriations as well as such provisions and regulations that govern how activities must be organized and carried out.
>
> (Prop. 1987/88:150, Appendix 1, p. 69)

The 1988 Supplementary Proposition furthermore states that the work of agencies should be conducted with 'a high degree of pragmatism' in which agencies should 'develop forms of a goal and result oriented control' (Prop. 1987/88:150, Appendix 1, p. 69). Through the 1988 declaration, a clear separation between the government and its agencies was implemented. The issue was further investigated in the early 1990s, when a governmental report (SOU 1993:58, p. 13) suggested that agencies should be responsible for managing their organizations and activities to a larger extent and another report suggested that agencies in central government should publish annual reports following GAAP (SOU 1990:64, pp. 9–10). The government acknowledged this and expressed it in the following terms in the 1994 Supplementary Proposition:

> Management by results should lead to a clearer division of roles between the Riksdag, the Government, and agencies and a clearer division of responsibilities between the state, municipalities, organizations, and individuals.
>
> (Prop. 1993/94:150, Appendix 1, p. 103)

The Nordic Council of Ministers commented on the use of management by results one year later by stating that:

> Management by results must be combined with a financial control that shall consist of a variety of tools that help the business managers to meet the objectives.
>
> (Nordiska Ministerrådet, 1995, p. 79)

By the mid-1990s, a number of reforms focused on marketization were implemented. Although this happened at the time when the conservatives were in power (1991–1994, see the discussion above), the reforms can be understood to be a consequence of the politics and reforms from the 1960s up until the 1980s.

In the following three sections, the findings in this chapter will be discussed from three different, although interdependent, perspectives: responsive reforms, constitutional traditions and the historicity of social democracy. Together these three perspectives enable an understanding about the emergence of the Swedish welfare state and how NPM has come to fit with the public sector.

Responsive reforms

Sweden has a long tradition of adapting and adopting techniques. Inspiration has been sought wherever opportunities presented themselves, meaning that other nations such as the US or the UK have certainly played an important role in which and how reforms have been implemented in Sweden. Other sources of inspiration have been in the private sector, where techniques for increasing efficiency have emerged. In the previous section a review of historical documents was presented, with the purpose of uncovering how policymaking has continuously been influenced by this latter criterion: increasing efficiency.

The emergence of social democracy in Sweden can be understood from a class perspective, in that the working class strived for equality and equity. The formation of SAP and LO in the late nineteenth century is in many ways a turning point in Swedish history. The tight connection between SAP and LO further spurred Swedish employers to form their own confederation, SAF, in order to create a balance. In this manner, politics could be handled in parliament, whereas conditions in the workplaces became delegated to LO and SAF. The December Agreement in 1906 and the Saltsjöbaden Agreement in 1938 are probably the more prominent outcomes of this separation.

Right through the twentieth century, Sweden has implemented a number of rather salient reforms, all of which have been subjugated to initial investigation and argumentation. From the texts presented above, it is interesting to see how the argument has in many ways been firmly grounded in efforts towards efficiency. These texts not only predate NPM as a concept but were also published under the leadership of SAP. Although seemingly contradictory, explanations can be sought in the manner of constitutional traditions as well as in the historicity of social democracy in Sweden.

Figure 3.1 summarizes some of the key findings presented in this chapter. It reveals how social democracy and managerial reforms have progressed simultaneously during the twentieth century.

Constitutional traditions as an explanation

The extent to which NPM reforms have become adopted can to some extent be explained through the constitutional tradition wherein they were implemented. In this respect, two conceptually different traditions are commonly portrayed (cf. Pierre, 1995; Pollitt and Bouckaert, 2011): Anglo-Saxon and continental European traditions. The Anglo-Saxon tradition is predominantly focused on preserving a personal interest, wherein individualism is cherished. These traditions do uphold the sovereignty of the state, but reduces the interference it can or should have on citizens' lives. The continental European tradition is, on the other hand, focused on upholding law and continuing the Rechtsstaat. Within such traditions the state's importance is sovereign to its citizens, meaning that the state exercises the right of interference to a much higher degree.

Historically, the Anglo-Saxon traditions have proven to be responsive to NPM reforms. Marketization has had an especially great impact on the public sector within these traditions. Within the continental European traditions, however, NPM reforms have proven to be difficult. One explanation for the failure in these traditions may reside in the perception that citizens are not sovereign to their state but subject to the laws and regulations within. Under those instances, reforms that are perceived as subjugating the state's ability to interfere with citizens' lives are chafing against some taken-for-granted assumptions about the role of the public sector. NPM, thus, is perceived as threatening the very core of the constitution.

In terms of constitutional traditions, the Scandinavian welfare states can be understood as being an anomaly. As argued by Pollitt and Bouckaert (2011), Scandinavian states are primarily understood as holding a pragmatic stance towards the two traditions. Sweden is perhaps the most pragmatic of them. The pragmatic stance has – in Sweden – resulted in a long and strong tradition of

SAP and (some) policy reforms	(Management) Reforms
	1634 Politicians cannot control the activities of civil servants (constitution of 1634)
	1719 Royal Declaration of Queen Ulrika Eleonora
	1809 The protection of higher civil servants from the King, established in the 1809 constitution
SAP was formed 1889	
LO was formed 1898	
SAF was formed 1902	
The December Agreement 1906 between LO and SAF	
Hjalmar Branting: party leader for SAP 1908	
	1911 Budget reform for central government
The 'Breaking Time' congress 1917	
General suffrage was implemented 1918	
8-hour work days were implemented 1919	
Per-Albin Hansson: party leader 1928 for SAP	
SAP gains 41.1% of the votes 1932 in general election	
Saltsjöbaden Agreement 1938	
	1949 The Rationalisation Investigation
General and mandatory pension 1950	
	1967 Programme Budgeting
40-hour work week 1970	
SAP loses to the Conservatives 1976	1975 SEA was launched
SAP regains power 1979	1979 The Management Investigation
Minister of Finance (SAP) launches 1982 'The Third Way Policy'	
The War of the Roses 1983	
	1988 Supplementary proposition
SAP loses 1991	
SAP regains power 1994	1994 Supplementary proposition

Figure 3.1 The progression of Swedish social democracy and some governmental (managerial) reforms.

neutral civil servants primarily adhering to the constitution rather than to politicians. This separation of politics and administration has in turn resulted in a responsive and flexible stance in which the citizens' well-being has become prioritized.

From a constitutional traditions perspective, the reforms portrayed in this chapter become more understandable. On the one hand, the combination of the Anglo-Saxon and continental European traditions has infused the welfare state with a pragmatic and flexible stance towards public administration. On the other hand, the pragmatism inherent in the policymaking of SAP during the twentieth century – especially with the construction of a People's Home, which virtually attacked the traditional class struggle in favour of equality for all – instigated a possibility of adapting and adopting new influences towards public administration.

Historicity as an explanation

Understanding the growth and intensification of certain reforms within the Swedish welfare state can be understood from a historicity perspective. According to this stance, social democracy in Sweden can in many ways be understood as a state bearing ideology that has helped to shape Sweden's modern welfare state.

The social democratic history is one in which the struggle for equality is central. During the nineteenth century the task of social democrats was therefore one of reallocating employers' power to organize and control the workplace to the employees. Around the turn of the twentieth century, this task was, however, seemingly overtaken by the union confederation in Sweden (LO). Social democracy in the form of SAP could thereby focus on other issues of policy implementation.

The pragmatic stance of SAP has been an issue throughout this chapter. According to Olofsson (1979), Swedish social democracy should be understood as political pragmatism, wherein socialism is combined with capitalism so that equality is favoured first. The open congress of 1917 (the 'Breaking Time'), in which the radical left-wing phalanx left the party, and the support of the 'Saltsjöbaden Agreement' in 1938 are indicative of such a stance.

With the end of World War II, Sweden was experiencing rapid economic growth. At the same time SAP was dominating Swedish politics, holding office largely uninterrupted between 1932 up until 1976.[6] This provided a good opportunity to expand the public sector and the general welfare. This is evident from the expansion undertaken during, in particular, the 1950s and 1960s, in regards to a general mandatory pension and the social insurance. Around that time, the Rationalisation Investigation was launched, searching for means by which the public sector could be organized and controlled in an efficient manner.

By the end of the 1970s, a number of things were happening to the public sector. One thing was that productivity within the public sector was declining (cf. Skr. 1984/85:202). Although it was expanding, it was doing so without retaining the efficiency in which welfare could be produced and offered to citizens in a sustainable manner. In addition, the oil crisis of 1973 had put serious restraints on the economic growth.

In a comparative analysis between Swedish and Danish social democracy, Green–Pedersen (2002) found that Sweden was more readily implementing NPM reforms – especially marketization – during the 1990s. Although the analysis focuses on the 1980s and 1990s, the explanation can be valid from a longer perspective. One conclusion held forth in Green–Pedersen's analysis was the responsibility of SAP as a state bearing party. Given its long reign of (political) power in Sweden, SAP was in large responsible for the expansion and development of the Swedish welfare state. That is, in many ways the Swedish welfare state was a project primarily owned by SAP. As the public sector became strained during the 1970s, SAP had an obligation to present valid alternatives.

In this precarious situation, SAP drew on a history of deliberation between socialism and capitalism – pragmatism and reformism functioning as a backdrop for equality without class struggle – and argued for implementing alternative techniques. That is, their choices, stemming from the 'Breaking Time' and the 'People's Home', paved the way for the possibility of SAP being influenced by how the private sector was undertaking issues of control and organization. Or, from another perspective, the pragmatic position, where socialism is combined with capitalism. The affirmation of acknowledging merits from the public sector as well as the private sector has been evident throughout the twentieth century, and became especially salient through the 'War of the Roses' during the 1980s.

Similar findings have been made in a study of the Finnish public sector. Yliaska (2015) found that in Finland the 1970s were characterized by a number of reforms innately implemented in order to increase efficiency. These reforms, had they been implemented today, would have been characterized as fitting firmly within the neo-liberal NPM paradigm. But the fact that these were implemented during the 1970s, predominantly under Social Democratic leadership, negates the neo-liberal explanation. In this case, the Finnish and Swedish progresses are similar.

The way forward

The main contribution of this chapter is an emancipatory confrontation of some established ideas concerning NPM reforms in Sweden: that it is primarily an effect of neo-liberal policymaking in the UK and USA. Several Swedish texts from the twentieth century suggest governmental reforms with clear inspiration from the private sector. In particular, the reforms during the 1950s and 1960s are indicative of an ambition to adapt and adopt. The implementation of reforms under the intention of achieving increased efficiency was progressed during a time period when social democracy dominated policymaking in Sweden.

NPM reforms that became observable, although not discussed in this chapter, during the 1990s in Sweden should not be understood as an emergence of something new but rather as an intensification of an already begun adaption and adoption of private-sector techniques. It was not so much a question of adopting techniques used within the UK and the USA as it was a result of historically embedded reform adaptability within the Swedish public-sector tradition. Interestingly in this respect, Lapsley (2008) found that the embedded nature of professional boundaries within the UK actually constrained managerial change, serving as an institutional hindrance for NPM to be implemented. In Sweden the contrary is suggested, leading to a situation wherein adaptability dominated resistance.

After this exposé one has to ask whether NPM reforms in Sweden really are a result of neo-liberal policymaking, or if this is a convenient way of masking a general distaste for reforms within the public sector in general. The merits of the criticism against NPM and its neo-liberal historicity have to be challenged and questioned. The distinctive nature of Swedish New Public Management and its historicity has been largely neglected in previous research. In this chapter it has been shown how Sweden has been a responsive context for a general dispersion of NPM.

Notes

1 Swedish: Socialdemokratiska Arbetarpartiet, SAP.
2 Swedish: Landsorganisationen, LO.
3 Swedish: Svenska Arbetsgivarförening, SAF.
4 Swedish: Statens ekonomiadministrativa system.
5 Swedish: Förvaltningsutredningen.
6 For a period of three months during 1936 the Agrarian Party led a minority government.

References

Almqvist, R. (2001) '"Management by contract": a study of programmatic and technological aspects'. *Public Administration – An International Quarterly*, Vol. 79, No. 3, pp. 689–706.
Almqvist, R. (2004) *Icons of New Public Management: Four Studies on Competition, Contracts and Control* (Stockholm: Stockholm University).
Bryntse, K. (2000) *Kontraktsstyrning i teori och praktik.* Dissertation, Lund University.
Byrman, Y. (2007) *Restaurangen har inga – Försäkringskassan har 9 miljoner: Bruket av och attityder till ordet kund* (Stockholm: Stockholm University Examensarbete).
Cheung, A. B. L. (1997) 'Understanding public-sector reforms: global trends and diverse agendas'. *International Review of Administrative Sciences*, Vol. 63, pp. 435–457.
Damm, M. (2014) *Läkarinfarkt: En effekt av new public management (npm)* (Lund: Studentlitteratur).
Drucker, P. F. (1954) *The Practice of Management* (New York: Harper & Brothers).
Funck, E. K. and R. G. Larsson (2014) 'The rise and fall of the balanced scorecard in municipalities and county councils in Sweden'. *Working Paper – Centre for Management Accounting Research (CMAR)* No. 2014:1.

Glenngård, A. H. (2013) *Objectives, Actors and Accountability in Quasi-markets: Studies of Swedish Primary Care*. Dissertation, Lund University.

Green-Pedersen, C. (2001) 'Welfare-state retrenchment in Denmark and the Netherlands, 1982–1998: the role of party competition and party consensus'. *Comparative Political Studies*, Vol. 34, No. 9, pp. 963–985.

Green-Pedersen, C. (2002) 'New public management reforms of the Danish and Swedish welfare states: the role of different social democratic responses'. *Governance*, Vol. 15, No. 2, p. 271.

Hood, C. (1991) 'A public management for all seasons?'. *Public Administration*, Vol. 6, No. 3, pp. 3–19.

Hood, C. (1995) 'The "new public management" in the 1980s: variations on a theme'. *Accounting, Organizations and Society*, Vol. 20, Nos. 2–3, pp. 93–110.

Huzell, H. (2005) *Management och motstånd: Offentlig sektor i omvandling – en fallstudie*. Dissertation, Karlstad University.

Karlsson, T. S. (2012) Organisering och styrning för ökad enhetlighet, in F. Andersson, T. Bergström, L. Bringselius, M. Dackehag, T. S. Karlsson, S. Melander and G. Paulsson (eds), *Speglingar av en förvaltning i förändring: Reformeringen av Försäkringskassan* (Stockholm: Santérus).

Karlsson, T. S. (2014) *Manager and Civil Servant: Exploring Actors' Taken-for-granted Assumptions in Public Administration*. (Lund: Lund University).

Lapsley, I. (2008) 'The NPM agenda: back to the future'. *Financial Accountability & Management*, Vol. 24, No. 1, pp. 77–96.

Modell, S. (2005) 'Students as consumers? An institutional field-level analysis of the construction of performance measurement practices'. *Accounting, Auditing & Accountability Journal*, Vol. 18, No. 4, pp. 537–563.

Modell, S. (2009) 'Bundling management control innovations: a field study of organisational experimenting with total quality management and the balanced scorecard'. *Accounting, Auditing & Accountability Journal*, Vol. 22, No. 1, pp. 59–90.

Modell, S. and F. Wiesel (2008) 'Marketization and performance measurement in Swedish central government: a comparative institutionalist study'. *Abacus*, Vol. 44, No. 3, pp. 251–251.

Nilsson, T. (1999) 'Staten och den oavsättlige ämbetsmannen – ett komplicerat förhållande'. *Statsvetenskaplig tidskrift*, Vol. 102, No. 2, pp. 113–137.

Nordisk Familjebok (1926) Trettiåttonde bandet supplement: Riksdagens bibliotek – öyen, in V. Leche, G. Nordensvan and T. Westrin (eds), *Nordisk Familjebok: Konversationslexikon och realencyklopedi*, Uggleupplagan, andra upplagan (Stockholm: Nordisk Familjeboks Förlags Aktiebolag).

Nordiska Ministerrådet (1995) *Effektivisering av välfärdsstaten: Rapport från ett seminarie 16–17 mars 1995, Reykjavik, Island* (Copenhagen: N. Ministerråd).

Ohlsson, P. T. (2014) *Svensk politik* (Lund: Historiska Media).

Olofsson, G. (1979) *Mellan klass och stat: Om arbetarrörelse, reformism och socialdemokrati* (Lund: Lund University).

Pierre, J. (1995) *Bureaucracy in the Modern State: An Introduction to Comparative Public Administration* (Aldershot: Edward Elgar).

Pollitt, C. (1993) *Managerialism and the Public Services: Cuts or Cultural Change in the 1990s?* 2nd edition (Oxford: Blackwell).

Pollitt, C. and G. Bouckaert (2011) *Public Management Reform: A Comparative Analysis – New Public Management, Governance, and the Neo-Weberian State* (Oxford: Oxford University Press).

52   T. S. Karlsson

Prop. 1987/88:150 *Regeringens proposition1987/88:150: Med förslag till slutlig reglering av statsbudgeten för budgetåret 1988/89 m.M. (kompletteringsproposition)*, Finansdepartementet (ed.) (Stockholm: Regeringen).

Prop. 1993/94:150 *Regeringens proposition: Förslag till slutlig reglering av statsbudgeten för budgetåret 1994/95, m.M. (kompletteringspropositionen)*, Finansdepartementet (ed.) (Stockholm: Regeringen).

Skr. 1984/85:202 *Regeringens skrivelse om den offentliga sektorns förnyelse* (Stockholm).

SOU 1950:8 *Rationaliseiringsverksamheten inom den offentliga sektorn* (Stockholm).

SOU 1967:11 *Programbudgetering (1)*, Statskontoret (ed.) (Stockholm).

SOU 1967:12 *Programbudgetering: Studier och försök (2)* (Stockholm: Statskontoret).

SOU 1967:13 *Programbudgetering: En sammanfattning (del 3)* (Stockholm: Statskontoret).

SOU 1979:61 *Förnyelse genom omprövning* (Stockholm: Huvudbetänkande från förvaltningsutredningen).

SOU 1990:64 *Årlig revision i statsförvaltningen* (Stockholm: Betänkande av revisionsutredningen).

SOU 1993:58 *Effektivare ledning i statliga myndigheten* (Stockholm: Betänkande av kommittén om förvaltningsmyndigheternas ledningsformer).

SOU 2007:75 *Att styra staten: Regeringens styrning av sin förvaltning* (Stockholm: B. A. Styrutredningen).

Wockelberg, H. and S. Ahlbäck Öberg (2014) *Reinventing the Old Reform Agenda: Public Administrative Reform and Performance According to Swedish Top Managers* (Cheltenham: Edward Elgar).

Yliaska, V. (2015) 'New public management as a response to the crisis of the 1970s: the case of Finland, 1970–1990'. *Contemporary European History*, Vol. 24, No. 3, p. 435.

4 Challenging the myth of NPM in Denmark

An argument from the health system

Nikolaj Kure and Margit Malmmose

Summary

This chapter presents a critical angle on New Public Management in the Danish health sector. While the Danish case is often associated with positive values, such as involvement, local democracy and dialogue, the current chapter aims at offering an alternative interpretation of the Danish NPM story as a story of invisible power operations. Based on the analysis of a performance measurement initiative at two hospital departments, the paper demonstrates how the departments are formally given the freedom to choose the indicators they prefer while in reality their freedom is restricted by what Foucault refers to as 'modern power'. Thus, we argue that the employees are made responsible for interpreting how top management views the world, which translates into the development of a set of performance indicators that looks suspiciously similar to the ones preferred by senior management. In this regard, the chapter contends that the myth of Danish democratic NPM processes blurs the power operations that do take place and that this blurring may imply an even stronger element of power than a top-down approach.

Introduction

Different accounts have been given as to how and when New Public Management (NPM) enters the Danish public scene. While Hood (1995) argues that Denmark gradually begins to display some NPM traits as soon as the early 1990s, Greve (2015) contends that the public modernization programmes carried out in the 1980s and 1990s, albeit ripe with NPM rhetoric, were in fact oriented towards collaboration and digitalization. As described by Jensen (1998), this may be down to strong local professional resistance against the entire idea of NPM, making the implementation process fraught with difficulties. Gradually, however, the resistance begins to falter and, in particular, the Structural Reform in 2004 paves the way for NPM as the dominant management ideology in the Danish public sector (Greve, 2006, Tanggaard Andersen and Jensen, 2010). The aim of this chapter is to describe how the introduction of NPM in Denmark, while maintaining a high degree of local decision autonomy, marks the beginning of a new type of power operations, one which relies on the ability of employees to actively anticipate the wants and needs of managers.

Different typologies have been proposed to classify how countries conceptualize and implement NPM. For instance, Pollitt and Bouckaert (2004, 2011) distinguish between marketizers and modernizers,[1] while Hood and Peters (2004) suggest a similar distinction between 'hares' and 'tortoises'. 'Hares', as the term connotes, are the countries that jump straight at it (sometimes overreaching themselves in the process), while the 'tortoises' apply a more cautious approach, introducing reforms in a more steady and often more successful manner. While these distinctions appear to be neutral reflections of how NPM practices are implemented, they often have an inbuilt normative bias towards one end of the extreme. To apply a modernization strategy, surely, is a much less brutal process than putting the raw market forces at play, as is proposed by the marketizers. And, similarly, a slow-paced tortoise-like strategy allows for citizens and employees to be heard in the decision process (as opposed to a 'hare strategy'), while a local anchorage of NPM processes stimulates a sense of ownership and responsibility. It seems that the one end of the theoretical extreme is discursively related to values that are deemed culturally 'good' (such as decentralization, consensus, delegation, self-determination, democracy, voluntary participation and bottom–up processes) while the opposite extreme is associated with practices and values that are considered problematic or bad (such as explicit power, instructions and central decision-making).

In the current storyline, Denmark is univocally placed at the preferred end of the scale. Largely, the Danish NPM story is about partnerships, low-paced democratic decision-making and decentralized processes (Kirkpatrick *et al.*, 2013, pp. S57–S58), which solidly places Denmark in the 'modernizing/tortoise' camp. Top rankings in OECD's Transparency Index[2] and Better Life Index[3] underline the argument, suggesting that the Danish case is indeed a 'good' case. Greve (2006) sums up the position with much precision:

> Denmark has 'modernized' to a great extent and 'marketized' to a lesser extent. Radical marketization strategies have been held back, as there has not been a majority in Parliament for such a strategy, and there is consensus on developing the public sector rather than dismantling or minimizing it.
>
> (Greve, 2006, p. 168)

While we certainly acknowledge that NPM processes in Denmark have been characterized by involvement and local democracy, we propose, in continuation of Kirkpatrick *et al.*'s (2013) concerns about the feasibility of implementing NPM in countries like Denmark, that a reinterpretation of the above story is needed. We suggest that the agreed-upon picture is too simplistic and too positive as it fails to grasp the complex power processes that actually take place in the field. In fact, we contend that, while we are led to believe that virtually no power relations are at play in the Danish context, the very fact that we believe this to be true creates even more space for what Foucault refers to as 'modern power' (Foucault, 1982). What appears to be a story of voluntary participation and self-determination is, we advocate, more accurately described as a myth, a fiction that paints a positive image of the Danish case and thereby obscures what we believe are very real and forceful power processes. In the current paper, we illustrate this alternative interpretation by means of a case study of the so-called 'New Control from a Patient Perspective' − a regional (RegionMidt) initiative that asks hospital departments to develop their own individualized qualitative performance measures.

The Danish health care sector: setting the scene

The Danish health care system consists of three different responsibility centres; the ministry, the regions and the municipalities. The ministry is in charge of resource allocation while the five regions are responsible for operating hospitals and for funding private practitioners. The municipalities are responsible for preventive medicine, health promotion and rehabilitation outside of hospitals (Strandberg-Larsen *et al.*, 2007; The Danish Health Ministry, 2004). Danish general practitioners, specialists and hospitals are free of charge and fully publicly funded. However, co-payments are expected for dentists, medicines and glasses (Olejaz *et al.*, 2012).

Historically, the Danish health sector has been managed according to principles of decentralization and local decision-making (Christiansen, 2002). In fact, the entire Danish labour market is regulated on a highly local basis as wage levels, working conditions etc. are negotiated locally by labour unions and employer organizations without the interference of the central government (Andersen *et al.*, 2010). This preference towards decentralization has been supported by a tradition of consensus law making (Kirkpatrick *et al.*, 2011) and a working culture that values agreements, unification and modesty (Nørreklit *et al.*, 2006). In the health sector, the trend has been further exacerbated by the existence of a strong and powerful medical profession (Dich, 1974; Jespersen *et al.*, 2002; Kirkpatrick *et al.*, 2011), which has been able to keep interference from national politicians and administrators at bay. Even the national quality model for hospitals[4] implicitly emphasizes the cultural value of decentralization in being an accreditation model that hospitals may or may not choose to comply with.

The decentralization embedded in the Danish system resonates well with the local anchorage of decision-making that is built into most NPM practices. However, while the NPM type of decentralization is driven by a desire to make local units accountable, the type of decentralization that is present in the Danish context is the result of a long historical and political process putting values such as democracy and self-autonomy at the heart of Danish institutions (Nørreklit *et al.*, 2006). Therefore, while NPM in an Anglo-Saxon context is often associated with a movement towards a higher degree of decentralization, the opposite seems to be true in Denmark. In fact, the implementation of NPM in Denmark has been pushed through by a number of centralized reforms that have passed parliament (Tanggaard Andersen and Jensen, 2010) in recent years (Olejaz et al., 2012; Vrangbæk and Christiansen, 2005). This trend towards centralization of decision-making has been powered further by a number of problems that become apparent around the mid-1990s. First and foremost, it becomes a political problem that hospitals are not able to reduce the length of their waiting lists (Pedersen et al., 2005). More and more people are faced with lengthy spells on waiting lists, resulting in public debates and a firm placement of hospitals' waiting lists on the news agenda. Additionally, Denmark is no exception to the escalating health care expenses that have tripled across OECD countries during the past 30 years (OECD, 2012).

These challenges stimulate a strict focus on productivity and costing in the health sector. This focus is particularly prevalent in the so-called 'Structural Reform' from 2004 (Malmmose, 2015a; Tanggaard Andersen and Jensen, 2010), which seeks to maintain a decentralized managerial sovereignty on the part of the hospitals (Bech, 2006) while also making the hospitals responsible for reaching specific levels of productivity. The basic idea is that the productivity level of any hospital department is established through a performance budget with an attached baseline demand (Felsager Jakobsen, 2014). The baseline is an activity level which is calculated from a specific population formula and is based on last year's activity plus 2 per cent (Dørken et al., 2012). In alignment with the global NPM trend (Malmmose, 2015b; World Health Organization, 1988), Diagnostic Related Groupings (DRG) are adopted from so-called 'best practices' (Forgione et al., 2005) to estimate the appurtenant costs by providing an average operating costs associated with a specific diagnosis. This, in combination with a governmental sanction-and-reward policy of adding/withdrawing 50 per cent of the relevant DRG level in the event of a deviating productivity level (Bilde et al., 2010), indicate that the health care system is perhaps the public service that has been pervaded the most in Denmark by the NPM logic.

In terms of productivity, the results have been unequivocal. The waiting lists have been reduced and the level of productivity has skyrocketed. While the treatment quantity, thus, has increased, a number of concerns have been raised about a simultaneous decline in treatment quality (Cardinaels and Soderstrom, 2013). Despite this type of criticism, the DRG calculations have been maintained as a resource allocation tool. However, a number of initiatives have been taken to address the question of treatment quality. Among these are an increased focus on quality data and the appointment of quality managers at all Danish hospitals. Furthermore, RegionMidt has called for all hospitals to supplement their financial reports with 12 quality measures, including the length of time from the patient's first encounter with the health system to a diagnosis being made (the aim is 30 days), a reduced use of force in the psychiatric ward, a reduction of mortality and a reduction of readmissions.

The legitimate case of 'New Control from a Patient Perspective'

Another significant quality initiative taken by RegionMidt, which has gained national as well international attention, is the so-called 'New Control from a Patient Perspective'. In 2013, when the initiative was launched, RegionMidt saw an opportunity to escape the unilateral focus on financial incentives. At the time, expenditure had been curbed and waiting lists had been significantly reduced, so now was the time to focus on quality in treatment. On top of this, the public debate demanded a focus on what appeared to be a decline in treatment quality. In this context, the New Control initiative was launched in an effort to develop a new type of incentive structure that increased quality while also sustaining current productivity levels. The concrete aim was to have a small number of hospital departments develop their own individualized incentive structure in order to generate a focus on both aspects of quality and productivity. The experiment was scheduled to run for two years, during which the DRG focus was suspended for the involved departments (starting 1 January 2014). In the course of this period, the departments were asked to develop and test 3–5 meaningful quality indicators that should ideally reflect the departments' aims and *raisons d'être* (Søgaard *et al.*, 2015). Nine neurological hospital departments were included in the initiative, of which five were situated at the same neurological centre at RegionMidt's university hospital. The four remaining departments were situated at three regional hospitals. Methodologically, the initiative took a bottom–up approach. Personnel with first-hand knowledge of patients' needs and hands-on treatment experience, i.e. doctors and nurses, were supposed to be in charge of the process. In this sense, the project reached back to the Danish decentralized consensus-seeking working culture with an interest in a united and concerted contribution to decision-making.

In December 2013, the two departments were asked to provide the first draft of the performance indicators. Therefore, a number of meetings/workshops were arranged to get the process started. As the project's overall intention was to unshackle the departments from the strict DRG focus, we would expect to see the development of indicators that highlight various qualitative aspects of hospital treatment, such as safety in treatment, thoroughness in treatment, individualized treatment etc. (Piligrimiené and Buciuniene, 2008). The findings, however, point to the opposite. As illustrated in Table 4.1, the departments surprisingly tend to select the exact measures that the initiative is meant to challenge, namely measures of productivity.

A closer look at Table 4.1 reveals a predominant focus on efficiency, with strong links to the original DRG focus. For instance, the intentions to decrease cancelled surgeries, increase outpatient treatments and decrease number of visits per patient signal a strong desire to optimize productivity and reduce costs. In fact, the Department of Ophthalmology has exclusively chosen targets of productivity while the Department of Oral- and Maxillofacial

Table 4.1 Developed indicators

Department	Indicator	Target	Realized 2014
Ophthalmology	Number of unique CPRs (social security numbers)	No decrease	Increase 2.1%
	Number of surgeries being cancelled	Increase	15.34% cancelled
	Number of outpatient visits per patient per year	Difference per diagnostic group	n/a
	Time from the patient's arrival to departure in the outpatient clinic	Decrease	n/a
Oral- and maxillofacial surgery	Number of unique CPRs (social security numbers)	No decrease	Decreased 4%
	Number of outpatient visits per treatment	Decrease	Increase 1%
	Number of patients having their surgery in the outpatient clinic (instead of inpatient)	Increase	Increase 28.9%
	Number of inpatient patients	Decrease	Decrease 16.2%
	Employee satisfaction based on 10 questions	No decrease	n/a
	Patient satisfaction based on five questions – just a particular patient group	Increase	The region has put it on hold[1]

Note
1 This measure was put on hold by the region, who wanted all departments to use the same standardized patient satisfaction survey. However, as each department had different views on what characterized a 'satisfied patient', the region didn't succeed in this.

Surgery has chosen three productivity targets out of five. Thus, the economic discourse is sustained, despite an explicit intention to develop a more patient-oriented and humanistic view on quality.

We find this extremely puzzling: finally, health care professionals are given the opportunity to return to their humanitarian roots and, bafflingly, they opt to follow an economic discourse of productivity? A possible explanation to this paradox is a purely discursive one: due to the power of calculative arguments (Miller and Rose, 1990) and audits (Power, 1997), the humanitarian language no longer works as a legitimate organizational discourse, making it virtually impossible to make references to a humanistic discourse in the development of new quality measures. The economic discourse dominates hospital language to the extent that no alternatives are readily available. While this explanation certainly has some merit and has been widely supported in research (Cardinaels and Soderstrom, 2013), we believe the argument can be extended further to a question of power: the absence of humanitarian quality measures is not only caused by the absence of a humanitarian language; it is also driven by subtle and invisible power processes that dispose health professionals to actively prioritize an economic reasoning at the expense of a humanistic one. To flesh out this argument, we build on Michel Foucault's notion of 'modern power' (Foucault, 1982).

The subjacent power at play

In a traditional understanding of power, the main distinction is one between coercion and freedom. Either you are forced to carry out actions by someone else or you are free to choose for yourself. While this distinction certainly has some explanatory value, it fails to tell the full story of how power works in the modern era. In fact, according to Foucault (1982), power, while often being confused with coercion, actually presupposes the very absence of coercion. In other words, power works when it manages to hide the fact that it is power. Therefore, modern power has no physical manifestations; it is invisible and operates without the use of traditional power tools, such as the physical presence of powerful persons, instructions and sanctions. This notion, which has been extensively highlighted in the accounting literature (see for example Miller and O'Leary, 1987, and Miller and Rose, 1990), enables the transfer of complexity from the part of the powerful to the part of the powerless (Åkerstrøm Andersen, 2009, p. 120). When everybody knows that the superior wants something but the superior does not make this explicit, it becomes the task of the powerless to anticipate what the superior wants. In this sense, modern power makes the powerless responsible for continuously interpreting how the world appears from the point of view of the superior, actively searching for ways of anticipating and handling this complexity. Thus, modern power feeds on both insecurity and freedom: when the powerless are insecure of what the powerful wants, they are effectively asked to use their apparent freedom to steer themselves on the basis of what they think their superiors want.

If we return to the two empirical cases, there can be no doubt that the hospital senior management teams are put in complex situations. On the one hand, hospitals are called on by the central government to develop strategies to handle the dual problems of efficiency and productivity. If hospitals fail to do this in a convincing way, they effectively shut themselves down as allocation of resources happens on the basis of levels of productivity. On the other hand, the region (i.e. the organizational level below the government) expects the hospitals to demonstrate an ability to integrate the patient's perspective through a qualitative performance measure system. As mentioned, this latter expectation is a part of a more pervasive macro-discourse of quality that has gained impasse in recent years in the Danish context.

It is important to note that the hospitals need to live up to both of these opposing expectations. The external environment demands both and so a hospital that puts emphasis on one aspect only is hardly legitimate in the eyes of external stakeholders (see Tanggaard Andersen (2010) for more elaboration on this topic in the light of the Danish Structural Reform in 2004). Thus, the hospital's senior management teams appear to be caught in what Gregory Bateson refers to as a 'double bind' (Jackson *et al.*, 1956). A double bind is a paradoxical communicative situation in which two expectations mutually exclude each other. In this case, when hospitals are both required to develop mechanistic systems that put unilateral emphasis on the quantity of services and to focus on the improvement of service quality they are effectively placed in a paradoxical communicative situation that cannot simply be solved by rational decision-making. It turns out that the situation is not just complex; it is paradoxical and therefore essentially impossible to dissolve.

What does one do when placed in such situations? Due to the decentralized management tradition in Denmark, Danish hospitals have a number of potential strategies at their disposal, including a strategy to balance the need for internal management autonomy with the external standards of productivity (Bech, 2006). In this case, however, the data suggests that senior management handles the paradox by transferring it to the departmental level. The departments are effectively asked to develop an incentive structure that deals with the paradoxical situation which was initially on the plate of senior management. The story is this:

Senior management knows that it has a paradoxical situation on its hands. Therefore, local workshops are organized where departments are explicitly asked to develop new qualitative measures for treatment. In this context, the message to the departments is quite clear: 'be free to develop the quality criteria that you see fit'. At the same time, however, a more subtle communicative stream flows through the workshops. In particular, two interesting communications stand out at the initial meetings between senior managers and department managers in 2013. First, department managers are told that the new measures should be in line with the so-called Triple Aim Strategy. The Triple Aim Strategy defines three overall targets: (1) to increase patient health, (2) to increase patient experience of treatment quality and, crucially,

(3) to control costs while doing (1) and (2). This means that participants are effectively asked to impose an economic logic on their quality criteria and thus the message to the departments seems to be: 'by all means, go ahead and develop new criteria of treatment quality but do so under strict consideration of the primary logic of productivity'. Second, department managers are given a very short time span (only a few weeks) to develop the new quality criteria and are also advised to reach consensus across the departments as to which criteria to select. This creates a pressure to pick measures that are already in place in the system, i.e. measures that are developed in the frame of the economic discourse. In any case, if the departments are to follow the guidelines it is nigh on impossible to develop entirely new and innovative performance measures. Neither the strict time frame nor the call for consensus allows this. Instead, the more likely interpretation is that senior management simply indicates that it wants the departments to develop measures that follow the efficiency logic already in place. It thus appears that hospital senior management's communication takes place at two distinct levels. At an explicit level (which Bateson refers to as the communicative level), senior management communicates a desire to have departments develop new qualitative criteria. At another, more implicit level (which Bateson refers to as the meta-communicative level), senior management indicates that it wants a focus on quantity.

By implication, this communicative pattern makes the departments responsible for handling the paradox which was originally on senior management's plate. The paradox is simply copied and presented to the departments as their problem. This, however, is bound to create a sense of insecurity at the departments: senior management does not make explicit whether it wants quality to be prioritized at the expense of quantity or the other way around – they simply demand both at the same time (which is equivalent to asking the departments to have their cake and eat it too). So what, if anything, does senior management really want from the departments? Naturally, we are unable to provide any definitive answers to this question but we may make a qualified assessment by means of theoretical deduction. Thus, if we follow Meyer and Rowan's (1977) seminal analysis of organizational legitimacy, senior managers' key concern is to construe legitimacy by adapting to so-called 'institutionalized myths' in the external environment. In our case, senior management is under pressure from the region to focus on quality and from the government to focus on quantity/productivity – and only if it succeeds in both tasks will the hospital as a publicly funded organization be considered legitimate. This means that senior managers are essentially unable to clarify what they want the departments to do: if senior managers make clear they want a stringent focus on quality, they do not live up to the 'institutional myth' of quantity; if they make clear that they want a unilateral focus on quantity, they do not live up to the standards of quality. In effect, top managers simply opt to demand both of the departments, thereby living up to both of the above legitimizing demands but at the unfortunate cost of displacing the paradox to the departmental level.

However, this is not the full story. As it stands, senior managers need cooperation from the departments if they are to succeed in their endeavour to construe external legitimacy. For instance, if workshop participants choose to expose or reject the paradox (which, at least in theory, was entirely possible) the entire 'operation external legitimacy' would be jeopardized. So, returning to the above question, what do the senior managers really want from the workshop participants? Again, we are unable to make too definitive claims but if we accept that top managers are preoccupied with external legitimacy it would undoubtedly suit them if participants took part in the workshops as if the aim were to develop quality indicators while in reality developing productivity indicators. In other words, senior managers' intention to develop external legitimacy would be supported if workshop participants enacted a play that appeared to be about quality but which, in reality, was about productivity.

The catch is that senior managers cannot specify this intention. Instead they need to rely on the ability of workshop participants to anticipate it. In Foucauldian terms, they need participants to voluntarily restrict their freedom by means of self-disciplinary measures. Apparently, as indicated in Table 4.1, the departments get the point. For example, when the incentive system is discussed in the workshops it is perceived to be of extreme importance that the indicators are already in place in the department's database. In fact, it appears to be a precondition that the measures are already there and, thus, the workshops play out as discussions of which of the existing measures to choose, not which new measures of quality should be developed. Furthermore, it is crucial for the department management that the indicators contain a potential for improvement. The interviews illustrate that the departments clearly understand that the most legitimate measurements are quantifiable in terms of improvements in productivity, thereby defeating the explicit (qualitative) purpose of the initiative. There is no doubt that departments attempt to 'do the right thing', i.e. develop quality criteria from the point of view of the patient, but both departments experience challenges in doing so as it hinders complying with the demands of the productivity discourse. Ultimately, the departments adopt an efficiency discourse which becomes discursively privileged to the patient perspective.

These and similar examples illustrate that the departments are not simply free to choose whatever they see fit. Put bluntly, employees and department managers are free to choose what they think their superiors want them to choose. This interpretation of Danish NPM practices challenges the story of the Danish consensus-seeking tradition and its partiality to democracy, delegation and autonomous decision-making as an unequivocal positive story. Instead, the case demonstrates that the delegated freedom has the full potential of manifesting invisible power operations that structure how employees make decisions. In this sense, the economic discourse seems to shroud its own significance by rearticulating patient-focused measures as questions of quantity and productivity. At a surface level, participants talk about quality but on closer inspection they really talk about quantity. It thus appears that the economic discourse has managed to naturalize and normalize itself as a perspective that cannot be questioned by health professionals. This invisible embeddedness in social practices is what Foucault refers to as 'the ultimate sovereignty' (Foucault, 1982; Foucault, 1991).

The way forward

The above case demonstrates an alternative interpretation of what is elsewhere characterized as a 'feel-good' democracy with delegated freedom and local responsibilities. It illustrates some of the underlying facets of power which result in limitations of freedom and demonstrates how the economic discourse of productivity is sustained despite an initial willingness to become more oriented towards quality. This finding is supported by Cardinaels and Soderstrom (2013), who show how the intention of focusing on quality often becomes secondary due to costing pressure. The current chapter illustrates how a highly wanted quality focus is effectively neglected and it pins down some of these contradictory processes. The hidden duality of the initial aim versus actual results adds a puzzling twist to the often positively connoted NPM modernizers. Kirkpatrick *et al.* (2013) highlight some of these challenges as a result of implementing NPM features in 'foreign' contexts like Denmark. By including the thoughts on desirability and feasibility, Kirkpatrick *et al.* (2013) suggest that the combination of wishing to implement a productivity focus and specific measurable indicators from a political level collide with values of consensus, dialogue and delegation, which is the problematic avenue that Nørreklit *et al.* (2006) warn us about. While the empirical cases illustrate the continuation of a new wish to implement post-NPM quality elements, they also point to the continuous challenges of adopting the NPM agenda to a working culture that is vastly different to the Anglo-Saxon one. By applying modern power as an analytical lens, it has been possible to highlight the forces that influence the contradictory results: how the integration of a patient perspective in a new management control system is diminished and an administrative and technical perspective on quality is sustained because the highly involved employees seek to accommodate senior management's dominating, yet partly hidden, wish for high productivity. These invisible underlying power currents are important to acknowledge and understand in a future wish to further implement the quality agenda. Politicians and senior management within the public sector should understand these subtle forces in their decision-making and their continuous wish to involve local management. In order to address this particular issue, more studies on power and legitimization in different 'foreign' contexts would be of great importance.

64   N. Kure and M. Malmmose

Notes

1 In their later version from 2011, these categorizations are developed further into the concepts of New Public Management, the Neo-Weberian State and New Public Governance.
2 www.transparency.org/research/cpi/overview.
3 www.oecdbetterlifeindex.org/#/11111111111.
4 www.ikas.dk/DDKM/ISQua-akkreditering.aspx.

References

Åkerstrøm Andersen, N. (2009) *Partnerships: Machines of Possibilities* (Bristol: Policy Press).
Andersen, T. M. F., H. Linderoth, V. Smith and N. Westergård-Nielsen (2010) *The Danish Economy: An International Perspective*, 3rd edition (Copenhagen: DJØF).
Bech, M. (2006) 'Kontraktstyring af sygehusene: Fra blød til hård kontraktstyring' [Contract management of hospitals: From soft to hard contract management]. *Tidsskrift for dansk sundhedsvæsen*, Vol. 10, pp. 343–346.
Bilde, L., A. R. Hansen and J. Søgaard (2010) Økonomi og styring i sygehusvæsenet [Economy and control in health care], in F.-F. O. A. Notat Udarbejdet for Foreningen Af Speciallæger, Hk/Kommunal, Sundhedskartellet Og Foreningen Af Yngre Læger (ed.) (Dansk Sundhedsinstitut).
Cardinaels, E. and N. Soderstrom (2013) 'Managing in a complex world: accounting and governance choices in hospitals'. *European Accounting Review*, Vol. 22, No. 4, pp. 647–684.
Christiansen, T. (2002) 'Organization and financing of the Danish health care system'. *Health Policy*, Vol. 59, pp. 107–118.
Dich, J. S. (1974) *Den herskende klasse: En kritisk analyse af social udbytning og midlerne imod den* [The ruling class: A critical analysis of social exploitation and the means towards it], 3rd edition (Copenhagen: Borgen).
Dørken, R., S. Feilberg, T. Buse, M. L. F. Jakobsen, T. Pallesen, X. B. Hansen, S. R. Kristensen and M. Bech (2012) *Takster i faste rammer – en analyse af takst- og økonomistyringen på sygehusområdet* [An analysis of activity rates and management accounting in health care] (KREVI, Aarhus University and Southern University of Denmark). Available online at www.kora.dk/media/276368/Rapport_-_Takster_i_faste_rammer.pdf.
Felsager Jakobsen, M. L. (2014) 'The patial adoption of performance budgeting at Danish hospitals'. *Danish Journal of Management & Business*, Vol. 78, no. 3/4 (2014) pp. 78–97.
Forgione, D. A., T. E. Vermeer, K. Surysekar, J. A. Wrieden and C. C. Plante (2005) 'Drugs, costs and quality of care: an agency theory perspective'. *Financial Accountability & Management*, Vol. 21, pp. 291–308.
Foucault, M. (1982) 'The subject and power'. *Critical Inquiry*, Vol. 8, No. 4, pp. 777–795.
Foucault, M. (1991) Governmentality, in G. Burchell, C. Gordon and P. Miller (eds), *The Foucault Effect – Studies in Governmentality* (Chicago: University of Chicago Press).
Greve, C. (2006) 'Public management reform in Denmark'. *Public Management Review*, Vol. 8, No. 1, pp. 161–169.

Greve, C. (2015) Sensemaking in Public Management Reform in Denmark, in S. Borrás and L. Seabrooke (eds), *Sources of National Institutional Competitiveness – Sensemaking in Institutional Change* (Oxford: Oxford University Press).

Hood, C. (1995) 'The "new public management" in the 1980s: variations on a theme'. *Accounting, Organizations and Society*, Vol. 20, No. 2–3, pp. 93–109.

Hood, C. and G. Peters (2004) 'The middle aging of new public management: into the age of paradox?'. *Journal of Public Administration Research and Theory*, Vol. 14, No. 3, pp. 267–282.

Jackson, D. D., J. Haley and J. Weakland (1956) 'Toward a theory of schizophrenia'. *Behavioural Science*, Vol. 1, No. 4, pp. 251–254.

Jensen, L. (1998) 'Interpreting new public management: the case of Denmark'. *Australian Journal of Public Administration*, Vol. 57, No. 4, pp. 54–65.

Jespersen, P. K., L.-L. M. Nielsen and H. Sognstrup (2002) 'Professions, institutional dynamics, and new public management in the Danish hospital field'. *International Journal of Public Administration*, Vol. 25, No. 12, pp. 1555–1574.

Kirkpatrick, I., B. Bullinger, F. Lega and M. Dent (2013) 'The translation of hospital management models in European health systems: a framework for comparison'. *British Journal of Management*, Vol. 24, pp. S48–S61.

Kirkpatrick, I., M. Dent and P. K. Jespersen (2011) 'The contested terrain of hospital management: professional projects and healthcare reforms in Denmark'. *Current Sociology*, Vol. 59, No.4, pp. 489–506.

Malmmose, M. (2015a) 'Management accounting versus medical profession discourse: hegemony in a public health care debate – a case from Denmark'. *Critical Perspectives on Accounting*, Vol. 27, pp. 144–159.

Malmmose, M. (2015b) 'National hospital development, 1948–2000: the WHO as an international propagator'. *Accounting History Review*, Vol. 25, No. 3, pp. 239–259.

Meyer, J. W. and B. Rowan (1977) 'Institutionalized organizations: formal structure as myth and ceremony'. *American Journal of Sociology*, Vol. 83, pp. 340–363.

Miller, P. and T. O'Leary (1987) 'Accounting and the construction of the governable person'. *Accounting, Organizations and Society*, Vol. 12, No. 3, pp. 235–265.

Miller, P. and N. Rose (1990) 'Governing economic life'. *Economy & Society*, Vol. 19, pp. 1–31.

Nørreklit, H., L. Nørreklit and P. Melander (2006) 'US "fair contract" based performance management models in a Danish environment'. *Financial Accountability & Management*, Vol. 22, No. 3, pp. 213–233.

OECD (2012) *OECD Health Statistics* (Paris: Organisation for Economic Co-operation and Development). Available online at http://stats.oecd.org/index.aspx?DataSetCode=SHA.

Olejaz, M., A. Juul Nielsen, A. Rudkjøbing, H. Okkels Birk, A. Krasnik and C. Hernández-Quevedo (2012) *Health Systems in Transition – Denmark Health System Review* (Copenhagen: European Observatory on Health Systems and Policies and the World Health Organization). Available online at www.euro.who.int/__data/assets/pdf_file/0004/160519/e96442.pdf.

Pedersen, K. M., T. Christiansen and M. Bech (2005) 'The Danish health care system: evolution – not revolution – in a decentralized system'. *Health Economics*, Vol. 14, No. S1, pp. S41–S57.

Piligrimiené, Z. and I. Buciuniene (2008) 'Different perspectives on health care quality: is the consensus possible'. *Engineering Economics*, Vol. 1, No. 56, pp. 104–111.

Pollitt, C. and G. Bouckaert (2004) *Public Management Reform – A Comparative Analysis*, 2nd edition (Oxford: Oxford University Press).

Pollitt, C. and G. Bouckaert (2011) *Public Management Reform: A Comparative Analysis – New Public Management, Governance, and the Neo-Weberian State* (Oxford: Oxford University Press).

Power, M. (ed.) (1997) *The Audit Society – Rituals of Verification* (Oxford: Oxford University Press).

Strandberg-Larsen, M., M. Bernt-Nielsen, S. Vallgårda, A. Krasnik and K. Vrangbæk (2007) *Health Systems in Transitions – Denmark: Health System Review* (World Health Organization, on behalf of European Observatory on Health Care Systems and Policies).

Søgaard, R., S. R. Kristensen and M. Bech (2015) 'Incentivising effort in governance of public hospitals: development of a delegation-based alternative to activity-based remuneration'. *Health Policy*, Vol. in press.

Tanggaard Andersen, P. and J.-J. Jensen (2010) 'Healthcare reform in Denmark'. *Scandinavian Journal of Public Health*, Vol. 38, No. 3, pp. 246–252.

The Danish Health Ministry (2004) *Agreement on Structural Reform* (Copenhagen: Danish Government).

Vrangbæk, K. and T. Christiansen (2005) 'Health policy in Denmark: leaving the decentralized welfare path?'. *Journal of Health Politics, Policy & Law*, Vol. 30, Nos. 1/2, pp. 29–52.

World Health Organization [WHO] (1988) *The Application of Diagnosis-related Groups (Drugs) for Hospital Budgeting and Performance Measurement*. Report on a WHO planning meeting, Cardiff, 23–25 November 1988.

5 Process orientation and management control in health care organizations

Gert Paulsson

Summary

The public sector in Sweden has been an early adopter of public management reforms and the health care sector has been in the forefront of the development. In recent years, process orientation has been one key component in this endeavour.

Studies in two health care organizations show that an increased focus on horizontal processes leads to changes in the management control system. However, it also shows that the vertical organization structure most often remains unchanged and that important management control devices like resource allocation in the budget process still are used in that structure. The management control devices that are focused on horizontal processes are mainly performance measurement systems.

In addition to that, other types of informal devices like fora for dialogue, joint projects across organizational borders and leadership become more important in the management of horizontal processes. This is a challenge since these types of devices, which seem to be important for process orientation, have, so far, not been used a lot in public management in Sweden.

Introduction

The public sector in Sweden was an early adopter of New Public Management (NPM) (see e.g. Andersson *et al.*, 2011; Lüder and Jones, 2003). This was not least the case in health care organizations, where far-reaching delegation of responsibility to lower-level organizational units, performance measurement, accrual accounting and budgeting, contracting out and internal markets were significant components in the reform agenda at the beginning of the 1990s.

At present, various kinds of process orientation are becoming more and more popular. The basic idea behind this is that traditionally management control has to a large extent been focused on the vertical organization structure, while the horizontal processes have been neglected. As a consequence of this, employees tend to do their best to optimize the activities in their own organizational unit, while no one focuses on optimization of the horizontal processes that are important for the patients. The phenomenon is often called 'silo mentality' (see e.g. Nylinder, 2012).

One common explanation of 'silo mentality' is that the medical sub-specialization leads to an increased focus on more and more narrow phases of the horizontal processes. Another explanation is that management control systems further reinforce a focus on the vertical organization structure (see e.g. Baretta and Busco, 2011). Thus, it may be that these systems hinder rather than support a focus on horizontal processes. Furthermore, this may be an even bigger problem in the health care sector in Sweden, in which decentralization to lower levels of the organization has been a key component in the development of management control systems.

It is a basic idea in the literature that management control systems must be designed in a way that makes them fit the internal and external context of the organization. Based on that idea, one important question is to what extent and in what ways management control systems become adjusted when health care organizations to a larger extent than before focus on horizontal processes. It is especially interesting to learn more about how management control systems can contribute to the success of these organizations. Van der Meer-Kooistra and Scapens (2008) make the following remark on that issue:

> We believe such organizations are likely to need rather different forms of control to those traditionally used in hierarchical organizations.
> (Van der Meer-Kooistra and Scapens, 2008, p. 366)

In spite of the long-lasting questioning of the ability of management control systems to contribute to improvement of horizontal processes, scholars argue that relatively little interest has been paid to this issue among academics (see e.g. Chenhall, 2008). This chapter tries to remedy this by looking into two Swedish health care organizations in which there has been an explicit ambition to focus more on horizontal processes, and where the design and use of management control systems have changed in connection with that development. The two cases are the Regional Cancer Center South (RCCs) and the TenHundred project (THp). The former is a virtual organization covering all cancer care in the southern region of Sweden, while the latter covers all health care and care for the elderly in Norrtälje Municipality (NM) in the northern part of Stockholm county. Before looking into the two cases, a brief note is made about the key concepts in this chapter – management control and process orientation.

Management control is presented in different ways in the literature. However, the following overall definition is relevant for this chapter:

> management controls include all the devices and systems managers use to ensure that the behaviors and decisions of their employees are consistent with the organization's objectives and strategies.
> (Malmi and Brown, 2008, pp. 288–289)

One important component in this definition is that management control ultimately has to do with influencing the behaviour of others. Thus, when designing and using management control devices in an organization it is important to focus attention on the 'signals' that are sent to the employees.

Furthermore, Malmi and Brown (2008) argue that the individual management control devices must support each other in order for the total system to contribute to the success of the organization. Therefore, they view management control as a 'package' of control devices, organized in certain groups – 'administrative controls' like governance and organization structure; 'cybernetic controls' like budgets and performance measurement systems; and 'cultural controls' like clans, values and symbols. Altogether, these groups of devices provide a rather broad picture of management control systems, which means that they extend the scope of the management control systems that are included in most standard text books on the subject.

In a general sense, *process orientation* has to do with a change in focus from the vertical organization structure to horizontal processes. There are different types of processes and one common distinction is made between sequential, pooled and reciprocal processes (see e.g. Westrup, 2002). Furthermore, the distinction between processes that take place within a single organization (intra-organizational processes) and processes that include several organizations (inter-organizational processes) is relevant, too (see e.g. Kurunmäki and Miller, 2011).

Based on the above discussion, it is interesting to look at *process orientation* and *management control*, and one key question is in what ways the design of management control systems is affected by an increased focus on horizontal processes. Two Swedish researchers summarized their view on this topic in the following way:

> MAS[1] should not be used for traditional control and coordination purposes but be replaced by managerial efforts to mould a culture focused on trust, competence empowerment, continuous improvement and cooperation.
>
> (Kastberg and Siverbo, 2013, p. 250)

In spite of this pessimistic view, previous empirical studies show that increased process orientation leads to either a development of the existing management control devices like budgeting and performance measurement systems or the introduction of new ones like fora for dialogue, trust making efforts and cultural control (see e.g. Carlsson-Wall *et al.*, 2011). Altogether, this supports a broadening of the concept of management control when we are studying process orientation and management control systems.

The empirical study that is presented in this chapter covers document studies, interviews with key persons in the two organizations and attendance in meetings.

Process orientation and management control –
two mini-cases

This section contains a presentation of two Swedish health care organizations – The Regional Cancer Center South (RCCs) and The TenHundred Project (THp) – that have implemented process orientation. Both organizations involve primary care units, hospitals and care for the elderly. Furthermore, both public and private providers are involved in the operations. Parallel to the implementation of process orientation, the RCCs and the THp have revised their management control systems. In that development, both organizations have experienced opportunities as well as challenges.

As mentioned above, Sweden was an early adopter of New Public Management. However, since the public sector in Sweden is decentralized there are substantial differences between different parts of the sector when it comes to public management reforms. Thus, it is not possible to present one single development in all parts of the sector. Nevertheless, both the southern region of Sweden and the Stockholm region have been in the forefront of developmental activities. Therefore, it is reasonable to say that the two projects that are presented in this chapter have taken place in regions where NPM is very present.

The Regional Cancer Center South (RCCs)

The RCCs was established in 2009. At first it was a project, but in 2013 it became a permanent organization in the southern health care region. The reason for the establishment of the RCCs was a general aim to improve the often complex processes in cancer (Regionalt Cancercentrum Syd, 2013b; Regionalt Cancercentrum Syd, 2013c). In addition to that, there was a political initiative in Sweden aiming at a national cancer strategy (SOU, 2009). The reason for this was a strong critique against the cancer treatment, focusing especially on inefficient patient processes. For example, several studies show that the time from the first visit to the setting of a proper diagnosis was far too long.

Since improved patient processes were one of the key ideas behind the establishment of the RCCs, the relationships between different organizational units was immediately focused. The reason for this is that cancer treatment often involves several providers, e.g. primary care, hospital care and care for the elderly, the latter traditionally being the responsibility of the municipalities. A further complicating factor in RCCs is that several county councils are involved, which means that there are inter-organizational relationships that have to be managed. Furthermore, as one part of the NPM movement in Sweden during the last decade, private primary care units and care for the elderly units have been established in all county councils in the southern region of Sweden. The concept of patient processes was defined in the following way at RCCs's web page:

By patient processes we mean all activities that together as long as possible takes care of the need the patient has when he/she contacts the health care organization. Patient processes include all activities that lead to the setting of diagnosis, treatment of the illness, as well as rehabilitation and, if needed, palliative care.

(Regionalt Cancercentrum Syd, 2013a)

The work on improved patient processes started in 2010, focusing on a few types of cancer diagnosis, and has continued since then. In 2013, there were 15 patient processes included in RCCs, covering around 70 per cent of all cancer treatment in the southern region. In the work on improved patient processes, the RCCs's role is to 'secure patient processes, provide education in process work, and openly present key performance indicators' (Regionalt Cancercentrum Syd, 2013a).

Parallel to the increased process orientation in cancer treatment in the southern region, the traditional hierarchical organization structure remained intact, with the same formal authorities and responsibilities as before. Furthermore, all personnel were still employed in the organizational units in this structure. This was expressed in the following way in the so-called Owners Directives:

RCCs is a network organization with responsibilities allocated to the processes, but without authority concerning the line organization. The assignment can only be carried out in close cooperation with a set of actors in the health care organization. This means that the success from a patient perspective to a large extent is dependent on the ability and will to cooperate across professional and organizational boundaries.

(Jansson *et al.*, 2013, p. 7)

The establishment of the RCCs is set in a written agreement between the county councils in the southern region. In addition to that, there is a board of directors with representatives from all county councils in the southern region, the faculty of the Scania University Hospital and various cancer patient organizations. The operations in RCCs are handled by a managing director and a small administrative unit.

The patient processes are managed by regional process owners, who are senior doctors. They, in their turn, have local process owners at each hospital. Furthermore, every employee who is involved in the treatment of cancer patients in the southern region is part of a multi-professional team. Finally, contact nurses and patient coordinators are responsible for contacts with the patients.

Altogether, the organization structure of the cancer treatment in the southern region of Sweden is similar to a matrix structure, even if that concept is not always used internally in the organization. The relationship between the RCCs and the organizational units in the vertical organization structure can be presented in the following way (see Figure 5.1):

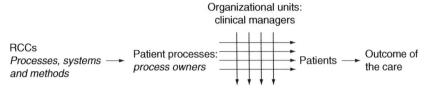

Figure 5.1 The vertical organization structure and horizontal processes.

An important issue in any management control system is the principles for the allocation of resources. In the southern health care region, this allocation takes place in the vertical organizational structure. Thus, resources are allocated to the organizational units, while the process owners have no budget on their own. The exception is the salary for regional and local process owners. The allocation of financial responsibility also means that the formal decision-making authorities rest within the vertical organization structure. Thus, it is sometimes argued that the horizontal processes in the RCCs have a 'supporting' rather than a 'steering' role (see Jansson *et al.*, 2013).

In the management control of cancer patient processes in RCCs, objectives and performance measures are important devices. Such objectives and measures are established in both the vertical structure and the horizontal processes. In the former they are common for all organizational units that participate in cancer treatment, while the objectives and performance measures in the horizontal processes are more or less unique for each patient process that is included in the RCCs. Furthermore, the ambition is that the objectives and performance measures in the horizontal processes should be openly presented so that the citizens can compare the care both between different units and over time.

Another device that is often mentioned in the discussion about management of the RCCs is the various kind of fora for dialogue between organizational units that participate in cancer patient processes, but also between regional and local process owners. These fora consist of, for example, meetings, workshops and joint projects.

In addition to that, proper information systems that can be used both internally among the persons involved in the patient processes and externally as a mode for communicating with the patients and the general public have been developed. A new website is one example of this.

Finally, in discussions with representatives from the RCCs 'professional self-control' has been highlighted. There is no clear definition of this concept, but it has been argued that it is important, in general, that professionals, e.g. physicians and nurses, have more control over the activities in the cancer patient processes, which also means that the traditional formal management control devices may become less important.

The TenHundred project[2] in Norrtälje

The TenHundred project (THp) was established in 2006 and has been extended several times. The site for the project is Norrtälje Municipality (NM), which is a relatively small municipality in Stockholm county. The project covers activities that are traditionally carried out in both the municipality – care for the elderly – and the county council – primary care and acute care at the Norrtälje Hospital.

The background to the project was that Stockholm County Council (SCC) planned to change the Norrtälje Hospital from being an acute care hospital to being a local hospital. The proposal was eventually withdrawn, but instead the Norrtälje Hospital faced a large decrease in funding from SCC. One consequence of this was that SCC and NM started to discuss the possibilities of handling the new situation by increased cooperation across organizational borders.

One important ambition in the THp was to improve horizontal processes that involve several organizational units. For example, in some formal documents there were discussions about 'activities without borders' and 'customer focus' rather than 'production focus'. One reason for this was that some patients obviously 'fell in-between the chairs'.

The THp concerns both the organization structure and the allocation of responsibility and authority. Furthermore, it concerns both the political and the non-political structure. The key organization unit in the political structure is the joint board for NM and SCC. From a formal standpoint, NM is 'hosting' the board in its organization structure, but it is a joint board in any practical respect.

The main responsibility of the board is to order health care and care for the elderly from private and public providers in Norrtälje. In order to handle this, the board has established an administrative unit. Furthermore, the public providers are to a large extent organized in a municipal corporation owned by the NM and the SCC. The corporation has about 2,300 employees, of whom about 1,500 were employed by NM and about 800 were employed by SCC prior to the establishment of the THp.

A key feature in the organization structure of the THp is the inter-organizational activity areas which have managers who are responsible for the performance in the area. In spite of that, the councils in SCC and NM have final responsibility for the operations. In order for the two councils to handle this, they appoint members to the joint board, issue directives and allocate resources.

The development of the management control system has been affected not only by the THp but also by other changes in the governance of the health care sector in Sweden. An example of such a change is the mandatory introduction of freedom of choice in primary care and care for the elderly, which has led to the establishment of many private actors in NM. This means that it is hard to distinguish between developments that are directly related to the

74   G. Paulsson

THp and developments that are related to other reforms in the health care sector.

The SCC and NM have chosen to use several types of device in order to handle the operations in the THp. 'Formal agreements' between the joint board and organizational units have been more common than before. In line with the introduction of inter-organizational activity areas, it would be reasonable to assume that the agreements focus on these areas. However, an evaluation shows that most of them are more 'silo-oriented' than horizontal, thus still focusing on organizational units in the vertical structure. However, there are exceptions, like parts of the care for the elderly.

The role of budgeting has been emphasized as important, and since the introduction of the THp there have been several changes in that device. One reason for this is that SCC and NM used different time frames for the budgeting processes before the establishment of the THp. In addition to that, in NM the budget included an overall cost frame, while the budget in SCC was calculated as the volume of services produced times a fee per service. The solution to these differences was a joint time frame for the budget process and a decision that SCC and NM should put in the same amount of money for activities that are included in the THp as they did before the project was launched. Thus, the THp got a 'pooled budget' which can be used in whatever way the THp board want. In spite of this, the experience is that the SCC part of the budget to a large extent is still used for the activities that were earlier on carried out by SCC, while the NM part of the budget is primarily used for the activities that were previously the responsibility of the NM. Furthermore, an evaluation of the THp (Sjögren and Åhblom, 2011) showed that the budget and the budget process had focused on relationships *between* different organizational units only to a limited extent. In spite of this, the new budget system was considered to function relatively well.

Performance measurement systems, which include formulation of objectives and follow-up against these objectives, are another device that has been highlighted in conjunction with discussions about the management control of the THp. Both SCC and NM had worked on these devices prior to the introduction of the THp, which meant that both organizations were familiar with the ideas and used some kind of 'balanced scorecard model'. That work continued when the THp was established and the new board started to use performance measurement systems focusing on citizens, patients, employees and finance (see e.g. TioHundranämnden, 2011).

In addition to the above-mentioned devices, representatives from THp emphasized the importance of networks, culture, leadership, communication and the development of administrative support functions. Networks and culture had long been an important tool in the cooperation between the SCC and the NM. However, when the THp was established it was highlighted even more. One example of this is the establishment of 'arenas' for meetings across organizational borders, e.g. 'the Forum for Psychiatry'. The purpose of that arena is to get employees from different organizational units who are involved in psychiatric care in Norrtälje to meet and share experiences (see e.g. Medical Management Centrum, 2011; Schön *et al.*, 2011, Sjögren and Åhblom, 2011). A seminar called 'Tear down the silos' is another example of such an activity. Finally, an organizational invention with the same purpose is that managers of all major organizational units are members of the board of the municipal corporation which is responsible for the care that is produced by the THp. One reason for this was that SCC and NM had very different cultures prior to the establishment of the THp (e.g. Sjögren and Åhblom, 2011; SKL, 2007).

Already in the early stages of the development of the THp, leadership was considered to be an important device. The interaction between the general managers for SCC and NM was considered to be especially important since they were expected to contribute to 'stability and security' in a potentially turbulent situation. This was stressed especially in connection with the merger, but also as a more long-term consideration (Anell and Mattisson, 2009; SKL, 2007).

Communication and information have been highlighted as important in the THp. It was considered to be particularly important during the merger process, but it has been highlighted as an important device in the long run, too, not least due to the nature of process orientation. The more practical work in this area has focused on things ranging from a forum for dialogue with the citizens to a new logotype for the THp.

Reflections on the development

It is a basic idea in this chapter that management control systems must be designed in a way that makes them fit the internal and external context. This means that a change in focus from the vertical organization structure to horizontal processes may require a change in the management control system as well. In spite of this insight, relatively little research has been done on the issue (see e.g. Chenhall, 2008). In order to contribute to our knowledge in the area, this section contains some reflections that are based on the developments in the two Swedish health care organizations that are briefly presented above.

We will look at the two cases by using the control package framework by Malmi and Brown (2008). The question is in what ways the different devices of the control package change when focus changes from the vertical structure to horizontal processes in health care organizations.

One overall group of devices that is included in the control package is the 'administrative controls', which include, among other things, governance and organization structure. In connection with the increased focus on horizontal processes, governance changed in the sense that new political bodies were established and various agreements were set. Examples of new bodies are the board of directors in the RCCs and the joint board of the THp, while the owners' directives in the RCCs and the 'formal agreements' in the THp are examples of the agreements.

When we look at changes in the organization structure, we can see both similarities and differences between the two cases. When it comes to similarities, it is, for example, obvious that increased process orientation hardly means that the vertical organization structure is removed. Rather, in both the RCCs and the THp, the vertical organization structure remains almost intact. Thus, the hospitals, primary care units and homes for the elderly are still important organizational units. What does happen is that horizontal agreements, like the process owners in the RCCs and the activity areas in the THp, are added. Thus, both organizations end up with some kind of matrix structure, including both the vertical organization structure and the horizontal patient processes.

Another group of devices in the control package framework is 'cybernetic controls', which focus on planning and control devices like budgeting, objectives and performance measures. Budgeting is basically intact in the vertical organization structure in the southern health care region of Sweden, despite the establishment of the RCCs. There have been discussions about whether or not to allocate resources to the process owners, instead of to the organizational units in the vertical structure, but the disadvantages of such a change have been considered to be larger than the advantages. Primarily, since there has been no discussion about removing the vertical organization structure, such a change would require either an extensive transfer pricing system in which the process owners would buy services from the organizational units that are involved in cancer treatment or some other kind of coordination mechanism, probably involving senior management.

The development of the THp was different when it comes to the allocation of resources in the budget process. The attempt with 'pooled budgets' is the most important example of this. However, it is evident from the interviews that this change in the cybernetic controls did not get the effect that was expected, i.e. a more unprejudiced use of the available resources. Rather, resources from SCC were primarily allocated to the organizational units that were formerly part of SCC, while resources from NM were primarily allocated to the organizational units that were formerly part of NM. This is interesting since allocation of resources in the budget process often is considered to be one of the most important management control devices in public-sector organizations.

Two other potentially important cybernetic control devices – objectives and performance measurement systems – support process orientation in a more direct way in both cases. First, there are several national databases with information about various aspects of cancer treatment that can also be used for management control in the RCCs. Second, the county councils in the southern health care region, as well as the SCC and NM, had already prior to the establishment of the RCCs and the THp introduced performance measurement systems that at least to some extent focused on the horizontal processes. Thus, there was a short but nevertheless strong history of using objectives and performance measures in both cases.

The final group of management control devices in the control package is 'cultural controls' like clans, values and symbols, but also other less formal devices that may affect the behaviour of the employees. When we look at the RCCs and the THp, we can see that both organizations use this kind of device in order to manage the horizontal processes. Examples of devices are fora for dialogue across borders, such as meetings, joint projects, networks, workshops and seminars. Furthermore, attempts have been made to further strengthen these activities by improved information systems like new websites. Finally, there is a general interest in other types of informal control, e.g. professional self-control, which is discussed extensively in the RCCs.

Taken together, the chapter shows that 'administrative controls' are changed, especially in the sense that some kind of matrix structure is established when focus changes from the vertical organization structure to the horizontal processes. 'Cybernetic controls' are still as important as before in the vertical structure, while they seem to have a less important role in the horizontal processes. The only exceptions are objectives and performance measures that focus on both structures, and they seem to be as important in the horizontal processes as they are in the vertical structure. Finally, there seems to be a growing insight that the so-called 'cultural controls' and other less formal control devices may have the potential to be very important if the management control system is going to support an increased focus on horizontal processes.

The way forward

The public sector in Sweden has long been active in public management reform, and was no doubt an early adopter of the ideas behind New Public Management. However, in Sweden public-sector organizations have a large degree of freedom when it comes to management reforms. This means that the reforms to some extent differ between different organizational units within the sector.

This is true also for the introduction of process orientation, which has been discussed in this chapter; though that kind of reform always has to do with a change in focus from the vertical organization structure to horizontal processes, there are ample room for variations. Nevertheless, the two cases clearly show that such a development always leads to changes in the conditions for management control. Not least does the management control system have to be designed in a way that motivates the employees to strive for well-functioning horizontal processes and not only well-functioning organizational units in the vertical structure.

An important question is then how public management reform in Sweden during the last decades has contributed to increased process orientation. One important component in these reforms has been a far-reaching delegation of authority and responsibility to low levels of the vertical organization (see e.g. Andersson *et al.*, 2011). This has been the case in the health care sector and has led to a strong focus on the organizational units in which the authority and responsibility rests and to which budgets, objectives and performance measures are attached, e.g. primary care units, hospitals, clinics and wards. Thus, the far-reaching delegation in the public sector in Sweden may actually support the 'silo mentality' that was discussed in the introductory section and hinder more focus on the horizontal processes.

One way to interpret this development is that there have been reforms in 'administrative controls' and 'cybernetic controls', while less attention has been paid to 'cultural controls'. Altogether there seem to be very limited experiences in the health care sector in Sweden to view 'cultural controls' as possible devices in the management of the sector. Rather, in health care organizations 'cultural controls' are most often related to professional norms, values and clans, and these controls are often considered by managers to constitute problems in the use of management control systems and contribute to 'silo mentality'.

There is no doubt that various kinds of process orientation will be important in the future reform agenda in the Swedish health care sector. Since the vertical organization structure is likely to remain, we will face some kind of matrix structure that has to be handled by the management control system. Thus, this structure will be an important part of the 'administrative controls'.

Drawing on the experiences so far, it seems reasonable to assume that the vertical organization structure will to a large extent still be managed by 'cybernetic controls', e.g. budgets and performance measurement systems. The latter will probably be useful in the management control of horizontal processes as well. However, that structure will require more 'cultural controls' and other less formal management control devices, and this will certainly be challenging for the health care sector in Sweden, since there are very limited experiences from such devices in that sector.

Notes

1 Management Accounting Systems ~ Management Control Systems.
2 The name of the project – TenHundred – is related to the one single telephone number 10100 that should be used whenever patients want to get in contact with the health care organization. The number, in turn, is related to the name of the historical area in which Norrtälje is located, Tiundaland.

References

Andersson, F., T. Bergström, L. Bringselius, M. Dackehag, T. S. Karlsson, S. Melander and G. Paulsson (2011) 'Organisatoriska vägval: En studie av försäkrings-kassans förändringsarbete'. *Nordiska Organisasjonsstudier*, Vol. 13, No. 4, pp. 53–76.

Anell, A. and O. Mattisson (2009) *Samverkan i kommuner och landsting – en kunskaps-översikt* (Lund: Studentlitteratur).

Baretta, A. and C. Busco (2011) 'Technologies of government in public sector's network: in search of cooperation through management control innovations'. *Management Accounting Research*, Vol. 22, pp. 211–219.

Carlsson-Wall, M., K. Kraus and J. Lind (2011) 'The interdependencies of intra- and inter-organisational controls and work practices – the case of domestic care of the elderly'. *Management Accounting Research*, Vol. 22, pp. 313–329.

Chenhall, R. H. (2008) 'Accounting for the horizontal organization: a review essay'. *Accounting, Organizations and Society*, Vol. 33, pp. 517–550.

Jansson, B. R., M. R. Wiren and H. Thulesius (2013) *Granskning av regionalt cancercentrum syd* (Malmö: TJP Analys och Utveckling).

Kastberg, G. and S. Siverbo (2013) 'The design and use of management accounting systems in process oriented health care – an explorative study'. *Financial Accountability & Management*, Vol. 23, No. 3, pp. 246–270.

Kurunmäki, L. and P. Miller (2011) 'Regulatory hybrids: partnerships, budgeting and modernizing government'. *Management Accounting Research*, Vol. 22, pp. 220–241.

Lüder, K. and R. Jones (eds) (2003) *Reforming Governmental Accounting and Budgeting in Europe* (Frankfurt am Main: Fachverlag Moderne Wirtschaft).

Malmi, T. and D. A. Brown (2008) 'Management control systems as a package: opportunities, challenges and research directions'. *Management Accounting Research*, Vol. 19, No. 4, pp. 287–300.

Medical Management Centrum (2011) *Från två till tiohundra – utvärdering av norrtäljeprojektets effekter och ekonomiska utfall* (Stockholm: Medical Management Centrum).

Nylinder, P. (2012) *Budgetary Control in Public Health Care: A Study about Perceptions of Budgetary Control among Clinical Directors* (Lund: Lund University).

Regionalt Cancercentrum Syd (2013a) Available online at www.cancercentrum.se/syd (accessed 1 April 2016).

Regionalt Cancercentrum Syd (2013b) *Bättre cancervård med patienten i fokus* (Lund: Regionalt Cancercentrum Syd).

Regionalt Cancercentrum Syd (2013c) *Årsredovisning 2012* (Lund: Regionalt Cancercentrum Syd).

Schön, P., L. Hagman and S. E. Wånell (2011) *Tiohundraprojektets effekter på vård och omsorg för målgruppen de mest sjuka äldre – utvärdering av tiohundraprojektet i norrtälje* (Stockholm: Äldrecentrum – Forskning & Utveckling).

Sjögren, E. and P. Åhblom (2011) *Hur har ledningsprocesser och system för ekonomistyrning bidragit till samarbete mellan sjukvårds- och omsorgsverksamhet? En utvärdering av tiohundraprojektet i norrtälje* (Stockholm: Stiftelsen Leading Health Care).

SKL (2007) *Tiohundra – kommun och landsting i samma båt* (Stockholm: Sveriges Kommuner och Landsting).

SOU (2009) *En nationell cancerstrategi för framtiden. SOU 2009:11* (Stockholm: Regeringen).

TioHundraförvaltningen (2011) *Verksamhetsplan TioHundranämnden 2011-2012* (Stockholm: TioHundranämnden).

Van der Meer-Kooistra, J. and R. W. Scapens (2008) 'The governance of lateral relations between and within organizations'. *Management Accounting Research*, Vol. 19, pp. 365–384.

Westrup, U. (2002) *Gränsöverskridande styrning: Om krav på ekonomisk styrning i social verksamhet inriktad mot barn och ungdomar*. Dissertation, Lund University.

6 The welfare state that wanted to keep track of its citizens

Personal identity numbers as administrative technology

Alexander Paulsson

Summary

The development of the Swedish welfare state is often characterized by several comprehensive social reforms and organizational changes. In previous research, as in the previous chapters of this book, scholars often tend to direct their interest towards these reforms. Often left out are the tacit administrative technological infrastructures that enabled these. The Swedish social security number, the person number, is such a tacit technology. Unlike similar personal identity numbers in other countries, e.g. the Social Security number in the USA and the National Insurance number in the UK, which were designed for administering specific welfare reforms, the forerunner to the Swedish person number was introduced in 1947 as a uniform number for universal personal identification. With this administrative technology, the state could produce bureaucratic knowledge by collecting demographic data, finding debtors, controlling spending and crosschecking entitlements to welfare benefits. And, equipped with their unique identity number, each citizen could claim the newfound social rights to which she was entitled. While simplifying state–citizen communication, the person number also opened up the possibility for authorities to crosscheck individuals' data in different registers. This sparked a heated debate in the early 1970s. To protect the personal integrity of the individual, the Data Protection Act (SFS 1973:289) came into force in 1973, making Sweden the first country in the world with such a legislative framework (Datainspektionen, 2016).

Introduction

Sweden is generally considered to be an elaborate and well-functioning welfare state. A plethora of bureaucratic routines, managerial procedures and administrative technologies has emerged over the years to ensure this. While several of these have been discussed elsewhere in this book, there is one administrative technological innovation that is rarely, if ever, discussed, namely the uniform social security number, or the person number as it is called in Sweden. This lacuna is surprising given the significant role the person number has had for effectively securing a person's identity in both the public and private sectors. Thus, the person number offers unique opportunities to explore issues of, and connections between, administrative technology and bureaucratic knowledge in welfare states.

The argument I will make in this chapter is as follows. In order to map an increasingly mobile population, the birth number was suggested in a bill proposal in the late 1930s, though it was not introduced as a uniform method for personal identification until 1947. For the state, the birth number quickly became an indispensable technological infrastructure for administering the social rights that came with the universal welfare reforms introduced during the 1950s and 1960s. Increased use of data processing technology eventually prompted changes to the way the birth number was written. In 1967, a new bill (SFS 1967:198) governing the population registration entered into force. A new 'control digit' was added to the birth number and it was also renamed the person number. This enabled different state authorities to crosscheck every citizen's personal information in different registries, but the person number also enabled each person to exercise the social rights she was entitled to. However, in the early 1970s a public debate arose that questioned the state's augmented ability to amass and crosscheck data on each citizen. This chapter expands on this argument in two ways: first, by returning to the political-legal discussions that preceded the introduction of the person number; and, second, by connecting how the widespread use of the person number led to the introduction of the Data Protection Act in 1973 (SFS 1973:289), the world's first law regulating the state's as well as private companies' right to create registers of personal information.

The person number is embedded in Swedish society. Not only does it work as an administrative technology for managing the social rights which practically make up the welfare state, it is also widely used in private companies, e.g. for accounting purposes and for managing customer relationships. It is, moreover, used in everyday life when one must prove one's identity. When opening a bank account, applying for a private insurance, applying for a library card, applying for housing assistance, applying to college, writing an exam or filing one's tax accounts, the person number is indispensable. Without the person number, one does not count as a legal person in Sweden. In fact, the tax authority assigns every newborn child a person number immediately after birth (Skatteverket, 2008). And the child's parents, too, need to obtain the child's person number in order to apply for parental insurance, another social right provided by the welfare state. Given the widespread use of the person number, it is not surprising to find that every Swedish citizen learns their person number by heart at an early age.

The *longue durée* of numbering bodies

There is a long history of scholarly work that seeks to study the ruler's relationship to its subjects. Within this long history, numerous studies have zoomed in on the modern state's attempt to draw boundaries around itself so as to determine its polity and within this establish some order. Foucault has shown how the modern state's administrative apparatuses recreate the conditions required for maintaining the social order. A decisive instrument in this was the development of state bureaucracies and their elaborate documentation practices. Echoing Weber's (1978) emphasis on files, rules and red tape as constitutive elements of the bureaucracy, Foucault argues that power in the modern state became exercised with and through certain innovations of 'disciplinary writing', which rendered the individual as a 'describable object'. Because of the 'accumulation of documents, their seriation, the organization of comparative fields' it was possible for the modern state 'to form categories, to determine averages, to fix norms' to which the individual, then, had to relinquish (Foucault, 1975, p. 190).

James C. Scott (1998), Michel Foucault (1975) and other likeminded scholars (e.g. Caplan, 2001; Miller and O'Leary, 1994; Noiriel, 2001; Torpey, 1997; Torpey, 1998) have described the twentieth-century practice of documenting populations as a political and administrative method for making 'legible' those persons, societies and cultures that developed without clear identity, hierarchical order or fixed geographical borders. With the aid of administrative methods like censuses and public health investigations, social order, Scott (1998) argues, could be established, borders fixed and knowledge about persons and society produced. All the while, this contributed to making society more manageable. As the modern state moved from counting people to collecting and aggregating data on the population's health status and mental well-being, a new type of power emerged, according to Foucault. As this power concerned the administration of life and of the biological features of both the human body and the body politic, he subsequently termed this 'biopower' (Foucault, 1978).

But there is another side to this story. The twentieth-century practice of numbering and counting people, as well as of spreading numeracy, is closely connected to democracy (e.g. 'one man, one vote'). As Rose (1991, p. 675) argues, there is a 'constitutive interrelationship between quantification and democratic government' because the numbers are intrinsic to the forms of 'justification that give legitimacy to political power in democracies'. While speaking more broadly about the linkages between the emerging modern state and the numbering of bodies, Rose also writes that

> Democracy requires citizens who calculate about their lives as well as their commerce. Henceforth, the pedagogy of numeracy was an essential part of the constitution of subjects of a democratic polity. If government was to be legitimate to the extent that it was articulated in a discourse of calculation, it was to be democratic to the extent that it required and sought to produce responsible citizens, with a subjectivity disciplined by an imperative to calculate.
>
> (Rose, 1991, p. 683)

Social order could be established and maintained in an increasingly secular community with the aid of numeracy, quantification and accounting. But, while numbers represent the demos, the process of quantification inevitably also reduces societal and spatial complexities. Following Foucault, Rose argues that statistical data and censuses require the establishment of social categories, allowing quantities both to serve to represent the social phenomenon behind the data and to reproduce expectations and beliefs about the very categories which the quantities represent. In addition to providing aggregate knowledge about society for use in the state bureaucracies, censuses also meant that knowledge about what constituted the common good could be produced.

Establishing the Swedish model – the interwar period

At the beginning of the twentieth century, Hjalmar Branting, the leader of the Social Democratic Party, published a massive two-volume book titled *The Century of Social Democracy*. The prophetic title turned out to be largely true. The Social Democratic Party has dominated the political landscape in Sweden since the beginning of the last century. From having first worked together with the Liberal Party in order to introduce universal suffrage, the Social Democrats started to collaborate with the Agrarian Party during the 1920s and 1930s. This stabilized the political landscape and several reforms were undertaken despite the Great Depression. 1934 saw the introduction of support for housing construction as well as the introduction of a specific unemployment insurance. 1935 was the year of a considerable increase in basic pension support and in 1937 means-tested maternity care was introduced. A statutory two-week vacation came in 1938. The same year, the Saltsjöbaden Agreement created amity in the labour market without government intervention.

In less than a decade, the political as well as the economic landscape had largely stabilized. This provided the sufficient support in parliament for the initial welfare reforms mentioned above. To ensure the financing of these reforms, the government wanted to modernize the tax collection organization. So, on 28 February 1936, the Social Democratic government appointed a committee

> with the mission to investigate and come up with suggestions concerning the manner of collecting debts and taxes, census data, as well as associated organizational and other issues.
>
> (SOU 1938:41, p. iii)

The committee was led by Thorwald Berquist, a liberal lawyer who was frequently involved in committees investigating legal and administrative issues. Two years later, in 1938, the committee published their report, *The Reorganization of Tax Collection and Population Registry* (SOU 1938:41). It suggested one major administrative reform: the merging of the tax collection and the population registration organizations. This would substantially simplify the state's tax collection, the committee argued, as debtors would be easily located. But, in this proposed reform there was another small, more technical reform too, which would have far-reaching consequences later, namely the introduction of the birth number. The birth number would eventually change the citizens' understanding of themselves as citizens of a welfare state, and also their relationship with the large, bureaucratic and impersonal entity that the modern nation state evolved into during the twentieth century.

Administrative reforms – from the clergy to the state

For several centuries, the Swedish church had registered the civilian population in terms of births, deaths, marriages, migrations, occupations and literacy (Kälvemark, 1979). The Tax Collection and Population Registry committee now suggested a break with this tradition. The civilian population should be registered by the state only, not the clergy, they argued. Should this break materialize, the committee wrote, the population registration could be efficiently reorganized into a hierarchy, beginning with the current accounts at the municipal level, then above this the tax registers at the county level and, then, at the top of the hierarchy, the national register.

While the responsibility for collecting data about the population would remain decentralized, much of the data was supposed to flow upwards in the informational hierarchy and be re-registered at different levels in different state authorities. Together with one's place of birth, current place of residence and information about property holdings, the birth number would constitute a line of information in the population registration records, thereby securely linking persons to their data in this proposed informational hierarchy (SOU 1938:41, pp. 10–13).

The birth number only played a minor role in the proposed reform. It was mainly seen as a new administrative technology to be used by bureaucrats in different state authorities, far away from the everyday life of the majority of citizens. The committee meticulously explained the uniform method for writing the birth number in official documents. It should be, they wrote, 'a whole number and a fraction', of which the whole number signifies the birth year; the numerator the serial number on which the person is recorded in the local birth registry; and the denominator one or more letters, denoting the county in which the birthplace is located, along with the number of the birthplace in that county. The three examples below are included in the bill proposal (SOU 1938:41, p. 145) in order to illustrate how the number was supposed to be written and understood.

$$1942 \frac{14}{B18}$$

This number represents a person born in 1942, with the numerator showing the serial number 14 in the local birth registry, B denoting the county in which the person was born and 18 the place of birth within that county.

There were a couple of exceptions, though. For persons with unknown place of birth or immigrants, the numerator should denote the serial number given to that person when recorded, either in the ledger of persons with unknown place of birth or in the immigration registry ledger.

$$1942 \, \frac{10}{Rf}$$

This example represents a person with unknown place of birth. The denominator shows the ledger where this person was registered and the numerator shows the serial number in that ledger.

$$1904 \, \frac{28}{Inv.42}$$

This example represents a person born in 1904 who immigrated to Sweden in 1942. The denominator denotes the ledger of immigrated persons in 1942 and the numerator the serial number, 28, in that ledger.

Information about geographic origin was considered important. But neither sex nor date of birth was included in the birth number. This information was still supposed to be entered in the bound ledgers maintained by the clergy. With this report, though, the first step towards a uniform method for personal identification had been taken in Sweden.

Merging the tax collection and population registration organizations was deemed necessary by the committee as the population was on the move, with large groups moving to the cities. Since the population had become more mobile, the committee deemed the current practice, in which the clergy registered births, deaths, migrations and property holdings, to be unfeasible, at least from a long-term perspective. Though the parishes had the capacity to keep track of their own local populations, they lacked capacity in two major respects according to the committee. First, the clergy did not have the same capacity as the state to rapidly disseminate information about individual citizens to different state authorities and government agencies. Second, the clergy was not obliged to search for non-existent persons. Current practice was so that the clergy listed so-called non-existent persons in a specifically designated ledger. A person was non-existent if (1) they had moved without notification to the clergy, (2) they had been registered twice in the registers, or (3) was non-existent because of other errors in the documentation practices. Someone who had been missing for three to five years, and whom the priest had heard nothing of or whose whereabouts the priest had not obtained knowledge of, was listed in the ledger of non-existent persons.

In light of this, the parishes were considered unable to keep up-to-date records of their current residents. This meant, among other things, that creditors had difficulties in tracking down debtors. The lack of a national register, or a common registry for all records in which all people were registered, made business for creditors difficult. Finding current addresses to evasive debtors was both a cumbersome and a time-consuming process (SOU

1938:41, pp. 294–295). Obviously, the state was ready to assist the creditors, though the state, too, wanted to find ways to track down individuals who avoided paying tax or had outstanding tax liabilities. Should the detailed information in the parishes' registers be forwarded to a centrally placed national registry, however, no person would be non-existent and hence not constitute a problem to the tax authority (SOU 1938:41, p. 42).

In Sweden, committee reports and proposals for new legislative reforms, like the one discussed here, are circulated for review to affected state authorities as well as to other interested organizations. Should the majority of the reviewing organizations be opposed to the suggested proposal, then the government may choose not to proceed with it. Occasionally, a single negative review may halt the whole process, e.g. when a committee proposal includes reforming a state authority, which itself is not in favour of the proposed reform. This is precisely what happened to the bill proposal in this committee report (SOU 1938:41). It was considered, inter alia, to be too complicated, cumbersome and costly. Heaviest criticism came from the authority responsible for producing official statistics, the National Bureau of Statistics, which saw no immediate benefits with the proposed reorganization. In its review, it contended that the clergy should remain responsible for registering the local population in bound ledgers. The clergy agreed. The Chapter of Visby argued, for example, that, as long as the state used the church 'as a means for the spiritual care of its people', the priests must obtain knowledge about the people the state has obliged the church to take spiritual care of. And, to this end, the church should manage the population registries (SOU 1944:52, p. 137). In other reviews by the clergy, it was clear that they could not see themselves *not* collecting data about the population.

However, a few small and less influential authorities espoused the committee's bill proposal. The National Board of Health and Welfare argued that the reorganization would lead to a considerable increase in effectiveness, while also facilitating 'the modern society's adaption to its social tasks' (SOU 1944:52, p. 138). In contrast to many of the bill proposal's critics, the National Board of Health and Welfare argued in their review that 'duplication of records' would actually be beneficial since it would lead to, or create better conditions for, increased control (SOU 1944:52, p. 139). The National Commission for Economic Defence, too, stressed that the suggested reorganization would be important, especially in case of a consumption cap during wartime or in time of crisis. Also, the military defence would benefit from a central vocational and employment registration, as the civilian population could be 'more rationally employed to fill the functions of military service and agricultural production' (SOU 1944:52, pp. 134–135).

The annual census – minor miscalculations and human errors

Several influential authorities and clerical institutions disputed the claim that there were substantial problems with the current organization. Discrepancies in data provided by the county tax offices and the parishes for the annual census, for example, were not substantial. The National Bureau of Statistics argued that miscalculations were minor and also that the discrepancies had decreased from 6.06 to 0.68 per thousand only in one year (1935). Since the miscalculations were not directly related to any problems with the current organizational arrangements, the National Bureau of Statistics explained them as being caused by human errors or other factors, which never could be fully controllable anyway (SOU 1944:52, p. 130).

Of the reviewing organizations, the National Bureau of Statistics was the most critical. The clergy ought to remain responsible for the registration of the population, they wrote in their review, since the clergy had the right knowledge and the best tools for this demanding task. Instead, they concluded, the state should seek to improve its civil registration (SOU 1944:52, pp. 132–133). The committee noted, though, that none of the reviewing authorities directly reflected upon the idea of introducing the birth number (SOU 1944:52, p. 140).

This indicates, among other things, that the birth number was overshadowed by the proposed merger. As it aimed at simplifying the communication between the clergy and the state, not the state and the citizen, the latter was largely missing in these discussions. Because of the heavy criticism against the proposal, especially from the National Bureau of Statistics, the merger never materialized. Instead, as has often been the case in Sweden, a new committee was appointed to investigate the issue further.

World War II and a renewed interest in numbering bodies

In September 1941, World War II had been going on for two years and the coalition government decided to appoint a new committee to investigate, once again, how the population registration and tax collection could be reorganized, preferably by merging them into one organization. The investigation was based on the government's need for 'reliable census data', which had 'expanded considerably since the outbreak of the war', as well as for saving purposes (SOU 1944:52, p. 145). A comprehensive accumulation of 'rational, modern census data' would generally contribute to demographics, social statistics and all other statistics that rely on, or benefit from, aggregated individual data (SOU 1944:52, p. 146). With more reliable and detailed data, the social statistics would 'in many areas serve as a better knowledge tool than ever before', the new committee wrote (SOU 1944:52, p. 146). In many respects, the new committee recycled its predecessor's proposal in so far as a unique birth number, one for each citizen, would be introduced here too.

As different authorities wanted to gather more and more data about the population, the new committee feared that the clergy would be burdened with an increasing amount of reporting obligations to the state in the near future. For example, the conscription enlistment of 1943 forced the clergy to communicate every change in a person's occupation to several different state authorities. Notifications of migration were becoming a heavy burden for the clergy also. A couple of County Administrative Boards had on their own initiative already established continuously updated records of persons' current places of residence (as opposed to previously, when these records were updated annually). Given the clergy's obligations to continuously report changes in their ledgers to various state authorities, the new committee asked:

> Why not make this notification as complete as needed from different viewpoints but limit the notification obligations to this one and only, and put all other notification obligations to the authority, responsible for the [here proposed] Central Registry?
>
> (SOU 1944:52, p. 152)

The clergy would now report changes in their ledgers to *one* state authority only, which would then forward information to other relevant state authorities. This also sought to solve another problem. Previous attempts at transferring the task of registering the population from the church to the state had met heavy criticism. To avoid being at odds with the clergy, the division between church and state had to be clearly demarcated. The new committee demarcated this division by arguing that, even though the birth number would be beneficial for both civil and military purposes, it would be of 'less importance in the ecclesiastical registries, as the possibilities already offered by the church records in this respect are sufficient' (SOU 1944:52, p. 168). Consequently, the clergy would continue to enter information about the population in their bound ledgers. This would be supplemented, however, by an additional associated ledger in which a replaceable card, called 'the personal file', would represent each citizen (SOU 1944:52, p. 5 and p. 16).

As the clergy would communicate births, marriages and deaths, as well as notifications of non-existent persons and migrations, to *one* state authority, a new authority set up to receive this data had to be established. The committee named it the National Registration Office. This authority would be the central node in the new organization of population registration (SOU 1944:52, p. 52). The National Registration Office would, moreover, establish the series of birth numbers and keep track of it, unless the County Administrative Boards were given this task (SOU 1944:52, p. 52). The government went for the latter proposal. The County Administrative Boards were to manage the data provided by the clergy as well as the series of birth numbers. A new index card system would be created also, and all data in this new system would effectively radiate around, and become accessible through, the birth number. For it to work as planned, though, it had to be uniformly written.

> The birth number consists of four with hyphens separated groups of numbers, written in sequence and containing; first, the person's year of birth, written with four digits; second, his month of birth and; third, his

day of birth, each written with two digits, while the fourth group consists of a three-digit number, odd for males and even for females, which also represents the person's serial number the day he or she was born.

The same number shall not represent more than one person; neither shall any one person be represented by more than one number.

(SOU 1944:52, p. 2)

Writing the birth number in fractions was now seen as inappropriate. A birth number based on the date of birth would be much easier to memorize for each citizen. It would, moreover, be written on a straight line. In the bill proposal, two examples are used to illustrate this (Kungl. Maj:ts proposition, 1946, pp. 43–45).

1 A male born on 9 January 1925 is given the birth number 1925-01-09-037.
2 A female born on 29 December 1928 is given the birth number 1928-12-29-002.

The three additional digits effectively turned the birth number into a personal series of digits, which is easy to memorize. The very last digit denotes whether the person is male or female: odd for men, even for women. Data on place of birth, so important in the earlier proposal, had now been abandoned. Knowing only a person's birth number would be enough to locate her current place of residence. In order not to burden the clergy, the clergy were instructed only to enter the entire birth number in the newly proposed 'personal file', not in other bound ledgers.

Since the County Administrative Boards were to manage the series of birth numbers, the digits at the end of the number, 001–999, had to be divided into smaller quotas for each County Administrative Board. In the unlikely event that a county would run out of numbers, e.g. due to too many babies born on the same day, additional numbers would be provided from a reserve series, managed by the newly launched National Registration Office. The same procedure would apply to immigrants.

For each church-registered person in the kingdom there shall be one, in ordinance with the King's decision and by the county office or the national authority established birth number, odd for men and even for women, a birth number which is intended to, in conjunction with the date of birth, be used as a means for personal identification.

(Kungl. Maj:ts proposition, 1946, p. 2)

When reviewing the bill proposal, many ecclesial and civil authorities suggested amendments. For example, month and day ought to change places, as was common practice already. For a man born on 9 January in 1925 as the thirty-seventh person that day, his birth number would be written like this:

25 9/1 37. Another idea was to add the county's official letter at the end of the birth number: *1925-01-09-C.* Not only would this designate the person's place of origin, it would also make the reserve series unnecessary. The pastor's office in the City of Vallentuna was more critical. They argued that a number ought not to replace one's name where 'it would be natural' (Kungl. Maj:ts proposition, 1946, p. 41).

After decades of discussions, the birth number was finally implemented on 1 January 1947. It served several purposes. In addition to simplifying tax collection and securing the citizen's identity, it also facilitated reliable and inexpensive demographical data and social statistics. With this administrative technological infrastructure a new regime of personal identification had emerged, by which the citizens could exercise their social rights as long as they utilized the technology provided by the state to prove their identity. This new regime emerged during wartime, a time when the coalition government undertook several administrative and organizational reforms that would have been unthinkable otherwise. After the war, the Social Democratic government decided to proceed with the committee's suggestions and most parts of the bill proposal. The Act of National Registration (SFS 1946:469) came into force on 1 January 1947 (Kungörelse 1946:783). Should a person migrate, decease or turn out to be non-existent, the clergy simply posted the replaceable 'personal file' in their bound ledger to the County Administrative Board, which then forwarded the information to other state authorities.

Golden Age of Capitalism and the growth of the welfare state

Just after World War II ended, many predicted a period marked by economic decline and perhaps even a second Great Depression, similar to the development post World War I. How wrong they were. Although inflation rose drastically, the post-war period stands out in the history books due to its unprecedented dual development: on the one hand the Golden Age of Capitalism, and, on the other hand the growth of the welfare state. In Sweden, many of the social reforms that today characterize the welfare state were implemented during the 1950s and 1960s. While the welfare state grew, it also changed direction and scope. Esping-Andersen (1994, p. 90) has argued that many reforms after World War II aimed at moving away from the ideal of 'minimalist equality', i.e. equal access, fair opportunities and non-discrimination, to 'maximalist levelling', i.e. equal outcomes and empowering of disadvantages groups. Both the new pension system and the health care insurance system were universal, incorporating all citizens, but geared to benefit the working class and the middle class. Benefits were also adjusted so as to meet each citizen's income and expectations. All this led to a significant increase in government spending and taxes during the 1960s.

By this time, computers were commonplace in the larger corporations and in some public organizations for automated data processing (ADP) (SOU

1961:4, 1961; SOU 1962:32, 1962). The National Bureau of Statistics informed the government that they needed ADP to process large amounts of data. By entering demographical data on punch cards, the pace of, and accuracy in, the computations would improve dramatically. Soon after the National Bureau of Statistics had voiced this desire, a committee was appointed to investigate how ADP could equip both the population registration and the tax collecting organizations (SOU 1961:18). Several state authorities were in favour of implementing ADP as the use of 'hard data' in social planning had expanded drastically over the last years. Demographic data was also seen as pivotal for achieving the expected results in the welfare reforms concerning health care, elderly care and education (Kungl. Maj:ts proposition, 1963, p. 39). Just as before, though, the County Administrative Boards would remain responsible for gathering data from the clergy, but now they were given the additional task of operating the ADP technology (Kungl. Maj:ts proposition, 1963, pp. 44–45).

A parliament decision in 1963 stated that the whole state apparatus should adopt this new technology. The County Administrative Boards should purchase the mechanical, punch card machines, while a central facility should be constructed, common for the whole country, for electronic data processing (EDP). This prompted changes to the way the birth number was written. But there were additional reasons for changing it. A coherent definition of the birth number was lacking both in ordinary language and in state authorities. Different authorities used different concepts. Some had developed a definition in which only the last three digits referred to the birth number. Other authorities included the date of birth also in the birth number (SOU 1966:16, p. 155). To clean up the language and make it suitable for ADP, a new name was suggested: the person number. Another suggestion was the self-number. But, in the bill proposal the person number was chosen and defined as:

> For each person a person number shall be established as marker of identity. The person number shall consist of the date of birth, a birth number and a control digit.
>
> The date of birth shall be written with six digits, two for the year, two for the month and two for the day, written in the order now mentioned.
>
> The birth number consists of three digits, odd for men and even for women.
>
> (Kungl. Maj:ts proposition, 1967, pp. 3–4)

Due to this new technology, standardization became necessary. To further reduce the risk of human errors and mistyped or incorrect numbers, a control digit was added using the Luhn algorithm. For the citizens, the change from the birth number to the person number only meant that one additional digit had to be memorized and used when proving one's identity to state authorities and corporations (SOU 1966:16, p. 155).

The summer of personal integrity

The population and housing census of 1970 marked the beginning of a public debate on how data about people's living conditions and attitudes could potentially be used by the state. Public awareness about the massive amount of data collected and the vast bureaucratic knowledge processed and stored sparked a lively debate. Earlier similar administrative reforms and censuses had not encountered public protests. Though different state authorities had been able to map the population prior to the 1970 census, too, the ADP technology together with the person number opened new possibilities for the state to crosscheck different forms of personal data in several registers. As the opportunities for selecting, sorting and comparing data improved, numerous ways of exploiting the data quickly materialized. At the same time, the files and documents created with ADP technology became available to the public. Since these files and documents were subject to the law regulating public access to official documents, private corporations could access and even purchase large series of personal data from state authorities, e.g. for marketing purposes (SOU 1972:47, pp. 41–43; SOU 1978:54, pp. 33–34).

As in many other Western European countries, leftist sentiments swept across Sweden during the late 1960s and early 1970s. Though the debate surrounding the 1970 census was sparked by people on the left, it did not generate a popular critique against the state. Instead, the issue of privacy entered into the parliamentary and public debate. This eventually led the Social Democratic Party to implement the world's first Data Protection Act (SFS 1973:289), which regulated both public and private registers containing personal data. To enforce the new legislation a new authority under the Ministry of Justice was constructed: the Swedish Data Inspection Board (Datainspektionen, 2016). This board was also given the task of compiling lists of all registers in the country that used the person number.

The way forward

Since the person number is the most significant administrative technology for proving one's personal identity, it has increasingly been abused and involved in identity thefts, often for purchasing goods online. Insurance companies and retailers have pressured the state to improve the regulation of person number, e.g. by introducing the possibility to block the person number for certain usages (Syrén and Geijer, 2015).

The tax authority has warned that the person numbers will eventually run out, mainly due to the fact that many immigrants are registered as being 'born' on the first of January. In light of this, the question has been raised whether the person number must be linked to the day of birth or if it is possible to issue randomized person numbers.

The government appointed a committee to investigate the use of the person number in an increasingly digital society (SOU 2007:47). Although the person number is identified as one of the key methods for quick and easy personal identification, it must be complemented by additional security measures when used in ICT.

This chapter has investigated the introduction of the person number as an administrative technology that enabled the emerging welfare state to map individual citizens as well as its entire population. Both the birth number and the person number were introduced so as to administer the extensive social reforms implemented both before and after World War II. As Garland (2001) and Higgs (2001) have suggested, personal identification tends to become pivotal the moment the government decides to enhance controls on spending. In Sweden, however, securing tax revenue was the prime impetus behind the introduction of the birth number and the person number. Despite several proposals, the merger of the state's tax collection organization and the clergy's population registration did not materialize until the year 2000.

During the Golden Age of Capitalism, the person number was geared to be a form of registration as well as an instrument for the documentation of every citizen liable to pay tax. Not only did it work as an instrument in the administration of retirement benefits and other welfare reforms, it also worked as a uniform method for the citizens to claim their social rights. According to Foucault, the examination system and its disciplinary power are exercised as part and parcel of the administration of the documents concerning the individual. Statistical surveys, as well as the way bureaucratic knowledge is used, force the individual into predetermined categories and place them in special compartments, simultaneously constituting the person as a subject in a certain fixed position (Steinwedel, 2001). But this does not hold true in this case. The person number effectively turned individuals into legal persons, while connecting it to citizenship, that is, the right to have rights. In this sense, the person number was crucial both for the welfare state and its population, as entitlements to basic social rights required citizenship.

The parliamentary and public debate following the 1970 census revealed a fear of the state having too much knowledge about people's lives and attitudes. The concept of privacy entered the public consciousness as a consequence of this. A new bill was also introduced, the Data Protection Act (SFS 1973:289), which would protect individuals against privacy violations by the state or corporations.

References

Caplan, J. (2001) 'This or That Particular Person': Protocols of Identification in Nineteenth-century Europe, in J. Caplan and J. Torpey (eds), *Documenting Individual Identity: The Development of State Practices in the Modern World* (Princeton, NJ: Princeton University Press).

Datainspektionen (2016) *Historik. Datainspektionen 1973–2011.* Available online at www.datainspektionen.se/om-oss/historik).

Esping-Andersen, G. (1994) Jämlikhet, effektivitet och makt, in T. Per and K. Östberg (eds), *Den svenska modellen* (Lund: Studentlitteratur).

94   *A. Paulsson*

Foucault, M. (1975) *Discipline and Punish: The Birth of the Prison* (New York: Random House).

Foucault, M. (1978) *The History of Sexuality Vol. 1* (New York: Parthenon).

Garland, D. (2001) *The Culture of Control: Crime and Social Order in Contemporary Society* (Oxford: Oxford University Press).

Higgs, E. (2001) 'The rise of the information state: the development of central state surveillance of the citizen in England, 1500–2000'. *Journal of Historical Sociology*, Vol. 14, No. 2, pp. 175–197.

Kungl. Maj:ts proposition (1946) *Proposition (1946:255) till riksdagen med förslag till folkbokföringsförordning, m m.* (Stockholm: Riksdagstryck: Bihang till riksdagens protokoll år 1946, 1:a saml., 14:e band, C 14.).

Kungl. Maj:ts proposition (1963) *Proposition (1963:32) till riksdagen angående riktlinjer för organisationen av folkbokförings- och uppbördsväsendet, m m* (Stockholm: Riksdagstryck: Bihang till riksdagens protokoll år 1963, 1:a saml., 7:e band, C 7.).

Kungl. Maj:ts proposition (1967) *Proposition (1967:88) till riksdagen med förslag till folkbokföringsförordning, m.M.* (Stockholm).

Kungörelse 1946:783 (1946) *Kungörelse (1946:783) med vissa bestämmelser om födelsenummer.* Report for Riksdagen (Stockholm).

Kälvemark, A.-S. (1979) The Country That Kept Track of its Population. Methodological Aspects of Swedish Populations Records, in J. Sundin and E. Söderlund (eds), *Time, Space and Man. Essays on Microdemography* (Uppsala: Almqvist & Wiksell).

Miller, P. and T. O'Leary (1994) Governing the Calculable Person, in A. G. Hopwood and P. Miller (eds), *Accounting as Social and Institutional Practice* (Cambridge: Cambridge University Press).

Noiriel, G. (2001) The Identification of the Citizen: The Birth of Republican Civil Status in France, in J. Caplan and J. Torpey (eds), *Documenting Individual Identity: The Development of State Practices in the Modern World* (Princeton, NJ: Princeton University Press).

Rose, N. (1991) 'Governing by numbers: figuring out democracy'. *Accounting, Organizations and Society*, Vol. 16, No. 7, pp. 673–692.

Scott, J. C. (1998) *Seeing like a State: How Certain Schemes to Improve the Human Condition Have Failed* (New Haven, CT: Yale University Press).

SFS 1946:469 (1946) *Folkbokföringslag (1946:469).* Available online at www.riksdagen.se/sv/Dokument-Lagar/Lagar/Svenskforfattningssamling/Folkbokforingslag-1967198_sfs-1967-198.

SFS 1967:198 (1967) *Folkbokföringslag (1967:198).* Available online at www.riksdagen.se/sv/Dokument-Lagar/Lagar/Svenskforfattningssamling/Folkbokforingslag-1967198_sfs-1967-198.

SFS 1973:289 (1973) *Datalag (1973:289).* Available online at www.riksdagen.se/sv/Dokument-Lagar/Lagar/Svenskforfattningssamling/Datalag-1973289_sfs-1973-289.

Skatteverket (2008) *Skatteverket (2008). Personnummer. Skv 704 utgåva 8.* Available online at www.skatteverket.se/download/18.1e6d5f87115319ffba380001857/1359707375938/70408.pdf.

SOU 1938:41 (1938) *Statens offentliga utredningar (1938:41). Omorganisation av uppbördsväsendet och folkbokföringen m.M. Del ii: Folkbokföringen.* Report for Regeringen (Stockholm).

SOU 1944:52 (1944) *Statens offentliga utredningar (SOU) 1944:52. Omorganisation av folkbokföringen.* Report for Regeringen (Stockholm).

SOU 1961:4 (1961) *Automatisk databehandling inom folkbokförings- och uppbördsväsendet. Del i.* Report for Regeringen (Stockholm).

SOU 1961:18 (1961) *Statens offentliga utredningar (SOU) 1961:18 automatisk databehandling inom folkbokförings- och uppbördsväsendet. Del ii. Datamaskiner hos länsstyrelserna.* Report for Regeringen (Stockholm).

SOU 1962:32 (1962) *Statens offentliga utredningar (SOU) 1962:32. Automatisk databehandling.* Report for Regeringen (Stockholm).

SOU 1966:16 (1966) *Statens offentliga utredningar (SOU) 1966:16. Ny folkbokföringsförordning m.M.* Report for Regeringen (Stockholm).

SOU 1972:47 (1972) *Statens offentliga utredningar (SOU) 1972: 47. Data och integritet.* Report for Regeringen (Stockholm).

SOU 1978:54 (1978) *Statens offentliga utredningar (SOU) 1978:54. Personregister – datorer – integritet.* Report for Regeringen (Stockholm).

SOU 2007:47 (2007) *Statens offentliga utredningar (SOU) 2007:47. Den osynliga infrastrukturen – om förbättrad samordning av offentlig it-standardisering.* Report for Regeringen (Stockholm).

Steinwedel, C. (2001) Making Social Groups, One Person at a Time: The Identification of Individuals by Estate, Religious Confession, and Ethnicity in Late Imperial Russia, in J. Caplan and J. Torpey (eds), *Documenting Individual Identity: The Development of State Practices in the Modern World* (Princeton, NJ: Princeton University Press).

Syrén, A. and P. Geijer (2015) *Personnummer måste kunna skyddas bättre* (Stockholm: SvD).

Torpey, J. (1997) 'Revolutions and freedom of movement: an analysis of passport controls in the French, Russian, and Chinese revolutions'. *Theory and Society*, Vol. 26, pp. 837–868.

Torpey, J. (1998) 'Coming and going: on the state monopolization of the legitimate "means of movement"'. *Sociological Theory*, Vol. 16, No. 3, pp. 239–259.

Weber, M. (1978) *Economy and Society. An Outline of Interpretative Sociology* (Los Angles and Berkeley, CA: University of California Press).

Part II

Governance and modernization

'Governance' preserves order and continuity, but is not necessarily the maintenance of the status quo.

(Dunsire, 1990, p. 18)

Order and continuity, but also change and improvement. This is one way to attach meaning to this 'magic concept' (Pollitt and Hupe, 2011). Societal order and predictability may be key to trust, something that needs to be earned and maintained. Many countries, not least the Scandinavian ones, have seen Supreme Audit Institutions (SAI) strengthened or introduced as a consequence of an increased focus on public-sector performance and NPM reforms. Performance auditing has become a key aspect of public-sector governance and, as the public sector moves from traditional public administration to a system aimed at governing diverse actors on the basis of market forces, trust in these institutions is imperative. It is suggested here that the distinctive positioning of Scandinavian SAIs may be of particular interest to countries which are or aspire to be egalitarian countries like the Scandinavian ones.

It has been suggested (Grindle, 2011) that we need new ways of governance in the public sector. The Scandinavian way offers an alternative to the neo-liberal model. Trust is a fundamental property of the Scandinavian public sector. In Sweden, the governance and performance of the public sector is signified by far-reaching autonomy in both government agencies and local governments. Since 1720, Swedish government agencies have constitutionally been 'semi-autonomous' in relation to the government. This, however, is not a static relation. From a system-wide perspective, we can illustrate how relations between agency management and parent ministry, the relation between agency management and employees (street-level bureaucrats) and the relation between the agency and the citizenry vary over time and with the individuals involved. It is indicated that constitutional and institutional arrangements are systems within systems – delicate, trust-related interactions between director-general, agency and ministry all affect one another. Similarly, in the world of higher education. The strategic plans of Lund University are analysed and show how NPM has also influenced how this sector is governed. As in many other contexts, two dominant logics – collegiality and managerialism – appear in conflict. The university governance, in terms of arranging and coordinating incumbent actors, becomes a matter of the vice chancellor handling these logics and making sense of ambiguity, inconsistency and paradoxes. The case illustrates a process, perhaps typically Swedish, of finding a middle way of 'muddling through' between two logics.

One key governance issue in Scandinavia and Sweden is how to arrange and coordinate service provision under conditions where demographics change quickly. Inter-municipal cooperation becomes increasingly important in municipalities in Sweden. The challenges are upholding welfare services and governing new relations while still maintaining citizens' trust. In relation to the 'hybrid' municipal company with a board, the determination of board positions raises issues over the fairness of appointment processes.

References

Dunsire, A. (1990) 'Holistic governance'. *Public Policy and Administration*, Vol. 5, No. 4, pp. 4–19.

Grindle, M. (2011) 'Governance reform: the new analytics of next steps'. *Governance: An International Journal of Policy, Administration, and Institutions*, Vol. 24, No. 3, pp. 415–418.

Pollitt, C. and P. Hupe (2011) 'Talking about government. The role of magic concepts'. *Public Management Review*, Vol. 13, No. 5, pp. 641–658.

7 The unfolding of agency autonomy over time

The Swedish Social Insurance Agency 2003–2015

Louise Bringselius

Summary

The literature on agency autonomy typically assumes that agency autonomy is relatively stable over time and that it unfolds primarily in the relation between agencies and their parent ministries. This chapter challenges these assumptions. It explores how agency autonomy unfolds over time from a system-wide perspective, including the relation between the agency and its parent ministry, the relation between management and employees and the relation between the agency and the citizenry. Data from a qualitative case study of the Swedish Social Insurance Agency (SIA), covering the 12-year period 2003–2015, is reported. Observations indicate that the agency/ministry relation has changed with each director-general but they also indicate that there is a delicate interaction between the three relations, where they all impact on one another. This suggests that agency autonomy may be best understood as volatile and formed in a complex web of relations.

Introduction

Until the 1980s, in the OECD countries public-sector organizations were typically incorporated into the realms of the political administration in central government. This allowed policymakers extensive influence over the policy process, including policy implementation. However, it also entailed the risk that policy implementation would become politicized – and, as a consequence, possibly also inefficient. This concern contributed to a long series of reforms, still ongoing today, where many OECD countries have chosen to transfer responsibilities for policy implementation to semi-autonomous bodies at arm's length from central government and its ministries. This shift is sometimes referred to as *agencification* (O'Toole and Jordan, 1995; Pollitt *et al.*, 2001; Pollitt *et al.*, 2004; Van Thiel and Yesilkagit, 2011).

The increasing interest in the agency model is coupled with a more general trend towards decentralization and disaggregation in the public sector. However, the opposite trend, namely reforms focused on centralization and the (informal) reduction of agency autonomy, can today also be found in the public sector. In a few cases, this involves not only the informal relations between the agency and its parent ministry, but also the formal-legal relation between these (legal autonomy). Some of these cases are found in Sweden. This is not very surprising, considering that Sweden was also one of the first countries in the world to adopt the agency model. This means that Sweden also has had time to experience the downsides of it. As with any type of reform, in particular when these are taken very far, it will eventually tend to result in new problems and issues. This is also the case with the structurally disaggregated design of the administration. This has resulted in, for example, fragmentation, weakened political control and blame-avoidance issues (Christensen and Lægreid, 2006; Pollitt, 2006; Verhoest *et al.*, 2012; Yesilkagit and van Thiel, 2008). Against this backdrop, there is a growing acceptance for the idea that there is a need to reassert the state and regain some of the control over the administration that has been lost during all the years when structural devolution has been the general fad.

In Sweden, an example of a reform aiming to reduce, rather than increase, formal-legal agency autonomy was implemented in 2005. This was the last fully autonomous executive agency under the government and it was transformed into a semi-autonomous agency, meaning that it had a status equal to that of other executive agencies in Sweden. One of the aspects that make this case interesting is the model of corporatism that characterizes Sweden and the other Nordic countries. This means that there is a high level of involvement of various external stakeholders in the work of the administration. This indicates, we argue, that there may be a need to explore not only the relation between the agency and its parent ministry but also other relations when trying to understand how de facto agency autonomy unfolds over time. This study focuses on three relations: (1) the relation between ministry and agency director-general; (2) the relation between the director-general and the street-level bureaucrats within the agency; (3) the relation between the agency and the citizenry (clients and potential clients). The agency autonomy literature is today primarily preoccupied with the first of these relations, but this chapter wishes to broaden this perspective and also include other key relations. This chapter describes and analyses how the three relations mentioned above change over time, and how they interact. It builds on the case study of an executive central agency in a context of corporatism. The case selected for this study is interesting in particular because of its transformation from full autonomous status to semi-autonomous status, but also because it has undergone a major crisis, challenging trust in many different relations: the Swedish Social Insurance Agency (SIA).

The study builds on document studies and interviews. Observations suggest that the relation between the agency and its parent ministry changed with each director-general, suggesting that agency autonomy may be highly volatile with interpersonal relations or individual agendas. Observations suggest that there is a need to also understand other agency relations when trying to understand how agency autonomy unfolds over time. This may be of particular relevance in countries characterized by a high degree of corporatism, meaning that stakeholders are an important source of legitimacy.

The reformation of the SIA 2003–2014

For many years, the SIA had been something of an 'odd bird' in the Swedish administration. While other traditional agencies (not including the National Audit Office or the Central Bank) were semi-autonomous, this was the only agency which enjoyed full autonomy, although it was funded by the government. The reasons for this could be found further back in history, when the social funds were set up.

The social insurance administration was launched as a citizen movement. The first law governing sickness benefit funds was passed in Sweden in 1891. Its purpose was to support the existing voluntary sickness benefit funds. All registered funds were provided with public subsidies and advice. At this time, only a small proportion of the population, about 3 per cent, was insured through the sickness benefit funds, but this number increased rapidly, in particular following the introduction of centralized benefit funds in 1933. In 1955, a law making health insurance public was passed and social welfare services were now provided to all citizens. The social insurance administration consisted of 21 County Sickness Insurance Offices (CSIO) and a central agency, the National Social Insurance Board (Swedish: *Riksförsäkringsverket*), also reporting to the Ministry of Health and Social Affairs. This agency provided with recommendations to the county funds and with reviews and other data to the ministry. The CSIOs, however, enjoyed a unique legal status among the executive agencies in central government, making them the only legally autonomous bodies under the central government. However, it was the ministry that provided them with their funding. The CSIOs were represented by a shared interest organization, the Association of Social Insurance Offices (Swedish: *Försäkringskasseförbundet*).

For many years, there had been an ongoing debate concerning the need for a reformation of the social insurance administration. One of the reasons for this was the soaring costs for early retirement pensions and long-term sickness allowances. With its widespread presence throughout the country and its special legal status, the SIA had turned into a political tool in regional unemployment politics, in the sense that citizens who were not able to gain access to the labour market were often offered long-term sickness pension or early retirement, instead of remaining in the unemployment insurance system for a long time (Eriksson *et al.*, 2008). Early retirement pensions could be used to push the costs of long-term unemployment on from municipalities to central government.

In addition, a culture had developed, since the early days of the agency (when it was a voluntary fund established by the citizenry), where some social security officers saw themselves as partners to the insured (here referred to as the citizen/citizenry). Instead of making decisions that the citizen disliked, they could approve generous allowances and pensions.

In 2003, a column in one of the major Swedish newspapers summarized the background to the SIA reform in the following way.

> Most people would probably assertively respond yes to the question if the social insurance office is a state agency. But it is not. From an administrative perspective, it rests on two legs, who often wish to go in different directions.
>
> One leg is the National Social Insurance Agency, a state agency. The other leg is the 21 social insurance offices, one in each county, and the Association of social insurance offices, their employer.
>
> The social insurance offices are not state agencies, but independent and legally autonomous institutions with their own boards who decide how the state money should be used. It is an unorthodox solution. A model that has developed through history, but that encompass obscurity, conflict and unequal treatment.
>
> In the boards of the social insurance offices, there are local policymakers who have a vested interest in pushing costs over to the state. Rather early retirement paid by the state than measures funded by the municipality or county.
>
> The National Social Insurance Board and the social insurance offices have been in conflict for many years. They struggle over how allowance policies shall be interpreted, and what data decisions should be based on.
>
> Our right to have social insurance allowances is governed by laws that should be equal to everyone, all over the country. But the social insurance offices apply these laws differently. The system hinders the rule of law.
>
> When the National Social Insurance Board, for example, scrutinized how the social insurance offices handled six different types of benefits, the handling of four of these failed. Out of almost 800 requests for early retirement pensions or sickness allowances, every third decision was incorrect. The social insurance offices had not followed the law when it stipulated that all possibilities for rehabilitation had to be investigated. During only one quarter, up to 6,000 people may have been granted early retirement or had sickness benefits on the wrong basis.
>
> Complaints over the decisions of the social insurance offices are numerous with the Parliamentary Ombudsman and in its reports, the National Audit Office has conveyed the image of a relation of distrust between the National Social Insurance Board and the social insurance offices.
>
> The best thing would be to nest the social insurance offices under the governmental ministries and to organize it all as one coherent state agency.
>
> This is also what a governmental commission suggested in 1996. Practically all bodies considering the proposed legislation applauded the suggestion. Except for, not very unexpectedly, the Association of Municipalities, the Association of Regional Councils, the Association of Social Insurance

Offices, and all the social insurance offices. Facing this special interest, the Government backed off. The structure remained intact...

Pressured by the high sickness rates, the Government launched a new commission in April. As Dagens Nyheter has explained, the commissioner is expected to suggest that the social insurance agencies are transferred to a state agency and becomes a part of the National Social Insurance Board, that their boards are abolished and that the influence of local policymakers is reduced. Is it finally time for a reform?

(*Dagens Nyheter*, 19 August 2003)

In the directives (Dir. 2002:166) for the commission preceding the parliamentary decision in May 2004, problems such as inefficiency and lack of proper documentation for decisions were raised. In particular, however, these directives emphasized the problem that the same type of allowance requests was handled differently in different counties and by different officials. Citizens could not be sure that they were treated equally. The commission came to go under the name of the ANSA Commission (Swedish: *Utredningen angående socialförsäkrings-administrationen*).

With the parliamentary decision in May 2004 it was agreed that the 21 autonomous county offices, together forming the SIA, would be merged with the National Insurance Board, which already served as a semi-autonomous agency under the Ministry of Health and Social Affairs. The reform would take place on 1 January 2005. A new commission now worked on outlining how the reform should be implemented from an organizational point of view. This commission was referred to as the GEORG Commission (Swedish: Försäkringskassans genomförandeorganisation). In its final report (SOU 2004:127) it emphasized that changes had to be incremental in order to ensure that everyday operations were not disturbed.

This was also how the reform initially was rolled out, by the new director-general, Curt Malmborg. As the reform was implemented, the new management team was requested to provide the ministry with a report on how they planned to continue developing the organization in order to ensure a high level of confidence in the social administration and social policy and to ensure that the social insurance administration was aligned with legislation and public policy while treating citizens equally across the country, and in order to improve efficiency. According to the response from the SIA management team (Dnr 83686–2005), the plan was to continue working towards these goals in accordance with the ideas that were outlined in the previous commission (the GEORG Commission).

However, in 2007, a more ambitious change plan was set up. As opposed to the ideas of the GEORG Commission, this was designed and implemented in a highly centralized fashion, with little transparency and scarce opportunities for the various internal and external stakeholders (including unions) to object. A small group of people from the agency management formed a secretariat, called the 'change programme'. They had a series of changes rolled out at a rapid pace. In particular, the model with county offices was now abandoned and national insurance centres were formed. The change programme also included time-measuring procedures, continued work on standardized protocols, office shutdown and mergers, personnel cuts and general budget cuts. All employees at the agency (circa 14,000 people) were disconnected from their previous positions and had to apply for a position again. Many employees were made redundant. In addition to this, a new and more restrictive sickness insurance policy was passed through parliament and the SIA was required to implement this. There was a rage of protests from all sides. The director-general worked closely with the ministry, who had recruited him, to handle these protests and continue with the reform. However, there was also a rapidly growing discontent against this close collaboration. Social security officers and citizens were both upset and there were thousands of critical reports in the media, focusing both on the reform process and on those people who were no longer entitled to sickness allowances.

The change management programme eventually lost control over the vast changes included in the reform programme. The time that citizens now had to wait for a decision from the SIA on their applications, questions etc. had now been extended to weeks – far beyond what was required by the SIA in the government directives. In addition, it turned out that the SIA would run out of funding several months before the end of the budget year. The situation had now come to a point where the director-general had to resign from his position. Instead, Adriana Lender was quickly assigned to the post by the ministry. She had worked in top positions at the SIA for many years. She wanted to restore the relationship between the management team and the social security officers within the SIA and improved communication in various ways. However, she was more distanced in relation to both ministry and citizenry, emphasizing that this was a bureaucracy and that their primary task was to implement public policy – not to challenge it or to interpret this according to their own liking. In the media, she challenged the ministry by pointing critics to them and explaining that the SIA merely implemented the directives given by them. In this way, her approach was different from that of her predecessor, who had worked closely with the ministry and avoided confronting or blaming the ministry in the public debate.

The ministry became increasingly annoyed with this attitude from the director-general and, with only a few months left of her appointment, the ministry had her replaced with a new director-general, Dan Eliasson. He had previously been the director-general of the Swedish Migration Board (Migrationsverket), meaning that he was well known to the government. Dan Eliasson talked about the importance of empathy with those seeking allowances from the SIA and he also started a campaign seeking suggestions from citizens and social security officers on how public policy could be changed in order to reduce administration for the SIA. This resulted in a list of suggestions to the government (Försäkringskassan, 2012); the SIA suggested 30 changes and the work has continued since then. This list was also advertised in the media, making it explicit that the SIA wanted to collaborate both with citizens and with the ministry to improve the situation for all. In 2014, Dan Eliasson was appointed director-general of the Swedish Police when this was about to undergo a major reform. By this time, the SIA was generally understood to be a well-functioning agency and the flood of critical reports in the media had basically ebbed away.

A model to understand the reformation process

The reformation of the SIA unfolded over a long period of time, as the account above shows. In particular, the relation to both ministry and citizenry, but also within the agency, shifted over time and with the different directors-general. The visions and attitudes of the directors-general shape the relationships of the agency. These visions also include ideals in terms of the identity of the agency. What should the agency be and what role should it take in different relations?

Figure 7.1 outlines how the reformation process during the years 2003–2014 can be understood as consisting of four phases. Each phase ends with a new director-general being put into office. Phase 1 ends when the reform is implemented.

The figure suggests that the SIA functioned as a Citizen Partner before the reform, with a distanced relation to the ministry. Building on the history of the social insurance administration as a citizen movement, local social insurance officers focused on meeting the requests of those insured, rather than challenging these requests. A more restrictive approach to the social insurance was requested by the ministry.

Directly after the reform had been implemented, the new director-general and the ministry worked closely together, but instead a divide in relation to social security officers and citizens emerged. Many officers

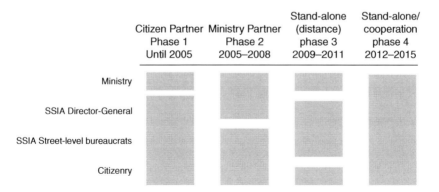

Figure 7.1 Relations during the reformation of the Swedish Social Insurance Agency (2003–2014).

wanted to preserve their role as Citizen Partners and this was also what many citizens expected. By working closely together, the SIA management and the ministry tried to communicate a new approach to the sickness insurance, emphasizing that this should build on an evaluation of the individual work capacity rather than whether or not the individual could be classified as 'sick'.

After the administrative crisis in 2007, a new director-general came into office. She wanted the SIA to function as a classic bureaucracy, and emphasized that the SIA should simply implement public policy, but otherwise its relation to both citizens and ministry should be distanced. She was not prepared to let the SIA take the blame for the new restrictive sickness insurance policy but pointed towards the ministry when approached by the media in this matter.

Finally, when Dan Eliasson began as director-general, the SIA started cooperating more closely in all these relations. This also included cooperation on public policy and a friendlier and more collaborative tone in marketing campaigns.

This process can also be summarized according to Table 7.1. This includes the names of the directors-general and also a brief account of what happened during each phase.

Table 7.1 The first 10 years at the Social Insurance Agency, outlined as four phases

	Time period	Director-general	Role	Brief
Phase 1	2003–2005	Katrin Westling Palm	Citizen Partner	Preparation for the reform. Some protests, but also support. Soaring sickness allowances creates momentum.
Phase 2	2005–2008	Curt Malmborg	Ministry Partner	Implementation of the reform (2005). New sickness insurance policy. Major change programme. Major protests from clients and officials.
Phase 3	2009–2011	Adriana Lender	Stand-alone/ distance	Continued budget cuts. Improved administration. Distance and conflict agency/ministry.
Phase 4	2012–2014	Dan Eliasson	Stand-alone/ cooperation	Improved administration. Improved relationship with ministry and citizenry. Increased policy collaboration

Below I will describe in more detail what happened during each of the phases.

Phase 1: Citizen Partner

The formal aims with the reform were to 'create greater uniformity throughout the country, reinforce the due process of law and shorten processing times' (Försäkringskassan, 2011, p. 7). However, the reform also reflected an ambition to reduce fragmentation and increase political control over the sickness rehabilitation area. A commission from 2000 (SOU 2000:78) established that the public responsibility for rehabilitation was highly sectorized, meaning that it was divided between four different sectors, which were poorly coordinated. These were the social insurance administration, health care providers, social services and the unemployment administration. In a report from a new government commission, issued two years later, it was suggested that the CSIOs were transferred into 'the normal agency structure' (SOU 2003:63, p. 131). Soon after this, a government commissioner was appointed to outline a general plan for the reform, including a plan to improve coordination between the social insurance administration and the unemployment administration.

Again, the reform was coupled with the intention to implement a more restrictive praxis in the SIA with regard to these benefits. A couple of weeks before the reform an article in one of the major newspapers in Sweden reported:

> Within a few years, the new Social Insurance Agency will provide service and efficiency in world class. But one of the most important prerequisites for this to succeed is a considerably stricter implementation of the sickness insurance policy.
>
> (*SvD*, 17 December 2004)

The commissioner being interviewed, Jan Ryd, explained that the concept of sickness allowance was problematic because it led people to believe that any sick person could have this, but what it really should focus on was rather people's work capacities. The sickness insurance policy did not need to change – the rules were already in place, he explained – but what had failed was the implementation, which had to become more restrictive.

In general, the commissioner estimated that it would be possible to cut costs by around 20 per cent per year after the SIA reform. During the first years, however, these savings would have to be redistributed to other activities within the agency, such as the development of new routines and IT systems. After these initial years, however, it would probably be possible to reduce the agency budget, according to the commissioner.

Another article, about the same time, described the problems at the SIA before the reform as follows.

The old organization has been subjected to heavy criticism for long waiting times for administrative processes, late payments and for not reaching goals in terms of helping people back to work after rehabilitation. Standards have varied from county to county.

(*SvD*, 16 December 2004)

Thus, there was also an ambition to achieve a quicker and more standardized process for the administration of allowance requests as the reform was implemented. Whereas there was broad political support for the reform, however, unions and representatives for the Association of CSIOs were highly critical to the it and objected in various ways. A newspaper article reads:

The social insurance offices of the country fight tooth and nail against the proposition to merge and form a state agency together with the National Social Insurance Board.

– You will lose the democratic dimension on the county level. All the matters that the boards of the social insurance offices decide on today, would be made somewhere else, says Marianne Stålberg, Chairman of the Association of Social Insurance Offices.

(*Dagens Nyheter*, 19 August 2003)

During the years preceding the reform, the SIA served as a partner to the citizen. This partnership meant empathy and flexibility towards the requests and needs of the citizen, but also to the wishes of other local stakeholders (in the local social security boards), were considered central. Table 7.2 provides an overview.

Phase 2: Ministry Partner

The governmental commission (SOU 2003:63) preceding the merger explained that there would be no major restructurings in connection directly to the merger and this was also the way that the reform was implemented in

Table 7.2 Characteristics of the citizen partner phase during the SIA reform

		Citizen Partner
Values	**Agency identity**	Unique partner to the citizen
	Key value	Empathy and flexibility*
Organization	**Central part**	Local offices
	Central mechanism for coordination	Adjustment (bottom-up)
	Central mechanism for control	Collegial control

Note
* Towards individual needs and regional circumstances.

2005. It was emphasized that it was primarily the headquarters that would need to undergo fundamental changes (SOU 2003:106, p. 105f.).

However, in the year after the formal implementation of the reform, plans for major restructuring were presented. This change programme was rolled out to start in 2007. This was called 'the largest government agency reorganisation in modern times' (Försäkringskassan, 2011, p. 7).

Implementation was characterized by limited transparency, a top-down approach (Andersson *et al.*, 2012; Försäkringskassan, 2009a). Standardized protocols for the work of the sickness insurance officers were implemented, along with time-measuring procedures (Bringselius, 2012a). The whole change process was handled by the director-general and a small team of three to four other people and consultants from a major consultancy firm. Decisions were made rapidly within this team and other people from the management team were rarely involved or informed (interview no. 17; Försäkringskassan, 2009b).

The new organization design meant that the former regional offices were abolished and a new regional level was created. Many local offices were also abandoned and some were newly created. In some cases, this meant that employees, in order to stay at the agency, had to commute for hours every day. The change programme meant that around 10,000 employees were requested to change work tasks and many of these also had to work in a different city. A member of the agency management team referred (interview no. 2) to the restructurings in terms of 'a palace revolution' (Swedish: *palatsrevolution*), admitting that these radical changes also were implemented in a top-down fashion. He explained:

> This is on top management level. The Government's goal of becoming an agency of world class will not be achieved by fine-tuning the organization which we have had since the 1950ies. Instead, we have blown up the whole structure. No one requested this, but this was something we decided. There were those who thought things were governed very much from [the head office in] Stockholm – and they were.
>
> (Interview no. 2)

The quote suggests that the interviewee saw the radical change process as justified by the ministry's request for a world-class agency. As a partner to the ministry, it may have been that those in charge of this process, including this interviewee, would be excused by the ministry for any problems that could occurred along the way.

The interviewee (interview no. 2) continued and explained that complaints from employees were natural and usually passing. This resistance always followed the same phases, he explained, and described a model with four phases which ended up with acceptance. Implementing changes bottom-up simply did not work, he maintained. Employees cannot see as far as the management, he explained, adding that 'It is not their job either'.

>There are no changes bottom–up. It does not work that way. Either you
>change because you are in a deep crisis, or because you, as a management
>team, can see beyond the problems which the employees can see right now.
>
> (Interview no. 2)

The change approach lead to major protests from unions, employees and other stakeholders. Protests from citizens often concerned the new, more restrictive public policy, implemented in 2008, for the sickness insurance. However, citizen protests also concerned new agency procedures. For example, after the reform all officials were meant to be anonymous in their contact with clients and it was no longer possible to call a specific official to discuss a specific decision. Instead, clients were requested to write or to contact the SIA call centres. Officials were requested to comply with the new standardized protocols, designed by a team at the head office, in their everyday work. Many officials complained that these protocols were often unrealistic or bad but they had little response and this led to increasing problems with compliance (Bringselius, 2012b). They also complained over the harsh and impersonal approach that they were requested to adopt in the contact with citizens, regardless of their personal situation (Bringselius, 2012b).

In autumn 2008 the agency experienced a major financial and administrative crisis. It started with a highly critical article in the news journal *Computer Sweden* (22 August 2008), disclosing the soaring costs for the new IT system at the SIA, which had exceeded budgets by a large margin. A highly critical report on this subject was presented six months later by the Swedish Supreme Audit Institution (Riksrevisionen 2009:2). The article was followed by a number of other disclosures concerning the chaotic situation at the SIA. In October/November 2008 it turned out that the SIA was rapidly running out of funding and that it would not be able to fund the last month of the budget year. It was lacking almost one billion Swedish Krona. Yet the ministry had been informed in continuous meetings with the SIA director-general that restructurings continued more or less according to plan (interview no. 116). Also, the chair of the SIA board explained that they had been misinformed (interview no. 28) and a blame-avoidance game started, channelled through the media (Bringselius, 2012b).

At the same time as the financial deficit was disclosed in autumn 2008, it became evident also that the SIA was no longer anywhere near the previous deadlines for the management of benefit requests and payments. Citizens reported how they were forced to take bank loans for their daily expenses as benefit payments were delayed for months. In December 2008 the director-general resigned and a new director-general was put in place in January 2009.

The phase as Ministry Partner involved a shift in several regards. It meant that efficiency and correctness replaced empathy and flexibility as key values. It meant that focus shifted from the local offices to the head office, as many decisions were centralized. Top-down authority replaced adjustment, and standardization replaced collegial control. The latter had typically also involved external stakeholders, such as local policymakers, before the reform took place. The characteristics of this second phase are outlined in Table 7.3.

Table 7.3 Characteristics of the first two phases of the SIA reform

		Citizen Partner	Ministry Partner
Values	**Agency identity**	Unique partner to the citizen	A lean and agile tool of the ministry
	Key value	Empathy and flexibility★	Efficient (1) and correct (2)
Organization	**Central part**	Local offices	Head office
	Central mechanism for coordination	Adjustment (bottom–up)	Authority (top–down)
	Central mechanism for control	Collegial control	Standardization

Note
★ Towards individual needs and regional circumstances.

Phase 3: stand-alone/distance

The management staff later explained (Försäkringskassan 2009) that an important explanation for the crisis was the management culture around the director-general, a culture which did not allow for dissent. In interviews (e.g. interview no. 71, December 2009), people at the SIA headquarters described how the former director-general had tried to convey a success story that everyone within the agency knew was untrue. This undermined confidence in him.

With the new director-general, the SIA culture gradually shifted towards more openness and the relationship between management and employees was improved. For example, she opened up opportunities for employees to chat with her over the internal web (the intranet) and she went back to a procedure where many matters were subjected to open internal discussions prior to management decisions. She emphasized that this was part of the tradition in central government. The administrative routines were gradually improved and an investigation of the performance of the SIA during the years 2000–2009 showed that efficiency had indeed increased (ISF, 2010). Another report (Statskontoret, 2009) described how the work load had gradually decreased between 2008 and 2009 and how there were many signs of an improved situation in terms of employee satisfaction.

Tensions between the SIA management and the ministry remained, in particular in issues concerning funding. The SIA relationship with clients was also improved, as the director-general repeatedly explained that they merely implemented public policies, pointing at the ministry and government. In an article from October 2010 in one of the major Swedish newspapers, *Dagens Nyheter*, the director-general also emphasized that the SIA must not be blamed when the government was responsible for public policy (Lender, 2010).

The relation between the ministry and the director-general became increasingly tense and with only a few months left of her appointment she was removed and replaced by a new director-general, who started in October 2011.

The third phase of the reformation process, stand-alone/distance, was characterized by a focus on both correctness and efficiency, but particularly the first. Quality and correctness were now also increasingly emphasized in management decision-making. Stakeholders were invited to express feedback and in general organizational transparency increased. Coordination was achieved through a combination of authority and dialogue and the ideal was the traditional Weberian bureaucracy, with neutrality and objectivity as core features (see Table 7.4).

Phase 4: stand-alone/cooperation

Towards the end of year 2011, Dan Eliasson was appointed the new director-general at the SIA, from the same position at another executive agency in Sweden. Soon after this, he was requested by central government to return

Table 7.4 Characteristics of the first three phases of the SIA reform

		Citizen Partner	Ministry Partner	Stand-alone/distance
Values	**Agency identity**	Unique partner to the citizen	A lean and agile tool of the ministry	Bureaucracy with integrity
Organization	**Key value**	Empathy and flexibility★	Efficient (1) and correct (2)	Correct (1) and efficient (2)
	Central part	Local offices	Head office	Head office
	Central mechanism for coordination	Adjustment (bottom-up)	Authority (top-down)	Authority and dialogue
	Central mechanism for control	Collegial control	Standardization	Standardization

Note
★ Towards individual needs and regional circumstances.

with suggestions as to how public policy can be changed in order to facilitate their work and the work of citizens in the social insurance area. In a response in April 2012 (Försäkringskassan, 2012) the SIA suggested 30 changes and the work has also continued after this, while encouraging SIA officials to contribute suggestions. On the SIA web page, citizens are also encouraged to come up with suggestions. Just one month after the SIA suggestions were presented to central government, a minister explained that he would proceed immediately with one of them.

This cooperation on policy level has also characterized the work of the Swedish Tax Agency (interview no. 39), which often has been presented as a success story among Swedish agency mergers. The Swedish Tax Agency also cooperates closely with its parent ministry in matters of policy design. In Sweden, this kind of cooperation is generally common (Verhoest *et al.*, 2012).

Consequently, the relationship between the SIA and its parent ministry was gradually improved, as was the relationship between the SIA and the citizenry. According to results from an annual survey of citizen attitudes to the SIA, there has been a positive trend in this regard since year 2010. See Figure 7.2.

The relation between the social insurance officers and the agency management were also improved. Major internal projects focused on organizational values were started. The new director-general built on the idea of a formalistic and distanced bureaucracy, but he also talked about empathy with the citizen and tried to build a culture of collaboration.

The values of the final phase during the period included in this study are outlined in Table 7.5. The SIA had now begun to cooperate in all types of relations – while still emphasizing its integrity, however. Dialogue was a key value and focus again shifted back to the local offices.

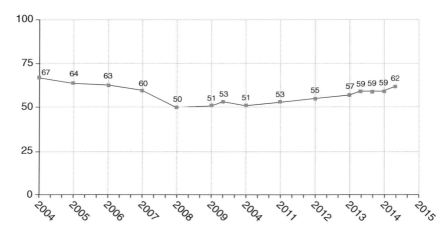

Figure 7.2 The development of the customer satisfaction index for the SIA 2004–2014 (Försäkringskassans kundundersökning, 2014).

Table 7.5 Characteristics of the four phases of the SIA reform

		Citizen Partner	Ministry Partner	Stand-alone/distance	Stand-alone/collaboration
Values	Agency identity	Unique partner to the citizen	A lean and agile tool of the ministry	Bureaucracy with integrity	Collaborative bureaucracy with integrity
	Key value	Empathy and flexibility★	Efficient (1) and correct (2)	Correct (1) and efficient (2)	Combination
Organization	Central part	Local offices	Head office	Head office	Local offices
	Central mechanism for coordination	Adjustment (bottom-up)	Authority (top-down)	Authority and dialogue	Dialogue and authority
	Central mechanism for control	Collegial control	Standardization	Standardization	Standardization

Note
★ Towards individual needs and regional circumstances.

Autonomy as unfolding in a network of relations

In the previous sections, I have blended empirical accounts with discussion and analysis. A framework to understand how the three relations have developed over time has been suggested, and I have argued that these relations have influenced one another in a complex interplay that this brief account only can capture to a limited extent. Observations indicate that agency autonomy may be best understood as played out within a web of relations. This may be typical, I argue, in particular of countries characterized by corporatism (Anthonsen *et al.*, 2011; Lundberg, 2014). Corporatism, or neo-corporatism, can be distinguished from pluralism. In neo-corporatist systems a limited number of organizations are allowed to influence the work of the administration, and these tend to build a close trust relation. In a pluralist structure, such as the USA, on the other hand, the number of interest organizations that are allowed to influence politics and administration is close to infinite (cf. Lundberg, 2014). This competition makes it difficult to build stable and close long-term relationships, but on the other hand the model signals transparency and trust for the system as a whole. Sweden is one of the more corporatist countries in the world and this may be one explanation for the fluctuations found in the SIA case, in terms of stakeholder relations.

The way forward

This chapter has described the changes that the SIA has undergone during the 12-year period 2003–2014, with special attention to three specific stakeholder relations: the relation between agency management and parent ministry; the relation between agency management and employees (street-level bureaucrats); and the relation between the agency and the citizenry. Two conclusions have been made. First, findings suggest that de facto agency autonomy may change as the relation between specific individuals and stakeholders changes. In this process, trust and personal agendas may play a central role. Second, it suggests that agency autonomy may be best understood as a relation formed in interaction with other relations, in a network where they all influence each other. This finding may be relevant in particular to countries characterized by corporatism, as is typical of the Nordic countries (Anthonsen *et al.*, 2011; Lundberg, 2014). More studies focused on the role of how agency autonomy unfolds over longer periods of time, combining this system-wide perspective, are welcome in future research on agency autonomy.

References

Andersson, F., T. Bergström, L. Bringselius, M. Dackehag, T. S. Karlsson, S. Melander and G. Paulsson (2012) *Speglingar av en förvaltning i förändring: Reformeringen av försäkringskassan* (Stockholm: Santérus).

Anthonsen, M., J. Lindvall and U. Schmidt-Hansen (2011) 'Social democrats, unions and corporatism: Denmark and Sweden compared'. *Party Politics*, Vol. 17, pp. 118–134.

Bringselius, L. (2012a) 'Gaining legitimacy as a public official: how to understand supportive employee attitudes to the standardization of work'. *International Journal of Public Administration*, Vol. 35, No. 8, pp. 544–552.

Bringselius, L. (2012b) Mergers of Authorities in Central Government: Role Ambiguities and Blame-avoidance, in H. Andersson, F. Nilsson and V. Havila (eds), *Mergers and Acquisitions: The Critical Role of Stakeholders* (London: Routledge).

Christensen, T. and P. Lægreid (eds) (2006) *Autonomy and Regulation: Coping with Agencies in the Modern State* (Cheltenham, UK, and Northampton, MA: Edward Elgar).

Computer Sweden (21 August 2008) Försäkringskassan blöder hundratals miljoner, *Computer Sweden* (21 August 2008).

Computer Sweden (12 September 2008a) Accenture sitter i förarsätet, *Computer Sweden* (12 September 2008).

Computer Sweden (12 September 2008b) Tio miljarder för SAP på Försäkringskassan, *Computer Sweden* (12 September 2008).

Dagens Nyheter (2003) Dubbelkommando på vinglig kurs, *Dagens Nyheter* (19 August 2003).

Dir. 2002:166 *Översyn av socialförsäkringsadministrationen* (Stockholm: Socialdepartementet).

Dnr 83686–2005 (2005) *Försäkringskassan: Försäkringskassans förändringsplan (sia)*.

Eriksson, U.-B., L.-G. Engström, B. Starrin and S. Janson (2008) 'Falling between two stools: how a weak co-operation between the social security and the unemployment agencies obstructs rehabilitation of unemployed sick-listed persons'. *Disability and Rehabilitation*, Vol. 30, No. 8, pp. 569–576.

Försäkringskassan (2009) *Åtgärder för effektiviserad ledning och styrning inom försäkringskassan*.

Försäkringskassan (2011) *Socialförsäkringen i siffror 2011* (Stockholm: Försäkringskassan).

Försäkringskassan (2012) *Socialförsäkringen i siffror 2012* (Stockholm: Försäkringskassan).

Försäkringskassan (12 April 2012) 'Försäkringskassans förslag på minskat krångel'. Letter to the Government. Dnr 84150-2011.

Försäkringskassan (2014) *Försäkringskassans kundundersökning 2014:2*. Available online at www.forsakringskassan.se/wps/wcm/connect/a494adc7-e2c4-490f-8c38-5c737d0ecd 0f/fk_kundundersokning_2014.pdf?MOD=AJPERES.

ISF (2010) *Effektiviteten i försäkringskassans administration 2000–2009. Rapport 2010:9* (Inspektionen för socialförsäkringen).

Lender, A. (2010) Bättre sjukförsäkringsregler politikernas ansvar, *Dagens Nyheter* (6 October 2010).

Lundberg, E. (2014) *A Pluralist State?: Civil Society Organizations' Access to the Swedish Policy Process 1964–2009*. Doctoral thesis, Örebro University.

O'Toole, B. J. and G. Jordan (1995) *Next Steps. Improving Management in Government?* (Dartmouth: Dartmouth Publishing Company).

Pollitt, C. (2006) 'Performance management in practice: a comparative study of executive agencies'. *Journal of Public Administration Research and Theory*, Vol. 16, pp. 25–44.

Pollitt, C., K. Bathgate, J. Caulfield, A. Smullen and C. Talbot (2001) 'Agency fever? Analysis of an international policy fashion'. *Journal of Comparative Policy Analysis: Research and Practice*, Vol. 3, pp. 271–290.

Pollitt, C., C. Talbot, J. Caulfield and A. Smullen (2004) *Agencies: How Governments Do Things through Semiautonomous Organizations* (New York: Palgrave Macmillan).

Riksrevisionen 2009:2. *Försäkringskassans inköp av IT-lösningar* [Procurement of IT solutions by the Social Insurance Agency] (Stockholm: Swedish National Audit Office).

118   *L. Bringselius*

SOU 2000:78 (2000) *Rehabilitering till arbete en reform med individen i centrum.* Report for Regeringen (Stockholm).

SOU 2003:63 (2003) *21+1–1 en sammanhållen administration av socialförsäkringen.*

SOU 2003:106 (2003) *Försäkringskassan – den nya myndigheten. Slutbetänkande från ansa* (Stockholm: Regeringen).

SOU 2004:127 (2004) *SOU 2004:127. Försäkringskassan. Betänkande från georg* (Stockholm: Regeringen).

Statskontoret (2009) *Den nya försäkringskassan – i rätt riktning men långt kvar.*

SvD (16 December 2004) Nya mål för Försäkringskassan. I dag: En skyhög egen sjukfrånvaro, *SvD* (16 December 2004).

SvD (17 December 2004) Hårda regler ska ge världsklass, *SvD* (17 December 2004).

Van Thiel, S. and K. Yesilkagit (2011) 'Good neighbours or distant friends?'. *Public Management Review*, Vol. 13, pp. 783–802.

Verhoest, K., S. Van Thiel, G. Bouckaert and P. Lægreid (eds) (2012) *Government Agencies: Practices and Lessons from 30 Countries* (Basingstoke: Palgrave Macmillan).

Yesilkagit, K. and S. van Thiel (2008) 'Political influence and bureaucratic autonomy'. *Public Organization Review*, Vol. 8, pp. 137–153.

8 Audit in a trusting climate

Åge Johnsen, Kristin Reichborn-Kjennerud,
Thomas Carrington and Kim Klarskov Jeppesen

Summary

Following the rise of performance management movements and New Public Management, many countries have established new or strengthened their Supreme Audit Institutions (SAIs) and introduced performance auditing. The outcome of this practice is, however, contested. In the UK, for example, Michael Power has labelled this development 'the audit society'. He argues that audit is shaping many organizations' practices and managers' everyday experiences but represents rituals producing comfort without furthering the improvement of the public sector or society at large. Alongside economic crises and public management reforms, the public sector worldwide has been under pressure to improve its performance and administrative accountability. Following the financial crisis in 2007–2008 there is an increased interest in finding out whether performance audit is 'delivering' on its promises. This chapter analyses comparative survey data on civil servants' perceptions of the audit process and the impact of performance audit on public administration in the Scandinavian countries. We consider four dimensions of impacts: perceived usefulness; holding ministers to account; causing changes; and making improvements in the audited organizations. In addition, the chapter discusses some institutional factors that may influence the impacts.

Introduction

Many Western societies developed welfare states after World War II. This development has necessitated enlarged public sectors with increased bureaucracies. With time big bureaucracies and prolonged periods with growth were suspected of causing inefficiency and red tape. There have therefore been various initiatives and reforms to trim and change the public sector in order to make it more efficient and effective (Pollitt and Bouckaert, 2011).

With the development of several performance management movements during the twentieth century and the rise of New Public Management (NPM) in the 1980s, Supreme Audit Institutions (SAI) have enjoyed increased importance (Put and Bouckaert, 2011). SAIs have, in the traditional governance system, been external controllers of the public administration. The SAIs traditionally emphasized accountability by controlling whether accounts were according to standards and whether activities complied with rules (White and Hollingsworth, 1999). Since the 1990s the SAIs have expanded their activities and taken on different roles, such as judges, public accountants and evaluators, with a mandate to assess whether the public administration works economically, efficiently, effectively and transparently. Sometimes auditors have also taken on a role as consultants for giving advice in implementing improvements (Pollitt *et al.*, 1999). This activity is called 'performance audit' and can be considered an evaluation in the context of institutional control (Barzelay, 1997). The name illustrates the purpose of assessing performance as well as accountability in the public sector. This is often in line with the NPM focus on managing performance, delegating and giving freedom to subordinate entities but controlling their results after the fact.

Whether audit, in practice, contributes to a more efficient and effective public sector or is merely a ritual of verification producing comfort in an 'audit society' has been a contested issue in public management since the mid-1990s (Lapsley, 2009; Morin, 2001; Power, 1997, 2005). Impact is nevertheless a complex issue, ranging from direct to indirect and from desired to undesired influences (Lonsdale *et al.*, 2011). Moreover, much of the literature on the audit society has studied audit and SAIs in other contexts than the Scandinavian countries, in particular the UK. The UK is commonly regarded as having a more individualistic and less trusting national as well as public management culture than many other countries (Hofstede, 1984; Hood, 1998). The context of the audit, including national and public management cultures, may affect the audit and its impact. It is therefore interesting to study the SAIs and their performance audits in the Scandinavian countries that are characterized by more egalitarian and less individualistic values, and which are possibly more transparent and trusting societies, than many other countries.

This chapter analyses the impact of the SAIs' performance audits of public administration in Denmark, Norway and Sweden. We analyse four different aspects of the impact of audit on public administration: usefulness, accountability, changes and improvement. Moreover, we discuss some institutional factors that may be important determinants for the impacts of the SAIs' performance audits.

Performance audit impacts and determinants

The impacts of performance audit can be conceptual, political and material. The performance audits may be perceived as useful in that they provide new knowledge in some respect for some actors. By providing new knowledge the impact of the performance audit resembles organizational learning, meaning that the information gives new insights into the potential for action

(Huber, 1991). This knowledge may be used for holding someone to account and making changes that may or may not make improvements for someone or something in society, but organizational learning on a conceptual level does not require any specific action or material improvement to take place. In the next sections we discuss some factors that may influence the different aspects of the impacts of performance audits.

Performance audit type. Performance audits may be negotiated and designed differently and oriented towards scrutinizing compliance to rules, activities and performance (Pollitt *et al.*, 1999). The type of performance audit may be chosen depending on many factors such as the perceived problem, auditor training, available resources for the audit, organizational strategy (Barzelay, 1997), the dominant public management culture (Hood, 1998) or governance paradigm (Osborne, 2006). In general, one could expect that performance-oriented audits are more useful for the auditees than activity (accountability) and compliance-oriented audits.

Administrative levels and tasks. Civil servants have different tasks and responsibilities. Civil servants in ministries are often closely involved in policymaking and need information on the execution of the policies or are close to politicians who will be made responsible for public policies (Wilson, 2000). Civil servants in ministries may therefore find performance audits especially useful, in particular when this information comes from a reliable and legitimate source.

Actor interests. Performance information may be formally made accessible to the public administration as well as the public at large at the same time. Providing information may in itself, however, be insufficient for the information to be put into productive use, holding someone to account or making changes. Publishing the information may give the opportunity for it to be used, but knowledge of the potential for usage may also give someone the motive (Hood, 1995) to factually use the information. The auditees are not only objects of the tools (Vakkuri, 2010). The auditees may use the performance audits intentionally. The assessment of improvement is (also) political (Boyne, 2003). When different actors use the information to pursue their interests, the audits may be used to hold someone to account or to make changes.

Audit process communication. The SAIs are independent bodies that give external assessments of the auditees' business. When selecting areas and methods for the audit the SAIs normally design the audit in such a way that the final report will contain material of interest to someone regarding economy, efficiency and effectiveness, including equity. When something is 'interesting' it often means that someone could be held accountable for something and that some issue is substandard and could be improved. In practice, the audit may result in 'blaming and shaming' (Hood, 2007; Justesen and Skærbæk, 2010; Skærbæk and Christensen, 2015), which may be discomforting for the auditee and the responsible minister. In order to produce a reliable and interesting audit and uphold high standards and integrity for their independence, it is important for the SAIs to ensure good communication, both during the production of the audit (Keen, 1999; Roberts and Pollitt, 1994) and in the dissemination of the audit results (Bringselius, 2014; González-Díaz *et al.*, 2013). In a good communication process during the production of the audit, the auditees will be given due opportunities for providing reliable data and correcting material errors in draft reports so that the final report is considered 'true and fair', even though it might produce discomfort (Carrington and Catasús, 2007). The auditees are therefore expected to find the audit reports more useful when there has been a good audit communication process than when the process has been bad (Reichborn-Kjennerud, 2013). SAIs pursuing the goal of improving public administration would be likely to emphasize working closely together with the auditees in order to get the auditees to psychologically 'own' the recommendations (Barzelay, 1997). Therefore, performance audits with good communication processes could lead to more changes and improvements than processes with bad communication.

Audit process strain. Performance audits, unlike financial audits, are conducted at irregular intervals. They are often large projects that can put heavy demands on the auditees. The auditees have to attend meetings, produce data, answer questions and comment on draft reports in order to make things auditable (Power, 1997; Skærbæk, 2009). If the audit process has put little strain on the auditees and the final report produced substantial new knowledge outweighing the costs associated with producing the information, then the auditees are likely to find the audit useful (Reichborn-Kjennerud, 2014a).

Audit quality. Performance audits are often large projects carefully designed with regard to both the selection of objects to be audited and the methods to be employed. Moreover, performance audits often investigate the implementation of specific policies or the use of certain policy tools in great detail. In contrast to financial audits, the feature of customized, almost 'tailor-made' performance audits requires that the auditors are highly skilled with regards to both audit methods and the policy area in question in order for the audits to have high quality and provide new and relevant information that is useful for the auditees (Keen, 1999; Pollitt *et al.*, 1999). Performance audits that have high quality with regards to the selection of object for audit, choice of method and, if relevant, advice may therefore be perceived as more useful, be used more for changes and result in more improvements than low-quality audits (Reichborn-Kjennerud, 2013).

Audit rigidity. Performance auditing is an evaluation activity (Barzelay, 1997), but some of the auditors and the routines employed stem from an accounting rather than an evaluation tradition. Often, explicit standards or specific criteria are used in the assessments. The use of such criteria makes it feasible for the auditors to assess and give advice on the issue in question without being regarded as subjective and arbitrary. In the audit process the auditors, therefore, often use checklists and demand detailed information, which may help the auditors in being as objective and systematic as they can, modelled after the accounting profession. Sometimes, however, the auditees see this procedure as formalistic and 'rigid' without adding value (Reichborn-Kjennerud and Johnsen, 2011). Rigid performance audits may be perceived as less useful than performance audits that are adaptable.

SAI legitimacy. SAIs are independent institutions, often providing audit information that can be 'bad news' for someone in a political context. The bad news for some could often be good news for others. The opposition can for example use the information to question the government's ability to execute policies properly or to challenge some minister's integrity and accountability. In order to be taken seriously by different stakeholders, the SAIs need legitimacy (Funnell, 2015; Guthrie and Parker, 1999; Jacobs, 1998; Lonsdale, 2008). This legitimacy may stem from avoiding political issues, being unpartisan, selecting 'interesting' objects for audit, employing sound methods and judgement and using proper communication strategies. SAIs that are perceived as having much legitimacy may therefore have bigger impact regarding perceived usefulness by the auditees, holding someone to account, making changes and making improvements than SAIs with little legitimacy.

Media attention. Public administrations are complex systems, executing a large number of programmes and utilizing a large number of tools. Public administrations often handle difficult issues – wicked problems – balancing the interests of a multitude of stakeholders, including powerful internal actors. Public administrations are therefore often operating in a delicate balance between opposing interests, many issues competing for attention and scarce resources. This delicate balance makes public administrations hard to change (Metcalfe and Richards, 1990; Wilson, 2000). There may be many well-prepared plans in public administration which for many reasons are not executed without external pressure. External shocks, crises and new external pressures can unsettle this delicate balance and trigger processes for reform and change (Jones and Baumgartner, 2005; Pollitt and Bouckaert, 2011). Performance audits that provide bad news, especially from SAIs with legitimacy, are very interesting for the media (Reichborn-Kjennerud, 2014b). The political agenda is often closely linked to what issues the media find interesting. When media find performance audits that document misconduct, misjudgement and improper use of public money, it could often be politically opportune to use this information for holding someone, often the minister in charge, to account. Therefore, performance audits that get much media attention may provide new external pressure and give the public administration impetus for change.

The Supreme Audit Institutions

The Scandinavian countries, Denmark, Norway and Sweden, are interesting to study because they share some common traits. They are small, unitary and democratic states, but are different in terms of their fiscal situations, the histories of their SAIs, and their public management reform trajectories.

124   Å. Johnsen et al.

The OECD mapped its member countries' policies for reviews and performance audits in 1996 and found that only 13 countries responded and 12 countries reported performance audit activities (Barzelay, 1997). Norway and Sweden were among the countries with the most active SAIs in performance auditing. (Denmark did not respond to that mapping.) The International Organization of Supreme Audit Institutions (INTOSAI) surveyed its members in 2007 and concluded that probably fewer than 30 SAIs had well-developed and stable approaches to performance audit work (Put and Bouckaert, 2011). At least two of the Scandinavian countries had conducted performance audits for a long time. This makes the Scandinavian countries suitable for empirical analysis of impacts.

Table 8.1 presents descriptive statistics for some demographic, economic and administrative issues in the countries. The Scandinavian countries share many demographic and political traits. They are small and democratic countries and are unitary states. The countries vary in population size, from 5 million in Norway to 9.5 million in Sweden (2012).

The countries' economies are also diverse and have been differently affected by financial crises, the most recent being in 2007–2008. Gross domestic product (GDP) per capita in 2014 varied from USD58,887 in Sweden to USD97,363 in Norway. Measured by average annual percentage change in GDP, Denmark had lowest growth and Sweden highest growth in the economy from 2005 to 2014. Norway, until the drop in the crude oil prices in 2014, has largely been sheltered from the most recent financial crisis.

The countries' administrative organizations are diverse with relatively old and new SAIs. The Norwegian SAI (Riksrevisjonen) was regulated in the constitution of 1814 and established in 1816, and formally became an independent institution reporting to parliament in 1918. The Danish SAI (Rigsrevisionen) was part of the Economy Ministry from 1976 to 1991 and then made independent under parliament in 1991. The Swedish SAI (Riksrevisionen) was formally established in 2003 when the Ministry of Finance's National Audit Office (Riksrevisionsverket, RRV) and the parliament's

Table 8.1 The Scandinavian countries and their Supreme Audit Institutions

	Population in millions, 2012*	Mean percentage annual change in GDP, 2005–2014**	GDP per capita in USD, 2014**	National audit established	SAI established
Denmark	5.6	0.2	60,634	1849	1991
Norway	5.0	1.4	97,363	1816	1918
Sweden	9.5	1.7	58,887	1961	2003

Notes
* Source: OECD.
** Source: World Bank.

parliamentary auditors merged. The Swedish SAI has nevertheless a long tradition of conducting performance audit as a distinct work since the establishment of the RRV in 1961 (Pollitt *et al.*, 1999).

Key findings

The empirical analysis is based on survey data of civil servants who have experienced performance audits. The first data collection took place in Norway in 2011, covering the public institutions that had experienced performance audits between 2005 and 2010. The data collection in Denmark and Sweden took place in 2013–2014 and covered all performance audits carried out by the SAIs between 2005 and 2012. In total, 579 civil servants responded to the surveys in the three countries. The response rate varied from 91 per cent in Denmark and 71 per cent in Norway to 65 per cent in Sweden. Due to missing data on some variables the number of usable responses may be fewer than 579 in the analyses.

Table 8.2 reports the main differences in the performance audits' emphasis, as perceived by the civil servants who experienced the audits. The Danish performance audits were more oriented towards activities, and the Swedish performance audits were less oriented towards checking compliance and more oriented towards results, than the performance audits in the other countries.

Table 8.3 documents some factors that may impede or improve the impacts of the SAIs' performance audits. Actors in Norway use the audit reports most in pursuing their own interests, according to the civil servants' perceptions. The audit communication process is regarded as good in all the countries and best and the least straining in Sweden. Norway and especially Sweden are perceived to have high-quality audit reports, which also coincides with high legitimacy of the SAIs in Norway and Sweden in particular. There is relatively little perceived media attention in the three countries, but there is most media attention in Norway.

We chose four variables for measuring the dimensions of the performance audits' impacts. These are perceived usefulness, holding to account, change resulting from the performance audit and improvements resulting from the performance audit. The first variable, *usefulness*, where we asked to what

Table 8.2 Civil servants' perceptions of different emphasis in the Supreme Audit Institutions' performance audits

	n	*Report mainly checking compliance*	*Report oriented to activities*	*Reports oriented to results*
Denmark	76	31.6%	38.2%	30.3%
Norway	321	32.7%	30.8%	36.4%
Sweden	89	15.7%	32.6%	51.7%
Total	486	29.4%	32.3%	38.3%

Table 8.3 Civil servants' perceptions of factors that are possible determinants of performance audit impacts

	Actors use the audit reports to pursue their own interests	Audit process communication (index)	Audit process strain (index)	Audit report quality (index)	SAI legitimacy (index)	Media attention
Denmark	2.84 (n = 69)	3.06 (n = 63)	2.73 (n = 61)	2.92 (n = 67)	3.27 (n = 93)	2.50 (n = 64)
Norway	3.05 (n = 228)	3.28 (n = 112)	2.42 (n = 167)	3.42 (n = 208)	4.00 (n = 328)	2.79 (n = 278)
Sweden	2.79 (n = 82)	3.45 (n = 27)	1.86 (n = 74)	3.46 (n = 79)	3.92 (n = 112)	2.26 (n = 84)
Total	2.96 (n = 379)	3.24 (n = 202)	2.35 (n = 302)	3.33 (n = 354)	3.86 (n = 533)	2.64 (n = 426)

Note

The original survey questions used Likert scales ranging from 1 (low/little) to 5 (high/much). The audit process communication index measures to what extent the audited civil servants felt that their comments have been taken into account in the performance audit process. The audit report quality index measures different aspects of the quality of the performance audit report as perceived by the civil servants. The performance audit rigidity index measures negative aspects of the performance audit report. The SAI legitimacy index measures the civil servants' perception of the SAIs' ability to contribute to improvement and prevention of corruption and mismanagement.

degree the civil servants perceived the performance audits as useful, is a proxy for conceptual impact. For the second variable, *holding to account*, we asked to what extent the reports were used to hold the minister to account. This variable works as a proxy for political legitimizing and tactical use. For the third variable, *change*, we asked the civil servants to what extent the audited entities made certain changes to their organization as a consequence of the assessments in the performance audit report. This variable is used as a proxy for instrumental use. For the fourth variable, *improvement*, we asked whether the report was used to make improvements in the audited entity. This variable is a proxy for the interactive impact, the performance audit report being but one source that is used to make improvements in the audited entity.

Table 8.4 reports the civil servants' perceptions of the impacts of the performance audits reports on the four dimensions. In total, the civil servants perceived the usefulness of the performance audits positively, but the civil servants in Norway and Sweden assessed the usefulness of the performance audits more positively than the civil servants in Denmark. The impact on accountability, when probed by asking if the performance audits were used for holding the minister to account, were modest, and lowest in Denmark. The civil servants perceived the impacts of the performance audit reports on making changes and contributing to improvements in the audited entities to be relatively large. The perceived impacts on making changes in Sweden and contributing to improvements in Denmark were positive but relatively small.

The survey also had questions on background variables, including questions on the civil servants' administrative affiliation. Table 8.5 shows how different affiliation, being a civil servant in a ministry or agency, affected the perceived usefulness of the performance audits in the three countries.

In addition to differences in perceived impacts between the three countries, there was also variation in perceived usefulness between administrative levels. Civil servants working in ministries and in agencies reacted differently to the reports in the different countries. Civil servants in the agencies in Norway perceived the reports to be more useful than civil servants in the ministries. In Norway, 70 per cent of the civil servants in agencies thought the reports were useful to a large or very large extent, whereas only 41 per

Table 8.4 Civil servants' perceptions of Supreme Audit Institutions' performance audit impacts

	Usefulness	*Accountability*	*Change*	*Improvement*
Denmark	2.85 ($n = 65$)	2.41 ($n = 66$)	3.25 ($n = 71$)	2.86 ($n = 66$)
Norway	3.61 ($n = 312$)	2.71 ($n = 231$)	3.33 ($n = 290$)	3.40 ($n = 267$)
Sweden	3.50 ($n = 90$)	2.69 ($n = 84$)	2.93 ($n = 86$)	3.19 ($n = 86$)
Total	3.48 ($n = 467$)	2.65 ($n = 381$)	3.24 ($n = 447$)	3.27 ($n = 419$)

Note
Survey questions using Likert scales ranging from 1 (to a very small extent) to 5 (to a very large extent).

Table 8.5 Civil servants' perceived usefulness of Supreme Audit Institutions' performance audits by country and administrative level (*n* = 342)

Country	Administrative level	*n*	Perceived usefulness		
			To a small or very small extent useful	*Neither to a small nor large extent useful*	*To a large or very large extent useful*
Denmark	Ministry	20	30.0%	45.0%	25.0%
	Agency	35	40.0%	37.1%	22.9%
	All	55	36.4%	40.0%	23.6%
Norway	Ministry	106	26.4%	33.0%	40.6%
	Agency	98	12.2%	17.3%	70.4%
	All	204	19.6%	25.5%	54.9%
Sweden	Ministry	5	0.0%	20.0%	80.0%
	Agency	78	20.5%	28.2%	51.3%
	All	83	19.3%	27.7%	53.0%
Total	Ministry	131	26.0%	34.4%	39.7%
	Agency	211	19.9%	24.6%	55.5%
	All	342	22.2%	28.4%	49.4%

cent of the civil servants in the ministries thought the same. In Denmark and Sweden, the civil servants in the ministries perceived the reports to be more useful than the civil servants in the agencies.

Overall, the SAIs' performance audits seem to have positive impacts on public administration on several dimensions. The results from the multivariate cross-tabulation in Table 8.5 show that almost half of the civil servants found the performance audits very useful, but there were notable differences between the countries. The majority of the civil servants in Norway and Sweden perceived the performance audits to be useful to a large or very large extent. In Denmark only a minority of the civil servants found the perform-ance audits useful to large or very large extent.

One explanation for these results is that the Scandinavian countries use dif-ferent public management models (Ahlbäck Öberg and Wockelberg, 2016). Sweden (along with Finland) uses the East Nordic model, with small minis-tries and very autonomous agencies. In Sweden, the performance audits may have been used relatively frequently for accountability by holding the minister to account and in particular for evaluation in order to learn about policy out-comes in this decentralized system. Denmark and Norway have the West Nordic model, which typically uses more administrative control than the East Nordic model. The majority of the civil servants in Denmark, however, did not seem to have perceived the performance audits as very useful. In Denmark, which has a compliance-oriented SAI, civil servants found per-formance audit least useful. Denmark may have emphasized the development of distinct performance audits the least among these countries (something the Danish SAI's non-response to the OECD survey in 1996 also may have sig-nalled). Type of performance audit and the SAIs' choice of role may be important factors for the audit impacts.

Another possible but speculative explanation for some of the differences in impacts between the countries is that Denmark was more severely hit by the financial crisis in 2007–2008 than Norway and Sweden. The audits in Denmark may have been used more as tools for checking economy and effi-ciency in public management reforms aiming for cutback management than in Norway and Sweden. The audits may for this reason not have been per-ceived as very useful by many civil servants in Denmark, being the 'victims' for some of this information, during our period of analysis. In Norway, by contrast, the Norwegian public administration did not emphasize cutback management in the period of analysis.

Moreover, in addition to differences in perceived impacts between the countries there were also differences in the perceived usefulness of the per-formance audits between administrative levels. In Denmark, and especially in Sweden, the civil servants in the ministries perceived the audits as more useful than the civil servants in the agencies. In Sweden, this may be due to the administrative structure, with very small ministries and autonomous agencies. In the Nordic countries, a division of labour between ministries as 'secretari-ats' for top politicians and more autonomous, specialized agencies serving the public has developed over the last few decades. Sweden is an exception to this development, having had autonomous agencies and small ministries in the East Nordic public management model over a longer period of time. Civil servants, especially in the Swedish ministries, may therefore not have the capacity to monitor, or have the detailed knowledge of policy implementation, that many of their colleagues in other Scandinavian ministries and in the Swedish agencies possess. The civil servants in the ministries in Sweden may therefore find it very useful to get an independent assessment from the performance audits of what is going on in the agencies. In Denmark, almost as many civil servants in the ministries as in the agencies perceived the reports to be useful.

In Norway, however, the civil servants in the agencies perceived the audits to be more useful than the civil servants in the ministries did. There can be several reasons why civil servants working in the agencies are the most positive to the SAIs' performance audits. One reason might be that civil servants working in agencies have more use of the reports, as they are more operational than civil servants in the ministries. Most of the SAI reports actually evaluate the work in the agencies. The objects of the investigations are seldom the ministries. To be the object of a performance audit report can be especially useful for agencies if it raises awareness of their policy area and thus heightens its priority. Civil servants in the ministries are maybe more negative because the audits often publish 'bad news' for them. The ministers are often held to account for the shortcomings. Civil servants, especially those working in ministries, get only to take the blame. They may therefore find the audits too discomforting or, in the case of senior managers with in–depth knowledge, too remote from the most salient administrative issues to find the audits very useful.

Another reason why civil servants working in ministries may take a dislike to the reports is that they have gradually evolved into secretariats for the political leadership. They are active in formulating and communicating the political measures chosen by the political leadership. Therefore, they may think that some of the SAIs' reports are interfering with political priorities. The civil servants in the ministries may also find the reports unbalanced and too focused on areas and implementation issues that are of less importance for the policymaking work in the policy area.

A third reason why civil servants in some of the ministries showed relatively little satisfaction with the usefulness of the audits is that civil servants in ministries are expected to be well informed about their field of responsibility. Therefore, they may already be aware of the situation documented in the audit report, and this is why they may consider the performance audits not to be so useful, as the audits tell them what they already knew or at least ought to have known. Even if there were some new information in the reports, the civil servants may often not be willing to admit this. It is therefore usually difficult to 'surprise' good experts in the ministries with performance audits. In these cases, the function of the audits is more to inform the public and parliament and to recommend improvements. As audits' recommendations are often not very detailed – at least in some countries the SAI takes the position that it cannot precisely prescribe to the ministries *how* to solve the problem in order to avoid problems related to independence in potential later audits – then the civil servants may find the audits of little use.

The way forward

This chapter has discussed the impacts of performance audit on public-sector organizations and some institutional factors influencing these impacts in the Scandinavian countries. The comparative analysis across different contexts shows that the SAIs' performance audits have positive impacts on perceived usefulness, accountability, changes and, to some extent, improvements. While many regard audits as having little beneficial impact on society, our analysis indicates that many civil servants who have experienced the performance audits perceived the audits to have positive impacts on several dimensions, especially on usefulness. The analysis also revealed some differences between the countries as well as between administrative levels. The performance audits had some impact on holding the ministers to account in Norway and Sweden but had less impact on contributing to the audited entities making improvements in Denmark. Sweden, which has the East Nordic public management model, with extensive devolution, might use the audits for holding the ministers to account and in particular for evaluating policy implementation and outcomes.

The discourse on the merits of audit in society has put much emphasis on the practice of making things auditable and the ritual aspects of the audit. The Scandinavian experiences of using audit in a trusting 'climate' also show different aspects of these issues. There were notable differences in how the civil servants perceived the audits' degree of strain, quality of communication in the audit process and rigidity in the audit. These factors may reflect dimensions of 'making things auditable', which have to be assessed alongside the beneficial dimensions of the audit. Empirical analysis of these relationships falls outside the scope of this chapter, but the important point is that these issues are amenable for empirical measurement and organizational design.

Many regard audit – and control in general – as management tools that are based on distrust and that have limited impacts. This is particularly the case in some countries with low levels of trust and high intensities of reforms. Our analysis indicates that audit is indeed used in the Scandinavian countries and has positive impacts. These countries have a high intensity of reforms but also a context of high levels of trust. Maybe the use of management models such as performance audit and evaluation is especially important in egalitarian countries with many public-sector reforms in order to maintain a high level of trust and transparency in the transition from traditional public administration to New Public Management and New Public Governance.

These results have several implications for policy and practice. The analysis shows that SAIs' performance audits largely have positive impacts on public administration, as perceived by the civil servants who have experienced the performance audits. Therefore, the underlying strategic choice of conducting performance audits, when the institutional arrangements are right, seems to be warranted. We therefore need more empirical research on the determinants of the different dimensions of performance audit impacts as well as the influence of performance audit on politics and the public debate.

Acknowledgements

This chapter is part of a four-year comparative project on the influence of performance auditing on politics and public administration in the Nordic countries. The project is financed by a research grant from the Joint Committee for Nordic Research Councils in the Humanities and Social Sciences (NOS-HS), project number 219574. Thanks to Louise Bringselius, Irvine Lapsley, Külli Taro and Jarmo Vakkuri for comments to drafts of this chapter.

References

Ahlbäck Öberg, S. and H. Wockelberg (2016) Nordic Administrative Heritages and Contemporary Institutional Design, in C. Greve, P. Lægreid and L. H. Rykkja (eds), *Nordic Administrative Reforms: Lessons for Public Management* (Basingstoke: Palgrave Macmillan).

Barzelay, M. (1997) 'Central audit institutions and performance auditing: a comparative analysis of organizational strategies in the OECD'. *Governance*, Vol. 10, No. 3, pp. 235–260.

Boyne, G. A. (2003) 'What is public service improvement?'. *Public Administration*, Vol. 81, No. 2, pp. 211–227.

Bringselius, L. (2014) 'The dissemination of results from supreme audit institutions: independent partners with the media?'. *Financial Accountability & Management*, Vol. 30, No. 1, pp. 75–94.

Carrington, T. and B. Catasús (2007) 'Auditing stories about discomfort: becoming comfortable with comfort theory'. *European Accounting Review*, Vol. 16, No. 1, pp. 35–58.

Funnell, W. (2015) 'Performance auditing and adjudicating political disputes'. *Financial Accountability & Management*, Vol. 30, No. 1, pp. 92–111.

González-Díaz, B., R. García-Fernández and A. López-Díaz (2013) 'Communication as a transparency and accountability strategy in supreme audit institutions'. *Administration & Society*, Vol. 45, No. 5, pp. 583–609.

Guthrie, J. E. and L. D. Parker (1999) 'A quarter of a century of performance auditing in the Australian federal public sector: a malleable masque'. *Abacus*, Vol. 35, No. 3, pp. 302–332.

Hofstede, G. (1984) *Culture's Consequences: International Differences in Work-related Values* (London: SAGE).

Hood, C. (1995) 'The "new public management" in the 1980s: variations on a theme'. *Accounting, Organizations and Society*, Vol. 20, No. 2–3, pp. 93–109.

Hood, C. (1998) *The Art of the State. Culture, Rhetoric, and Public Management* (Oxford: Oxford University Press).

Hood, C. (2007) 'What happens when transparency meets blame-avoidance?'. *Public Management Review*, Vol. 9, No. 2, pp. 191–210.

Huber, G. P. (1991) 'Organizational learning: the contributing processes and the literatures'. *Organization Science*, Vol. 2, No. 1, pp. 88–115.

Jacobs, K. (1998) 'Value for money auditing in New Zealand: competing for control in the public sector'. *British Accounting Review*, Vol. 30, pp. 343–360.

Jones, B. D. and F. R. Baumgartner (2005) *The Politics of Attention: How Government Prioritizes Problems* (Chicago: Chicago University Press).

Justesen, L. and P. Skærbæk (2010) 'Performance auditing and the narrating of a new auditee identity'. *Financial Accountability & Management*, Vol. 26, No. 3, pp. 325–343.

Keen, J. (1999) 'On the nature of audit judgements: the case of value for money studies'. *Public Administration*, Vol. 77, No. 3, pp. 509–525.

Lapsley, I. (2009) 'New public management: the cruellest invention of the human spirit?'. *A Journal of Accounting, Finance and Business Studies*, Vol. 45, No. 1, pp. 1–21.

Lonsdale, J. (2008) 'Balancing independence and responsiveness: a practitioner perspective on the relationships shaping performance audit'. *Evaluation*, Vol. 14, No. 2, pp. 227–248.

Lonsdale, J., P. Wilkins and T. Ling (eds) (2011) *Performance Auditing: Contributing to Accountability in Democratic Government* (Cheltenham: Edward Elgar).

Metcalfe, L. and S. Richards (1990) *Improving Public Management* (London: SAGE).

Morin, D. (2001) 'Influence of value for money audit on public administrations: looking beyond appearances'. *Financial Accountability & Management*, Vol. 17, No. 2, pp. 99–117.

Osborne, S. (2006) 'The new public governance?'. *Public Management Review*, Vol. 8, No. 3, pp. 377–387.

Pollitt, C. and G. Bouckaert (2011) *Public Management Reform: A Comparative Analysis – New Public Management, Governance, and the Neo-Weberian State* (Oxford: Oxford University Press).

Pollitt, C., X. Girre, J. Lonsdale, R. Mul, H. Summa and M. Waerness (1999) *Performance or Compliance? Performance Audit and Public Management in Five Countries* (Oxford: Oxford University Press).

Power, M. (ed.) (1997) *The Audit Society – Rituals of Verification* (Oxford: Oxford University Press).

Power, M. (2005) The Theory of the Audit Explosion, in E. Ferlie, L. E. J. Lynn and C. Pollitt (eds), *The Oxford Handbook of Public Management* (Oxford: Oxford University Press).

Put, V. and G. Bouckaert (2011) Managing Performance and Auditing Performance, in T. Christensen and P. Laegreid (eds), *The Ashgate Research Companion to New Public Management* (Farnham: Ashgate).

Reichborn-Kjennerud, K. (2013) 'Political accountability and performance audit: the case of the auditor general in Norway'. *Public Administration*, Vol. 91, No. 3, pp. 680–695.

Reichborn-Kjennerud, K. (2014a) 'Auditee strategies: an investigation of auditees' reactions to the Norwegian state audit institution's performance audits'. *International Journal of Public Administration*, Vol. 37, No. 10, pp. 685–694.

Reichborn-Kjennerud, K. (2014b) 'Performance audit and the importance of the public debate'. *Evaluation*, Vol. 20, No. 3, pp. 368–385.

Reichborn-Kjennerud, K. and Å. Johnsen (2011) 'Auditors' understanding of evidence: a performance audit of an urban development programme'. *Evaluation*, Vol. 17, No. 3, pp. 217–231.

Roberts, S. and C. Pollitt (1994) 'Audit or evaluation? A national audit office VFM study'. *Public Administration*, Vol. 72, No. 4, pp. 527–549.

Skærbæk, P. (2009) 'Public sector auditor identities in making efficiency auditable: the national audit office of Denmark as independent auditor and modernizer'. *Accounting, Organizations & Society*, Vol. 34, No. 8, pp. 971–987.

Skærbæk, P. and M. Christensen (2015) 'Auditing and the purification of blame'. *Contemporary Accounting Research*, Vol. 32, No. 3, pp. 1263–1284.

Vakkuri, J. (2010) 'Struggling with ambiguity: public managers as users of NPM-oriented instruments'. *Public Administration*, Vol. 88, No. 4, pp. 999–1024.

White, F. and K. Hollingsworth (1999) *Audit, Accountability and Government* (Oxford: Clarendon).

Wilson, J. Q. (2000) *Bureaucracy: What Government Agencies Do and Why They Do it* (New York: Basic).

9 Local government cooperation

A better way to respond to conditions?

Ola Mattisson

Summary

Studies have shown that all Swedish municipalities are involved in cooperation with other municipalities, most frequently in soft forms like agreements. Often each municipality has full control of its activities and then joins forces with others on the margin. However, in this chapter it is shown that this situation is undergoing a change. Municipalities facing a new landscape are looking for increased cooperation as a means of dealing with challenges. Over the last decade a great number of new and jointly owned municipal organizations have been created, in many cases with shared responsibilities. These new and bigger organizations are created predominantly for reasons of strategic choice, capacity to deliver and the supply of competence. Cost-efficiency is no longer the major argument for joining forces. A more extensive cooperation in the form of joint organizations brings challenges for the municipalities. It creates new structures for activities and for decision-making, causing a number of new issues to deal with when organizing for municipal services. Experiences and implications of these issues are discussed in this chapter.

Introduction

This chapter is about the Swedish municipalities' efforts with cooperation over the recent decades, the ways these efforts have been implemented and how the cooperative focus has changed over time. This includes a discussion of the experiences made and knowledge gained about the usability of cooperation as a way to develop the municipal supply of services.

As competition is getting more intense and scarce resources are perceived to be a growing problem, organizations in general seek ways to deal with the situation. One such approach is inter-organizational cooperation and the sharing of resources. The number of organizations joining forces is growing in extent. The research on inter-organizational cooperation is extensive and contributions stem from many academic disciplines such as economics, management and political science (Byrnes and Dollery, 2002; Huxham and

Vangen, 2005; Ring and van de Ven, 1994; Smith *et al.*, 1995). A vast array of potential advantages and benefits from cooperation is proposed, attracting both public and private organizations to make cooperative efforts.

Cooperation between local governments has been extensively discussed, both in Sweden and other countries (Anell and Mattisson, 2009; Bel and Warner, 2015; Dollery and Johnson, 2005). Inspired by the proclaimed benefits, local governments in many countries make joint efforts. Continuously growing needs and a grim financial situation make it challenging to fulfil the task and large-scale advantages to and possibilities of sharing critical resources and competencies are put forward as crucial arguments here (Bel and Warner, 2014). However, experiences show that it is a difficult approach and that these efforts often fail when implemented (Warner, 2011). Still, local governments in different countries appear to continue to pursue the path of cooperation in various ways.

Over time, different reforms have been introduced to deal with the most urgent challenges of the time. There is a constant problem of prioritization, as needs always tend to be bigger than available resources and the ability to arrange for supply. However, the last decade has shown new challenges in terms of an ageing population (more needs), a generation shift in the workforce (people retiring) and a moving population (supply of competencies/recruitments).

Swedish municipalities have developed a tradition of cooperation and sharing resources. In general, the climate is helpful and politicians as well as public servants express an interest and a willingness to cooperate. Studies show that all municipalities are involved in networks and exchanges with other municipalities (Mattisson, 2013). Some of them have been in effect for a long time, while others are more recent.

Local government cooperation – driving forces

In Swedish municipalities, cooperation has been a word of honour and a theme for improvement activities in the recent decades. A large number of municipalities claim that it is more and more difficult to fulfil their obligations and pursue their missions. Too many different tasks require too many different competences, which make a small municipal organization fragmented and less cost-efficient. Some municipalities even question if they are able to maintain the resources necessary to manage all their tasks (Knutsson *et al.*, 2008). In order to improve the scale of municipal activities, the actors put their faith in cooperative initiatives. The rhetoric calls that there is no need for a new structure (merging municipalities) but a higher degree of cooperation within specific supplies will give scale effects. Inter-municipal cooperation is seen as a central strategy to prepare the municipalities confronting the sector. Historically, most cooperative efforts have taken place in more or less temporary exchanges of resources (Anell and Mattisson, 2009). Normally, it is a matter of networks for exchanging information or expertise of different kinds. However, as the municipalities have been put under greater pressure, more radical approaches have to be considered (Mattisson, 2013). For municipalities, it is getting more and more difficult to make both ends meet.

The existing system for welfare production is questioned, and much work has been done in analysis and restructuring over the last two decades. The challenges are still extensive. Generally, cooperation has been regarded as an important way to enhance and increase efficiency, but the context has varied over time. In the 1990s it was described as an alternative to competition and privatization (Mattisson, 2000). However, during the last decade the focus has shifted towards being able to manage at all. In many municipalities there is a sense that it might be difficult to fulfil their obligations at all due to the lack of both financial and human resources. Cooperation is therefore regarded as a way to meet the challenges of today.

Within the municipal sector an increased horizontal cooperation is expected to be a crucial strategy for municipalities to develop. To realize large-scale advantages, a higher degree of mutual adaption and integration is needed. This cannot be done in terms of loose networks; it requires a more formalized merger into a joint resource pool to take responsibility for the things previously organized by municipalities on their own.

Historically, efficiency and better resource management were good reasons to justify the reforms in municipal organizations. This also applies to cooperation and Mattisson (2000) showed that efficiency is a central motive. In addition, there are also many advocates for cooperation as a means to creating better conditions for development and renewal. Still, this is a motive often put forward. Since the turn of the century, however, the supply of competences, skills and knowledge has been evident as a central motive for cooperation (Mattisson, 2013). Many municipalities have difficulties attracting and recruiting qualified staff. By creating larger organizations with more extensive activities, opportunities increase to offer interesting work, both for specialists and generalists. In the survey of the municipalities in the southern part of Sweden (Skåne), Fjertorp and Mattisson (2013) found recruiting and cost-efficiency to be the two central motives for cooperating. However, a number of other reasons for joining forces are also promoted. Several municipalities stress that an important objective is the stimulation of local economic growth and that it is impossible to do this as a single actor on the market. It is a problem that needs to be addressed regionally, i.e. in a joint organization. They also aim to improve their service to citizens by acting as a more competent supplier. Finally, more-similar local rules and regulations from municipal governing bodies will ensure equal treatment in matters that cross municipal borders, e.g. building permits and environmental issues.

Forms of cooperation

Cooperation means that the various parties will agree on how they should act together. This section will discuss the various forms of cooperation and the

138   O. Mattisson

legal frameworks for the agreements. From a legal point of view, three main forms of cooperation can be identified in the municipalities.

- Loose cooperation based on agreements but without legal regulation.
- Cooperation regulated by public law such as statutory joint authorities and joint boards.
- Cooperation regulated by private law such as contracts and limited liability companies.

A loose agreement without legal regulation is the most common form. Cooperation is then based entirely on mutual adaption on the basis of agreements, which requires a great deal of trust between the parties (often individuals). In terms of more developed inter-municipal cooperation, it is more common to use a legally regulated form. The need for a legal regulation often stems from a need for the shared financing of activities or investments, often resulting in the forming of new and joint organizations (privately or publicly regulated). The legal forms accordingly have some connection to the purpose and degree of cooperation. There are also examples of combinations where the same municipalities participate both in loose agreements in some areas and in several formal cooperation using joint organizations.

There is no complete list of the areas of cooperative projects in Swedish municipalities. The data available indicates, however, that this is an extensive phenomenon and that all municipalities are involved in several examples of inter-municipal cooperation (SKL, 2002). Surveys have shown that the most common form of cooperation is loosely organized through agreements and contracts. Different forms of loose or informal cooperation represent some 75 per cent of the cooperative initiatives (Andersson, 2007; Gossas, 2003; Håldal et al., 2005).

There are also good experiences from cooperation in the form of projects, agreements and contracts (Anell and Mattisson, 2009). Each organization can continue to operate independently but choose to cooperate on specific issues and projects. In principle, this may mean better overall effect of these interventions. As for inter-municipal cooperation, this may mean that the organization is revitalized, but the potential is limited. If each municipality continues to have its own organization, essentially designed to fulfil its major responsibilities, the cooperation will only cover a small portion of the costs and activities. To take advantage of the potential and realize the economies of scale, a firmer form of cooperation involving more of the total cost is required.

Therefore, the use of new and jointly owned organizations has increased since the turn of the century. These forms are not a new phenomenon. Whenever local governments are relatively small, there is a need to create joint solutions. When local authorities merged into bigger municipalities they became more capable and the joint bodies gradually disappeared. In 1985, there were only 19 statutory joint authorities left (SOU 1996:137). Since a new law was passed the number has increased to 94 statutory joint authorities in 2007 (Rosén and Wikell, 2007). The new law also made it possible to create joint municipal boards and in the first 10 years some 70 joint boards were created (Rosén and Wikell, 2007). During this period most local governments became members of one or more jointly owned organizations. In total, this caused a debate about the structure and the capacity of municipalities to fulfil their mission. The central government level initiated an extensive investigation about the structure and division of tasks between public bodies. The issues were controversial and after great turbulence only minor changes very suggested and even fewer were implemented (SKL, 2015). In 2013, there were 697 different organizations formally outside of the municipal organization but jointly owned by two or more municipalities (Mattisson, 2013).

Initiating and developing local government cooperation

So far we have seen that cooperation has existed for a long time and is increasing. Then the question is to what extent the desired effects have actually been achieved. Internationally, the experience of inter-organizational cooperation is that as a process it is complicated and difficult to run, regardless of context (Huxham and Vangen, 2005). The impressions from the local government level (i.e. municipalities) are that inter-organizational cooperation is perceived as more important but still difficult to achieve (Dollery *et al.*, 2007; Dollery and Johnson, 2005; Entwistle and Martin, 2005; Warner, 2011).

However, in Sweden there are numerous examples of inter-municipal cooperation that have worked very well. When the municipalities expanded in the 1960s and 1970s, they faced new demands on their capacity and technical expertise, e.g. environmental and technical demands. This required huge investments in infrastructure such as water and waste management. Since there was nothing, the conditions for creating new organizations with a mandate to invest in facilities were good. Characteristic of these projects is that they were large and had clearly identifiable benefits. At the same time, the newly created (joint) organizations did not threaten or replace any existing capacity. However, today the situation in Sweden is very different. At present the existing systems have well-functioning capacities and resources to deal with the supply.

Anell and Mattisson (2009) conclude by stating that the easy gains (large or small) of cooperation have already been realized. The sector's challenge is now about the increasing scarcity of resources and the development of the organizations' capacity to accommodate future requirements. Loose cooperation or minor contracts would not suffice. To realize the benefits and prepare for a new generation of supply-extensive coordination and restructuring is necessary. This means that cooperation affects priorities and individual interests. It requires a body entitled to decide and execute. It does not seem realistic to think that municipalities can do this by soft mutual agreements.

The development of common goals, i.e. ones that the parties agree on what should be achieved and how actions and benefits should be allocated, is often mentioned as a success factor. However, there are reasons to look realistically at the possibilities of creating entirely common goals. Cooperation initiatives between municipalities are often motivated by an ambition to make things 'better' in terms of both economy and quality. Indeed, more precise descriptions of the benefits to be achieved and how they should be monitored or measured are unusual. This can create problems if one of the parties is satisfied with the outcome while another on the basis of somewhat different expectations feels dissatisfied.

By far the most important driver for parties to agree on and get started with a joint solution is based on identified common external threats. Common examples of this include new legislation, the requirement for extensive changes (e.g. adapting to environmental concerns) or the requirement of the closing or restriction of operations. Furthermore, experience shows that it is important who currently undertakes the activities that the parties intend to cooperate on (Anell and Mattisson, 2009). As long as it is currently undertaken by 'somebody else' it is relatively easy to reach an agreement on how to form a joint solution. Thus cooperation involves an added value for everyone but that does not affect the parties' current operations. Moreover, it has proven particularly beneficial to start operations together or build a joint plant when this is in response to a common threat. Many regional facilities are examples of this, for example when more stringent environmental requirements have forced several municipalities to make big investments at around the same time.

It also appears that cooperation is easier to achieve if the purpose is to generate economic benefits that the parties can share without involving their own operations and resources. Otherwise, cooperation may have very negative consequences for their own operations due to cost-cutting and requirements for savings. When the cooperative initiatives affect 'somebody else' it is much easier to make all parties support a joint solution. It also explains why cooperation between partners on joint procurement and price pressure on suppliers is relatively unproblematic. The cases where the economic potential is most convincing are when they are clearly identifiable but where the consequences of change affect somebody else (other than the cooperating parties), e.g. less external purchases of services. Many examples of cooperation through agreements about joint buying devices are based on this view. Cooperation requiring changes or sacrifices in their own activities is more difficult to achieve. The argument to change your own operations is that the risk for changes in operations will be even greater if the external threat is not averted.

Analysing the potential

To succeed with the cooperation, it is important that the organizations have a common understanding of why they want to interact and what should be achieved, i.e. what is the potential to be realized. One way to achieve this common approach is to use the same language and a consistent set of concepts. Based on Mattisson (2000), the potential of a cooperative solution can be analysed in four dimensions:

- The nature of the potential.
- The size of the potential.
- The detectability of the potential.
- The distribution of the potential.

The nature of the potential

This refers to what type of gains or benefits is to be expected. Stakeholder expectations about the nature of the potential will affect their attitudes and the actions that stakeholders find appropriate to develop cooperation. Benefits can be described in terms of different types of synergy. Financial synergies can mean better access to capital or risk-sharing when facing major investments. Increased market power provides, for example, opportunities to get better rates or other terms from suppliers if they come together in a joint procurement. An example of competence synergies is when small municipalities join together to secure the supply of certain specialist skills or to achieve a better management of certain activities. Finally, operational synergies come in several different forms. The most common form is when partners work together to achieve economies of scale as a result of greater volume and/or coordinated production. Cooperation is then expected to achieve cost reductions and/or increased efficiency or quality of production.

Size and detectability

The second and third dimensions refer to the size and detectability of the potential. Anell and Mattisson (2009) summarize the alternatives (Table 9.1). Should it be possible to bring about a synergy it is usually required that all parties involved share a belief that the gains are fairly large and possible to realize. If the potential identified is both uncertain and small there is little prospect of achieving synergy. There is less of a problem if all parties make

Table 9.1 Contributions and gains from cooperation

Contributions	Potential gains	
	Small	*Large*
Small	Easy, but minor importance	Easy, first priority
Large	Not relevant	Difficult, but important

Source: Anell and Mattisson, 2009.

the same assessment. If there is consensus that the potential is small and uncertain, there are very good reasons not to invest in a joint process. Given that cooperation is difficult, profits need to be big enough and not achievable by other means for cooperation to be worthwhile. What is an acceptable size for profits cannot be determined in isolation but must be judged by the efforts required. Regarding ambitions to develop cooperation between two or more parties, the easiest profits are taken home first. For partners who have already cooperated for some years it is likely this has already been achieved. The challenges, then, are to develop synergies in areas with huge potential returns for which claims of stakes are also higher.

The extent to which identified potentials can be realistic and credible affects the ability to create support and commitment to cooperation. For those who want to achieve coordination it may therefore be tempting to exaggerate the size of the benefits and/or underestimate the problems to reach them. It will be important to find the gains that can be expressed in economic terms, and preferably in the form of money that cooperation partners can share. The party that does not wish to participate, on the other hand, may easily refer to that potential as 'unrealistic' or 'based on an optimistic calculation'. The actor who is sceptical about the cooperation therefore does not have to criticize the cooperation as such but may be content to conclude that the (demonstrated) potential is so uncertain and/or small that it does not outweigh the effort.

Distribution of contributions and potential benefits

It is relatively easy to handle a situation where all parties make the same assessment of the potential, the same assessment of the size and the same assessment of the efforts the various parties need to make. However, things get more difficult when the different parties make different assessments, both of the benefits and of the effort needed. This is probably also a more realistic situation. It may also be closer at hand to underestimate the efforts that need to be done by others rather than to underestimate the requirements of your own work.

In most practical situations, it is thus important to identify how the efforts and profits are allocated between different parties. Cooperation is often described as something that 'will benefit all' and is about 'give and take'. However, although the overall result may be desirable and effective, neither gains nor efforts need to be proportionately distributed. The potential can be both large and detectable, but cooperation will still not be achieved if the gains are not distributed in proportion to the effort. Seen from one party's perspective, the gains may be too small to be worth the effort, which in turn can prevent other parties from gaining much larger profits. Cooperation thus requires that the parties can find forms of distribution of both the gains and efforts. This is often very difficult because it is enough that one party does not 'see the benefits' to hinder a proposed cooperation.

In summary, the above discussion demonstrates that the benefits sought in cooperation may have very different characteristics and conditions. The party who intends to get involved in cooperation has reasons, together with the other parties, to go through these four dimensions. All indications point to the necessity of a common view on what is a priority and what should be achieved jointly.

Cooperation in a jointly owned organization – the next step?

The need to realize large-scale advantages increases the pressure on the municipalities to act and to act together. Since it is difficult to cooperate without a clear organizational form we now see local governments form jointly owned organizations. This requires the parties to choose a legal form. The reasons for choosing a particular legal form have varied over time depending on how the legislation has been designed at the specific time, as well as local conditions in the cooperating municipalities. For example, a variety of limited liability companies was formed during the 1960s, while a great number of statutory joint authorities has been created since the law was revised in 1998.

The argument for choosing the form of statutory joint authority is that it is possible to create a new joint organization but with separate economic units. It is perceived to have clear rules on political representation but still some flexibility in the selection of control forms (council or board). A common argument for engaging in a municipal association is that this is outside the Public Procurement Act. It is supposed to be possible for individual local authorities to hand over operations to the joint organization without prior competitive tendering. In the past decade, this has been cited as a key reason for the creation of several statutory joint authorities (Knutsson and Mattisson, 2006; Mattisson and Ramberg, 2004). The form is considered to work well when the number of cooperating parties is numerous and/or when it comes to significant resource commitments. Overall, the form of statutory joint authority is considered to work well but for smaller tasks, since the form may seem somewhat burdensome (Mattisson and Ramberg, 2015).

A central motive for choosing a joint board is that it constitutes a forum for political executive decision-making while requiring a minimum of formal administrative resources. In its context, the framework has been perceived to work well. There are good experiences in setting up a joint committee, particularly on sharing administrative functions or with talent management and recruiting (Rosén, 2005). There are also examples of services such as the collection of household waste that are carried out in a municipality on behalf of another, all within the framework of a joint board (Mattisson and Ramberg, 2004). A joint committee seems most appropriate for a small number of parties.

The reasons for choosing to interact in the form of a limited liability company is often said to stimulate professionalism and a businesslike approach.

The form is said to work well for cooperation within activities financed by user fees (Knutsson and Ramberg, 2005). User fees cannot be used outside the specific operation, whose finances are supposed to be kept separate. Since the money is not mixed with the owners' own funds, there is much less risk for conflicts and deviating priorities. In tax-funded activities it may be that an owner's specific needs (or problems) 'disturbs' the totality of the other owners, who do not simultaneously have the same issues to deal with. There has also been a general understanding among practitioners that it is impossible (illegal) to leave the task to a public company without prior public procurement, which is why the organization form is not common for tax-funded activities.

Cooperation in a jointly owned organization – some implications

Previously, we found that the number of joint organizations is increasing and the task they face is the restructuring and development of the supply of municipal services. Many municipalities operate under strong pressure to change, partly to keep the economy within the available budget and partly to be able to deliver at all. From earlier studies it is shown that there is a lack of knowledge about what particular effects we can expect from restructuring existing supply through a more extensive cooperation (Mattisson and Ramberg, 2015; Warner, 2011). However, there are some experiences of general interest from studies of cooperation within a jointly owned organization.

One distinct experience is difficulties in creating a good political representation from one municipality within the joint organization. In many processes of cooperation there have been reports of difficulties for the opposition and minorities to receive representation and transparency on, for example, an executive board or a board (Rosén, 2005). To remedy this, there are examples of attempts to broaden the base and increase the number of representatives by way of a council in a statutory joint authority. It is only possible if the two interacting partners agree. So, if the number of concurrent partners increases to four, the situation quickly gets complicated and hard to manage (Mattisson and Ramberg, 2015). Based on the expectation that more activity in municipalities will be held within the framework of common organizations, this will pose challenges to both individuals and the overall system. For individuals, it will make increasing demands on the transmission of information between individuals and institutions. At the same time, the issue of transparency and traceability also arises. On an organizational level, an increased number of joint bodies becomes more administratively demanding because decisions (appointments) are interdependent, both within the organization and in relation to others, e.g. the budget and investments.

Representation is also connected to transparency and accountability. The elected politicians are accountable towards the voters in their own municipality. Then it is crucial to decide which of the issues are to be dealt with in the joint organization and which ones are to taken care of within every single municipality (Mattisson and Ramberg, 2015). As the supply is transferred to, and executed by, a joint organization, access and transparency will become complicated. There are more events to keep track of. The municipal council is part of a process that can be difficult to discern, resulting in complicated questions about political influence and accountability.

Within the context of tax-funded activities it may be difficult to allocate resources and efforts. Although there are rational reasons for working in a larger organization, each municipality's politicians essentially strive to secure resources for their electorates. Tradition and history can make demands and requirements vary between different municipalities, which need to be handled within a common organization. Generally, the lesson is that it is challenging to cooperate on taxpayer-funded policies with obvious local character. To succeed, the parties must explicitly define the conditions for control of the common organization and its relations with the member municipalities (Knutsson and Mattisson, 2006). The need for each municipality to influence the level of costs and quality steer development towards a situation where the joint organization is becoming more of a joint producer. Then the economies of scale can be realized in production, while each principal in each situation can choose to order just as much as desired. This has proved to be problem-atic in at least two ways. First, it creates problems in the design of production and investment as it is difficult to predict the current priorities and redeploy-ments in the different municipalities. Second, it may be uncertain how well it fits within the framework of the Public Procurement Act.

Other issues focus on the interaction between the municipality and the joint organization. The experiences are that there is a great variety between different cases (Mattisson and Ramberg, 2015). When activities are politically delicate, the representatives of the individual municipalities are more active in safeguard-ing the terms for their own constituency. The existence of specific require-ments and conditions for individual partners could thus eliminate much of the sought-after economies of scale that were the basis for cooperation.

It has proved difficult to engage in activities that require facilities that are explicitly designed for a particular municipality (e.g. water supply) and its citizens. Historically, inter-municipal cooperation has involved capital-intensive investments that provide for all parties' needs (e.g. waste treatment plants or sewage treatment plants). This has brought clear economic benefits without restricting anybody's freedom of action. However, in the past decade there have been attempts to also cooperate on technical infrastructure invest-ments that are intended exclusively for only a very few municipalities. In order to distinguish the individual municipality's share in the joint organiza-tion (and at the same time escape the rules of the Public Procurement Act), different administrative structures have been tried.

Against the background of the formation of more and more common organizations, it seems interesting to follow more closely how these will be managed politically and how governance can be designed to be practical. In cases where activities and assets can only be used in a municipality, it will be crucial to find procedures that sort out what is common and that also allocate contributions, investment levels and decisions on tariffs. The joint organization (the cooperation) may require a greater degree of overview and consideration of the overall conditions (not just those from particular municipalities). The more parties that interact, the greater the risk of an individual municipality experiencing a deterioration, either in terms of increasing costs or in terms of decreasing quality. Local politicians may have a difficult time justifying this on their home turf.

The way forward

This chapter shows that inter-municipal cooperation is widespread and is growing in Sweden. Local governments facing problems to fulfil their obligations place more hope in the policy of cooperation. There is no clear pattern about which municipalities interact with each other. Instead, it appears that all types of municipalities are involved in cooperation and it is increasing in scope. From an operational viewpoint, the municipality's geographic boundaries are questioned and a growing interest in taking common action is expressed. Although all forms of cooperation increase, there is a clear focus on creating new and jointly owned organizations to address a common purpose. This brings difficulties to the municipal organizations, who then act in a context other than within their traditional geographical territory. Cooperation seems to work well as long as it is possible to distinguish (and separately report) individual collectives (municipalities) and their costs (and revenues). Then responsibilities and accountability remain in order. For tax-funded activities in which cooperation may involve common resources and common priorities, the distribution of responsibility and accountability becomes more complicated. There is a clear will to cooperate as long as it brings demonstrable benefits for all. In collaboration solutions when the benefits are not evenly distributed between the parties, it has proved very difficult to reach agreement.

An increased horizontal cooperation between local governments is expected to be a crucial strategy for municipalities to develop in the future. To realize large-scale advantages, a higher degree of mutual adaption and integration is needed. This cannot be done in terms of loose networks but requires a more formalized merger into a joint resource pool to take responsibility for the things previously organized by one municipality alone.

A clear indication is that municipal actors view cooperation as an effective strategy for dealing with the present challenges. The impression is that among practitioners it is understood as important to create new entities that cross municipal boundaries. Despite many efforts and unsuccessful attempts, the overall view is that it has brought significant benefits for citizens in terms of more efficient, better and less expensive supply.

Another reflection concerns the reasons for initiating cooperation. A substantial shift can be seen in the arguments for initiating cooperation. In the research studies of the 1990s, production conditions and economic benefits were emphasized. This can be compared with the reasons put forward during the last 10 years, where the urgency to secure competence and capacity to fulfil the municipal mission is stressed. The municipalities cannot handle the mission on their own but must interact. Another change concerns how municipalities perceive it as critical to be able to act together and unite towards other stakeholders. It is considered important to 'put the region on the map', to 'get help with infrastructure' and to 'be attractive towards citizens and businesses.' This type of 'strategic' work is today awarded considerably more importance than ever before.

The trend towards more municipal cooperation places the borders of municipalities under review. The variation in size and the varying conditions under which the different municipalities operate have raised issues about the realism of the idea that they should all provide an equivalent level of supply. Since the conditions are so different a high general level of municipal service offerings could be too much to ask for within the limits of available resources, monetary as well as human. So far the practitioners still believe a lot can be done through active strategic work and cooperation. Despite the somewhat disappointing experiences of cooperation (Bel and Warner, 2014; Huxham and Vangen, 2005), Swedish municipalities still continue to make joint efforts. But there are also limits to how far you can reach. The closer to these limits we get, the closer we come to a structural reform where the municipal borders will be revised.

References

Andersson, J. (2007) *Kommunal samverkan i skåne* (Öresundsinstitutet och Kommunförbundet Skåne).

Anell, A. and O. Mattisson (2009) *Samverkan i kommuner och landsting – en kunskapsöversikt* (Lund: Studentlitteratur).

Bel, G. and M. Warner (2014) 'Inter-municipal cooperation and costs: expectations and evidence'. *Public Administration*, Vol. 93, No. 1, pp. 52–67.

Bel, G. and M. Warner (2015) 'Factor explaining inter-municipal cooperation in service delivery: a meta-regression analysis'. *Journal of Economic Policy Reform*, pp. 1–25.

Byrnes, J. and B. Dollery (2002) 'Do economies of scale exist in Australian local government? A review of the research evidence'. *Urban Policy and Research*, Vol. 20, No. 41, pp. 391–414.

Dollery, B. and A. Johnson (2005) 'Enhancing efficiency in Australian local government: an evaluation of alternative models of municipal governance'. *Urban Policy and Research*, Vol. 23, No. 1, pp. 73–85.

Dollery, B., J. Byrnes and P. Allan (2007) 'Optimal structural reform in Australian local government: an empirical analysis of economies of scale by council function in new south wales'. *Urban Policy and Research*, Vol. 25, No. 4, pp. 473–486.

Entwistle, T. and S. Martin (2005) 'From competition to collaboration in public service delivery: a new agenda for research'. *Public Administration*, Vol. 83, No. 1, pp. 233–242.

Fjertorp, J. and O. Mattisson (2013) *Interkommunal samverkan. Reflektioner från observationer i skåne* (Lund: KEFU).

Gossas, M. (2003) *Kommunen som nätverksaktör. En kommunreform för 2000-talet* (Stockholm: Institutet för framtidsstudier).

Huxham, C. and S. Vangen (2005) *Managing to Collaborate. The Theory and Practice of Collaborative Advantage* (London: Routledge).

Håldal, L., M. Kastensson and M. Rosander (2005) *Kommunala samverkansmönster. En kartläggning av interkommunal samverkan i östgötaregionen* (Linköping: Centrum för kommunsrategiska studier).

Knutsson, H. and O. Mattisson (2006) *Bundsförvanter i bergslagen. Kommunalförbund för kommunalteknik* (Stockholm: Sveriges kommuner och landsting).

Knutsson, H., O. Mattisson, U. Ramberg and T. Tagesson (2008) 'Do strategy and management matter in municipal organisations?'. *Financial Accountability & Management*, Vol. 24, No. 3, pp. 295–319.

Knutsson, H. and U. Ramberg (2005) *Va i samverkan. Samverkansformer inom vatten- och avloppsförsörjning* (Stockholm: Sveriges kommuner och landsting).

Mattisson, O. (2000) *Kommunala huvudmannastrategier för kostnadspress och utveckling.* Dissertation, Lund University.

Mattisson, O. (2013) *Organisation och styrning på den lokala samhällsnivån – en forskningsöversikt om förändringar och utvecklingstendenser. Annex to SOU 2015:24, en kommunallag för framtiden* (Stockholm: Fritzes).

Mattisson, O. and U. Ramberg (2004) *När ett plus ett blir tre – om samverkan inom kommunal avfallsverksamhet. Rvf utveckling 2004:10* (Malmö: RVF Utveckling).

Mattisson, O. and U. Ramberg (2015) 'Co-owned local government organisations: conditions for strategy development'. *Financial Accountability & Management*, Vol. 31, No. 3, pp. 269–286.

Ring, P. S. and A. van de Ven (1994) 'Developmental processes of cooperative interorganizational relationships'. *Academy of Management Review*, Vol. 19, No. 1, pp. 90–118.

Rosén, T. (2005) *Samverkan pågår, möjligheter och begränsningar* (Stockholm: Sveriges kommuner och landsting).

Rosén, T. and S. Wikell (2007) *Kommunalförbund och gemensamma nämnder. Studie på uppdrag av kommunala kompetensutredningen* (Stockholm: Sveriges kommuner och landsting).

SKL (2002) *Interkommunal samverkan – en undersökning av samverkan mellan kommuner och landsting i sverige* (Stockholm: Sveriges kommuner och landsting).

SKL (2015) *Urbanisering. Utmaningar för kommuner växande och minskande befolkning* (Stockholm: Sveriges kommuner och landsting).

Smith, K. G., S. J. Carrol and S. J. Ashford (1995) 'Intra- and interorganizational cooperation: toward a research agenda'. *Academy of Management Journal*, Vol. 38, No. 1, pp. 7–23.

SOU 1996:137 (1996) *Kommunalförbund och gemensam nämnd – två former för kommunal samverkan* (Stockholm: Betänkande av Kommunala förnyelsekommittén).

Warner, M. E. (2011) 'Competition or cooperation in urban service delivery?'. *Annals of Public and Cooperative Economics*, Vol. 82, No. 4, pp. 421–435.

10 What about the boards?

Issues of transparency and accountability in board composition

Anna Thomasson

Summary

Sweden is generally regarded as a country with little corruption, equal rights for men and women and a strong emphasis on democratic values. Still, the appointment of political representatives to the boards of municipal corporations occurs without consideration of these values. One step towards increasing our knowledge about the governance of municipal corporations in Sweden is to look at how current governance processes affect accountability in relation to municipal corporations. Therefore, and with the discussion above as a backdrop, this chapter will be dedicated to opening up the 'black box' of the party organizations and shedding light on what the process of appointing board members actually looks like and how this process influences transparency and the ability to secure accountability in relation to the political corporate governance of Swedish municipal corporations.

This is in spite of the fact that issues concerning lack of transparency and corruption in municipal corporations have been raised over the last couple of years. In this chapter, the process of appointing members to the boards of Swedish municipal corporations is scrutinized, showing a lack of transparency in the nomination process as well as a lack of political responsibility when it comes to the overall composition of the board.

Introduction

Sweden is number three on the list of the least corrupt countries in the world according to Transparency International's Corruption Perception Index measuring (Transparency International, 2015). Sweden is also ranked number four on the World Economic Forum's Global Gender Gap list from 2015 regarding equalities between genders when focusing on factors such as health, economy, education and politics (World Economic Forum, 2015). With these figures as a backdrop it is surprising that there is no system in place that secures transparency and accountability when it comes to the appointment of candidates for the boards of municipal corporations.

In Sweden there are around 1,700 municipal corporations; this number is increasing and has done so since 2006 (SCB, 2011). Further, these municipal corporations had combined a turnover of around 200 billion Swedish Krona in 2010 (SCB, 2011). The estimated total value of their services and assets is 1,875 billion Swedish Krona (Andersson *et al.*, 2012). In spite of these figures, the control over one of the most important corporate governance mechanisms available to the owners, the board of directors, is handed over to the local branches of the political parties represented in the municipal council. The local branches are organized as small non-profit associations with individual members that through annual general meetings elect a board of representatives that plans and takes responsibility for the activities and economy of the organization and coordinates local general elections on behalf of the party. Some coordinating activities occur on regional and national levels prior to elections, but the local branches are to a large extent sovereign, including in the election of representatives to municipal boards and committees.

As a consequence, there is no one to take overall responsibility for the composition of the boards of municipal corporations in regards to, for example, gender equality and competence, or for securing that people appointed to the board aren't representing dual interests. The lack of a transparent system is even more apparent when considering the fact that the number of reported corruption cases has increased in municipal corporations since 2007 (BRÅ, 2012; Statskontoret, 2012), especially with the seven different indictments in the city of Gothenburg (Sweden's second largest city) that were a result of the exposure of corruption among their municipal corporations fresh in mind (Amnå *et al.*, 2013).

Further, research has pointed towards the lack of transparency in these organizations and the fact that, due to this, municipal corporations are subject to an increased risk of corruption (Erlingsson, 2006; Hyltner and Velasco, 2009; Statskontoret, 2012) and has thus not lived up to the legal requirements regarding transparency (Erlingsson *et al.*, 2014; Hyltner and Velasco, 2009).

Further, the number of women on the boards of municipal corporations is less than the number of women found in municipal committees and in municipal councils. In 2011 43 per cent of the members of the municipal councils were women and 44 per cent of the members of the municipal committees were women (SCB and SKL, 2012). This should be compared to the fact that according to a recent study women make up only 29 per cent of the boards of municipal corporations and 12 per cent of the boards have no female representation (Sundkvist, 2015). That almost 50 per cent of the members of municipal councils are women is the result of how political parties during the last decade have strived to present lists of candidates in local municipal council elections in which every other candidate is a woman. It is thus not possible to make a straight comparison of the figures. The numbers do however show how the efforts to secure gender equality on public lists have not had any effect on how branches of local political parties nominate their candidates. This in a time when politicians at the national level in Sweden argue for the need for quotas of women appointed to boards of corporations listed on the stock exchange.

The lack of transparency in municipal corporations combined with the recent discovered corruption problems point towards the need to further investigate the governance of Swedish municipal corporations, in particular with a focus on accountability. One step towards increasing our knowledge of the governance of municipal corporations in Sweden is to look at how current governance processes affect accountability in relation to municipal corporations. Therefore, and with the discussion above as a backdrop, this chapter will be dedicated to open up the 'black box' of the party organizations. The focus of the chapter will be to shed light on what the process of appointing board members actually looks like and how this process influences transparency and the ability to secure accountability in relation to the political corporate governance of Swedish municipal corporations.

Municipal corporations in Sweden

The presence of municipal corporations in the Swedish public sector is not a new phenomenon. The use of the corporate form among Swedish municipalities started to spread already in the 1940s (Hansson and Collin, 1991). Since then the number of municipally owned corporations has increased. The increase has mainly occurred during the last decades due to the influence of New Public Management (NPM), which, among other things, regards the private corporate form as a role model (Hood, 1995; Pollitt, 2000).

Today there are around 1,700 municipally owned corporations in Sweden (SCB, 2011). Related to the fact that there are 290 municipalities in Sweden, it is fair to say that the corporate form is a common way for Swedish municipalities to organize public services. The types of services most commonly provided by a municipal corporation are real estate, public housing and technical infrastructural services (e.g. water, gas, energy) (SCB, 2012). Consequently, there are not only a large number of corporations owned by municipalities in Sweden; they also provide a wide range of public services. Municipal corporations represent large values, provide a wide range of different public services and are large employers.

There are no specific laws or regulations for corporations owned by public authorities in Sweden. All corporations are subjected to the same legislation, Aktiebolagslagen (ABL, or the Swedish Corporate Law), regardless of whether they are listed on the stock exchange, family owned, state owned or owned by a municipality. This legislation provides the framework for corporate governance in Sweden and was developed with profit-oriented organizations in mind (Stattin, 2007). No consideration is thus taken in the Swedish legislation of the fact that the owners of companies owned by public-sector entities normally regard social values as more important than profit orientation (Stattin, 2007).

Besides ABL, Swedish municipal corporations are also subject to the laws and regulations regarding Swedish municipalities (Kommunallagen, KL). KL provides the guidelines for what type of services that municipalities can and should provide and also the specific regulations regarding for example transparency that public services are obliged to live up to. Municipal services that are corporatized are obliged to live up to what is stipulated in KL as well as in ABL. KL provides the framework for how municipalities provide public services, while ABL provides the framework for how to govern public services once they are organized in a corporation (Stattin, 2007). Municipally owned corporations are thus subject to two types of regulations, one developed for public services and one for profit-oriented services.

The framework provided by ABL is the foundation of the Swedish corporate governance system. The governance system concerns the division of responsibility between the different actors in the chain of command as well as how owners and other stakeholders can hold the board and the CEO accountable for how they govern and run the company (Aguilera, 2005; Ryan and Ng, 2000; Thomsen, 2008). When municipal services are corporatized, the role of owner is assumed by the municipal council. This council appoints representatives to the annual general meeting, who then elect board members and auditors. It is common that the municipal council delegates the main responsibility for the governance to the municipal board which also, according to KL, is obliged to supervise the corporations owned by the municipality.

The hybrid challenge

Municipally owned corporations are often referred to as hybrid organizations (Thomasson, 2009). The reason for this is that these organizations combine public-sector values and the political governance dimension with the management methods of private corporations. Studies conducted of the hybrid phenomenon show that there is a risk of goal conflict in these organizations due to the difficulty in combining public-sector values and interests with profit-oriented management (André, 2010; Bovens, 2009; Watson, 2003). It is especially difficult to live up to the expectations of stakeholders (Thomasson, 2009). It is however not only the ability to reach goal congruence that is problematic. How to secure accountability in relation to the political governance of these organizations has also proven to be difficult as the organizational form used is designed for profit-oriented private corporations and for securing transparency and democratic values (André, 2010; Luke, 2010; Watson, 2003).

Corporatization of public services has an impact on the governance of an organization since it affects the chain of command: the public service is removed from the municipal organization and put into a separate legal entity. Consequently, politicians lose some of their influence over the services produced and with that the ability to secure public values (Fimreite and Lægreid, 2009; Forrer *et al.*, 2010). Further, the corporatization of public services alters the relationship between elected politicians and citizens as well as how citizens can hold elected politicians accountable (Deleon, 1998; Romzek, 2000; Shaoul *et al.*, 2012; Sinclair, 1995). Consequently, there are now not only one but two systems for accountability in place at the same time (Grossi and Thomasson, 2015; Thomasson and Grossi, 2013). One is the traditional system between elected politicians and citizens – the so-called vertical accountability – and this is characterized by democratic values (Bovens, 2009; Greiling and Spraul, 2010). The other is the horizontal relationship between the local authority and the corporation owned by that authority (Hodges, 2012; Willems and Van Dooren, 2012). Transferred into the context of the Swedish legislative frame-work, the horizontal relationship is under the jurisdiction of ABL while the vertical relationship is under the jurisdiction of KL. As a consequence, the pres-ence of market solutions is by several scholars regarded as requiring an adaption of the system of accountability in order to secure vertical as well as horizontal accountability (see e.g. Grossi and Thomasson, 2015).

An adaption has however not occurred in Sweden. Issues regarding lack of transparency and problems with holding municipal corporations accountable have been raised by researchers and interest organizations as well as journalists (Erlingsson *et al.*, 2014; Hyltner and Velasco, 2009; Statskontoret, 2012) and the Swedish Association of Local Authorities and Regions (SALAR) (SKL, 2013). Further, actual cases of corruption in municipal corporations have been exposed over the last couple of years (see e.g. Amnå *et al.*, 2013). The need to look further into the governance of municipal corporations and how accountability can be improved is thus called for. One important aspect is the role of the board.

Why the board matters

The role of the board is to represent and to protect the interest of the owners. In Sweden there is a tradition of appointing elected politicians to the boards of municipal corporations as representatives of the owners (indirectly the citizens) (Thomasson, 2013). By appointing elected politicians to the boards of municipal corporations, the idea is to increase transparency and protect the public interest. This works well in theory, but in practice there are some complications.

One complication is Swedish legislation. According to the ABL, represent-atives on the board of a corporation are obliged to look after the interests of the corporation and are personally liable if they make a decision that in any way damages the corporation. This means that elected politicians cannot represent any other interests than that of the corporation when serving as a board member. This means that an elected politician who takes a seat on the board of a municipal corporation risks running into several situations in which he or she faces a conflict of interest. One such situation is when a decision that needs to be taken by the board that is in the best interest of the corporation runs against the ideological stance or the political programme of the party that the individual politician represents.

Another complication is that of disclosure and transparency. As a board member, the elected politician is not allowed to reveal information that might harm the corporation. However, as an elected politician representing the citizens and with a political interest, the individual politician is expected to be open with information when asked by citizens or other politicians.

A third complication is that many politicians in Sweden hold more than one seat within the municipality and that these different positions could be in conflict with each other in regards to the interest and degree of influence each position represents. Recent statistics show that as the number of people involved in party politics decreases, the number of politicians holding several different seats simultaneously increases. Recent figures point to the fact that around 15 per cent of elected politicians occupy more than three seats in Swedish municipalities (SCB and SKL, 2012). This opens up conflicts of interests because one politician could have a seat in the municipal council and/or the municipal board at the same time as he or she has a seat on a board of a corporation. This is a clear situation with conflicting interests since the municipal board is obliged by KL to supervise the corporations. Combining the role of supervisor and owner with that of board member therefore ought to be avoided. Still, it is not uncommon for local politicians to have this dual affiliation (Erlingsson *et al.*, 2014; Thomasson, 2013).

A fourth complication is the mere fact that there are elected politicians on the boards of municipal corporations in Sweden who do not secure transparency or accountability. Recent studies have shown how one in three municipalities do not evaluate their boards as they are supposed to (Levander and von Hofsten, 2013). In fact, private corporations are better at performing the mandatory self-evaluation process than municipally owned corporations are (Levander and von Hofsten, 2013).

Finally, the fifth complication and the issue in the focus of this chapter is the appointment of board members and the composition of the board. The process of appointing members to the boards of municipal corporations in Sweden is not transparent and protects neither the interests of the municipality nor those of the citizens. The whole foundation of the board and its role in the governance system can thus be questioned in relation to how municipal corporations in Sweden are governed. In the following sections the reason for why this is the case will be further elaborated and the process of appointing members to the boards of municipal corporations will be described.

A four-step process

Elections of members to the boards of municipal corporations in Sweden occur in what can be described as a process consisting of four different steps. The process commences after a general election is held. General elections in Sweden, for municipalities, regional authorities and the government alike, are held every fourth year.

The formal appointment of board members takes place at the annual general meeting following upon a general election. Even though the companies have annual general meetings every year, the custom (unless there are defections) is to appoint the board for four years (a term of office).

The *first step* of the election process consists of negotiations among the political parties in a municipality regarding how to divide seats on boards and committees among the parties. The *second step* of the process also concerns negotiations, but this time the negotiations occur within the respective local party organization. The second step leads up to a list from each party containing their nominees. The *third step* consists of when the municipal assembly (or, often, the nomination committee elected by the municipal assembly) decides, based upon the lists presented by each party, on the official candidates for seats on boards and committees. Finally, the *fourth step* consists of the annual general meetings, when the formal election of the boards takes place.

In the following sections, each of these steps and the processes leading up to them will be further elaborated. The description of the four-step process is based on observations and interviews conducted in Swedish municipalities. Observations of the political process have mainly taken place within one Swedish municipality, but interviews have been conducted with politicians from different Swedish municipalities. The interviews confirm the information gathered through observations.

Steps one and two: political negotiations are the key

The first step

The first step in the process contains the negotiations between the political parties. In focus for these negotiations are the degrees of influence each party will be given on different boards and committees in relation to the outcome of the election. The backdrop for the negotiations is thus the outcome of the general election and concerns which party gets which position among the governing parties as well as among the opposition parties. The governing majority is given the majority of the seats and also the positions as chairs of boards and in committees, while the opposition is given less influence.

Certain boards and committees are from a political point of view regarded as being more attractive than others based on, for example, the relevance of the issues dealt with, the media attention given to the issues dealt with, access to networks of importance and/or the size of the budget. Also, the position as chair or deputy chair is more valuable than ordinary seats. It is thus not only a discussion of the number of seats, but which seats and where.

The second step

After deciding which party gets which positions, it is time for the second step in the process. The second step also contains negotiations, but this time those negotiations take place within the parties and more specifically within the local branches of the party organizations.

The process of assigning seats to boards is, due to the fact that the process occurs within respective local branch of a party combined with the attractiveness of the positions, influenced by aspects other than each candidate's election results or competence and considerations of the overall composition of the board. Instead, other aspects influence the process.

One is the relationships between the members of a political party, especially those with prominent positions. Seats on boards are often assigned to people for long and faithful service or as a consolation prize. The latter is often meant to compensate someone who is overlooked when assigning seats to the most prominent positions in the municipality, for example the municipal board.

Another aspect is that the person elected for a position on a board or committee does not necessarily have to have been on a formal list of candidates disclosed to the citizen before the election. The political party is free to choose any member for those positions. One way to get a seat on a board could thus be by acquiring enough support from your peers and it is not uncommon that people are given positions based on the fact that they were able to rally up the largest support and that someone else loses that same position. Further, and on that note, there is a tendency for it to be the same people who get nominated to a position time after time, regardless of their individual performance or the audits evaluation of the governance of a board or the work on a committee.

That members of boards and committees are appointed by their peers, combined with the lack of transparency in the appointment process, also contributes to create a breeding ground for scheming, especially considering that seats on boards and/or committees provide a person with influence and some amount of income (the higher the position the higher the income and degree of influence). The keener someone is to keep their power and/or income the more inclined that person is likely to be to engage in scheming activities.

Steps three and four: formal decisions

The third step: overall composition not an issue

The result of the election processes taking place inside each local branch of a political party is a list with names of candidates from all parties who are nominated for positions on boards and committees. This list of names is then sent to the nomination committee under the municipal assembly. The nomination committee presents the names to the municipal assembly who in the case of candidates for boards of municipal companies confirms the list and sends the list to the annual general meeting. It is then the annual general meeting which makes the final decision. At that meeting, the owners are represented by politician/politicians from the municipal assembly. The municipal assembly does however have the possibility of delegating the latter to the municipal board.

There are generally no discussions in the municipal assembly regarding the overall composition of candidates before the list is sent to the annual general meeting. Rather, there seems to be, according to interviews with chairs of the municipal assemblies in municipalities, an informal agreement between parties not to question candidates nominated by other parties. This means that there is no discussion among the politicians within the municipal council regarding how representative the boards are of the general population in relation to gender, ethnicity and age. This observation has been further supported by a recently conducted survey focusing on how local politicians are elected to committees and boards.[1] Politicians in all of the 25 studied municipalities included in the survey stated that representatives were elected by their peers in the local branches of the different political parties. Consequently, there seems to be a general problem in Swedish municipalities with lack of transparency when it comes to how representatives on boards as well as committees are appointed. Further no one seems to take responsibility for the overall composition of the boards of the municipal corporations.

The fourth step: annual general meeting – merely a formality

After the decision in the municipal council, there remains one step, which is the formal decision taken by the annual general meeting. The people representing the owner, i.e. the municipality, in this meeting are representatives elected by the municipal assembly and normally those are either members of the municipal assembly or the municipal council. Hence, the decision taken by the annual general meeting is generally regarded as a formality.

In the end – what matters is the peers

There is in general no discussion regarding the overall composition of boards in municipal corporations in Sweden. Instead the process of selecting candidates for these positions (and other political positions alike) is a process that in Sweden normally takes place within the local branches of the political parties. Further, the process is not transparent to the general public and once the candidates are presented no political discussion takes place in the municipal council or at the annual general meeting. Consequently, no one takes responsibility for the overall composition of boards.

The application process and its implications for accountability

Public accountability is the essence of democracy and securing accountability is paramount to securing democratic control (Bovens, 2009). In the public sector it is the politicians in the government (local or central) who secure accountability based on performance and this takes place through the democratic system (Bovens, 2009; Skelcher, 2009; Watson, 2003). In the private sector, other systems are in place to secure accountability and one of them is the corporate governance system (Ryan and Ng, 2000; Thomsen, 2008).

The problem with the creation of hybrid organizations, of which the municipal corporation is one example, is that neither the democratic nor the private system for securing accountability is fully applicable (André, 2010; Grossi and Thomasson, 2015; Rhodes, 1994). Therefore, accountability can no longer be secured in the traditional way through the vertical relationship between citizens and elected politicians. Instead, new relations emerge between politicians, citizens and the civil servants working in the hybrid organizations (Grossi and Thomasson, 2015; Watson, 2003).

Consequently, and as pointed out by Watson (2003), Bovens (2009) and André (2010), this requires that the accountability issues with hybrid organizations are addressed and adhered to. As a response to this, accountability in relation to hybrid organizations has been discussed in previous research (André, 2010; Grossi and Thomasson, 2015; Luke, 2010; Shaoul et al., 2012). The tendency in previous research has however been to focus on the systems as a whole and not look at specific mechanisms within those systems and how those mechanisms apply in hybrid settings. The aim of this chapter was, by focusing on appointment of members to boards of directors of municipal companies, to shed light on one such mechanism within the system of corporate governance.

The example of the appointment process described here is not one of changing or adapting a mechanism of control and/or accountability to a hybrid context. The function of the board has not been altered or adapted to the municipal ownership in the Swedish system of corporate governance. Instead, the board has the same role as it has in a corporation in the private sector and the processes of appointing members to the board follows a similar process in the municipalities as in the private sector, with owners nominating candidates to the annual general meeting. The difference is that there is that the process is not open to the citizens, who are the actual owners. Not even the municipal council, which is directly elected by the citizens, takes full responsibility for the overall composition of the board.

The issue at hand is that, when transferring the same system and mechanisms as used in the private sector without adapting them to public-sector conditions, public-sector values in terms of transparency and accountability are not protected. Based on this study, however, it might not be necessary to go as far as suggested in some of the previous studies and develop a specific system for hybrid organizations. Instead, in this case it seems to be sufficient to adapting the appointment process in order to make it more transparent and based more on performance and less on social ties.

The way forward

The purpose of this chapter has been to highlight as well as discuss some of the corporate governance challenges in relation to how municipal corporations are governed in the Swedish public-sector context. More precisely, the focus has been on the appointment of board members and the lack of transparency in that process and how this lack of transparency affects the ability to hold politicians accountable, this in spite of the fact that Sweden generally is regarded as a country with low corruption and with equal rights for men and women.

It is fair to say that there is a clear discrepancy between the self-image of what is Swedish and what has been described in this chapter. On the one hand, the lack of transparency can be interpreted as politicians (and civil servants) taking time to adapt to the more market-based organizations that have emerged as a result of NPM. This would however be a benevolent interpretation. The problem here presented is not referable to the lack of systems in place to secure accountability in hybrid organizations. Rather, it is a problem related to a lack of ability to use existing systems in the right way. This assumption is supported by the fact that private-sector corporations are outperforming municipal corporations when it comes to implementing self-evaluation and codes of conduct. Private-sector corporations thus show how it is possible, within the governance system provided by Swedish corporate legislation, to improve accountability. Then why haven't we seen a similar development within our municipal corporations?

What we see in relation to municipal corporate governance is more likely explained as a problem in the culture and the general practice of the local branches of political parties. It is probably also a problem with a lack of understanding on behalf of governing politicians on municipal boards and councils regarding the importance of good governance in order to secure accountability.

The first things that are needed is therefore an adaption of the organizational processes to secure accountability and transparency in relation to how board members are appointed as well as the work of the boards. This is however not sufficient. Also needed is an increase of competence among politicians in municipalities regarding corporate governance.

Second, according to research on the issue of accountability, it is also necessary to determine the performance criteria against which an organization or, in this case, governing politicians are to be evaluated and judged (Bovens, 2009). No such criteria are in place when it comes to board processes in municipal corporations or, for that matter, the performance of the municipally owned corporations. All municipal corporations have mission statements, but few have performance criteria. The third issue that needs to be taken care of is thus how municipalities today evaluate and measure the performance of their corporations. This is especially important in the light of new legislation that will require an increase in the control that municipal boards exert over the corporations in the municipality.

To conclude, there are thus at least three things that need to be improved in the relation between municipalities and their corporations. These three things need to be improved in order to secure accountability and subsequently regain some of the legitimacy that municipal corporations have lost due to recent scandals. It is not only necessary to secure accountability and improve transparency, but also to secure the high values that these corporations represent. In other words, it is time to open up the black box of party politics.

Note

1 The survey was conducted by the author herself during autumn 2015/winter 2016.

References

Aguilera, R. V. (2005) 'Corporate governance and director accountability: an institutional comparative perspective'. *British Journal of Management*, Vol. 16, pp. 39–53.

Amnå, E., B. Czarniawska and L. Marcusson (2013) *Tillitens gränser: Granskningskommissionens slutbetänkande* (Gothenburg: Granskningskommissionen).

Andersson, L.-H., R. Dansell, S. Hubendick and S. Sen (2012) *Bättre styrelsearbete i offentligt ägda bolag* (Stockholm: SKL Kommentus Media AB).

André, R. (2010) 'Assessing the accountability of government-sponsored enterprises and quangos'. *Journal of Business Ethics*, Vol. 97, pp. 271–289.

Bovens, M. (2009) Public Accountability, in E. Ferlie, L. E. J. Lynn and C. Pollitt (eds), *The Oxford Handbook of Public Management* (Oxford: Oxford Handbooks Online).

BRÅ (2012) *Korruptionen inom kommuner och landsting* (Stockholm: Brottsförebyggande rådet).

Deleon, L. (1998) 'Accountability in a "reinvented" government'. *Public Administration*, Vol. 76, No. 3, pp. 539–558.

Erlingsson, G. Ó. (2006) 'Organisationsförändringar och ökad kommunal korruption: Existerar ett samband?'. *Kommunal Ekonomi och Politik*, Vol. 3, pp. 7–40.

Erlingsson, G. Ó., M. Fogelgren, F. Olsson, A. Thomasson and R. Öhrvall (2014) *Hur styrs och granskas kommunala bolag? Erfarenheter och lärdomar från norrköpings kommun. Rapport 2014:6.* (Linköping: Centrum för Kommunstrategiska studier, Linköping University).

Fimreite, A. L. and P. Lægreid (2009) 'Reorganizing the welfare state administration'. *Public Management Review*, Vol. 11, No. 3, pp. 281–297.

Forrer, J., J. E. Kee, K. E. Newcomer and E. Boyer (2010) 'Public–private partnerships and the public accountability question'. *Public Administration Review*, Vol. May/June, pp. 475–484.

Greiling, D. and K. Spraul (2010) 'Accountability and the challenges of information disclosure'. *Public Administration Quarterly*, Vol. Fall, pp. 338–377.

Grossi, G. and A. Thomasson (2015) 'Bridging the accountability gap in hybrid organizations: the case of Malmö-Copenhagen port'. *International Review of Administrative Sciences*, pp. 1–17.

Hansson, L. and S.-O. Collin (1991) *Kommunalt bolag? En studie av för- och nackdelar med bolagisering av kommunalteknisk verksamhet* (Stockholm: Svenska Kommunförbundet).

Hodges, R. (2012) 'Joined-up government and the challenges to accounting and accountability researchers'. *Financial Accountability & Management*, Vol. 28, No. 1, pp. 26–51.

Hood, C. (1995) 'The "new public management" in the 1980s: variations on a theme'. *Accounting, Organizations and Society*, Vol. 20, No. 2–3, pp. 93–109.

Hyltner, M. and M. Velasco (2009) *Kommunala bolag: Laglöst land?*, Den nya välfärden.

Levander, H. and A. von Hofsten (2013) Våga utvärdera bolagsstyrelserna, *Dagens Samhälle*.

Luke, B. (2010) 'Examining accountability dimensions in state-owned enterprises'. *Financial Accountability & Management*, Vol. 26, No. 2, pp. 134–162.

Pollitt, C. (2000) 'Is the emperor in his underwear? An analysis of the impacts of public management reform'. *Public Management*, Vol. 2, pp. 181–199.

Rhodes, R. A. W. (1994) 'The hollowing out of the state: the changing nature of the public service in Britain'. *Political Quarterly*, Vol. 65, No. 2, pp. 138–151.

Romzek, B. S. (2000) 'Dynamics of public sector accountability in an era of reform'. *International Review of Administrative Sciences*, Vol. 66, No. 1, pp. 21–44.

Ryan, C. and C. Ng (2000) 'Public sector corporate governance disclosures: an examination of annual reporting practices in Queensland'. *Australian Journal of Public Administration*, Vol. 59, pp. 11–23.

SCB (2011) *Offentligt ägda företag 2010. Statistiska meddelanden, oe 27 sm 1101* (Stockholm/Örebro: Statistiska Centralbyrån).

SCB (2012) *Näringsverksamhet, statistisk årsbok 2012* (Stockholm/Örebro: Tillväxtverket och Statistiska Centralbyrån).

SCB and SKL (2012) *Förtroendevalda i kommuner och landsting 2011, demokratisk rapport 12* (Stockholm: Statistiska Centralbyrån and Sveriges Kommuner och Landsting).

Shaoul, J., A. Stafford and P. Stapelton (2012) 'Accountability and corporate governance of public–private partnerships'. *Critical Perspectives on Accounting*, Vol. 23, pp. 213–229.

Sinclair, A. (1995) 'The chameleon of accountability: forms and discourses'. *Accounting, Organizations and Society*, Vol. 20, No. 2/3, pp. 219–237.

Skelcher, C. (2009) Public–Private Partnerships and Hybridity, in E. Ferlie, L. E. J. Lynn and C. Pollitt (eds), *The Oxford Handbook of Public Management* (Oxford: Oxford handbooks online).

SKL (2013) *Lekmannarevisionen i praktiken: Demokratins granskning av kommunala bolag* (Stockholm: Sveriges Kommuner och Landsting).

Statskontoret (2012) *Köpta relationer: Om korruption i det kommunala sverige* (Stockholm: Regeringen).

Stattin, D. (2007) *Kommunal aktiebolagsrätt: Bolagsrätt och bolagsstyrning för kommun- och landstingsägda bolag* (Solna: Nordstedts Juridik AB).

Sundkvist, F. (2015) Hälften av styrelserna tomma på kvinnor, *Svenska Dagbladet Näringsliv*.

Thomasson, A. (2009) 'Exploring the ambiguity of hybrid organisations: a stakeholder approach'. *Financial Accountability & Management*, Vol. 25, No. 3, pp. 353–366.

Thomasson, A. (2013) *Styrning av offentligt ägda bolag* (Studentlitteratur, Lund).

Thomasson, A. and G. Grossi (2013) Governance and Accountability of Joint Ventures: A Swedish Case Study, in P. Valkama, S. J. Bailey and A.-V. Anttiroiko (eds), *Organizational Innovation in Public Services: Forms and Governance* (Basingstoke: Palgrave Macmillian).

Thomsen, S. (2008) *An Introduction to Corporate Governance: Mechanisms and Systems* (Copenhagen: DJÖF).

Transparency International (2015) *Corruption Perceptions Index 2015*. Available online at www.transparency.org/cpi2015.

Watson, D. (2003) 'The rise and rise of public private partnerships: challenges for public accountability'. *Australian Accounting Review*, Vol. 13, No. 3, pp. 2–14.

Willems, T. and W. Van Dooren (2012) 'Coming to terms with accountability: combining multiple forums and functions'. *Public Management Review*, Vol. 14, No. 7, pp. 1011–1036.

World Economic Forum (2015) *The Gender Gap Report 2015*. Available online at http://reports.weforum.org/global-gender-gap-report-2015.

11 Leadership and strategy in a transforming academic field

Christine Blomqvist

Summary

The academic field in Sweden is in a state of transformation. Demands for change are facing universities and colleges. Drawing on empirical illustrations from the public debate in Sweden and from strategic plans of Lund University, analysis shows the prevalence of two dominant logics in the field – collegiality and managerialism. Leadership becomes a matter of handling these logics and making sense of ambiguity, inconsistency and paradoxes. It can be seen as a process of finding a third way between two logics, of 'muddling through' in a traditional Swedish way.

Introduction

Within the academic field,[1] leadership has often been equated with collegiality. Collegial leadership has been a key historical characteristic in academia, for higher education as well as research. Collegiality, or faculty governance, defines the relationship among colleagues at a university and refers to a structure as well as a culture (Björck, 2013). Academia, however, is no exception to the changing landscape of public administration. Several trends are visible in this transformation, for example an increased focus on performance and evaluation measurements and, as in Sweden, the Autonomy Inquiry (SOU, 2008). This reform aimed at increasing the freedom for state universities and colleges, within the framework of the current official form. In the bill, the government presented proposals and made assessments involving extensive deregulation of the internal organization and teaching positions. So far, academic organizations have not taken advantage of this increased organizational leeway. Despite the sometimes agitated discussions, often on the pros and cons of NPM as opposed to traditional perspectives on academia, it has been more or less taken for granted that the notion of collegiality stands out in its positive connotation. Even in governmental reforms, as in the autonomy reform, there is confidence in the collegial values (Björck, 2013; Sundberg, 2013). Moreover, collegiality is usually perceived as more or less the basis for academia, as it is one of the core values that academic organizations have been built on from the very beginning. To put collegiality into question is sometimes the same as challenging the very identity of academia.

Still, a public debate on the meaning and means of collegiality has emerged among academic professionals as well as other stakeholders within the academic field. Collegiality, or, rather, collegial leadership, has often come to be placed in opposition to NPM and its 'managerial' leadership when it comes to governing within the academic field. It is, of course, a tricky business to disentangle this debate and account for the various voices. Nevertheless, I will take the risk of 'lumping' together the different voices and opinions and treat them as two main logics. The aim of this chapter is to outline these two dominant logics visible in the academic field today – collegiality and managerialism – and to roughly describe and elaborate them in order to understand what characterizes the transformation as well as what possible implications it has for leadership.

The empirical foundations are of two kinds. I start with sketching a background consisting of the ongoing debate in Sweden. A second empirical source is made up of strategic plans for Lund University, starting with the first plans made in 1995 and continuing to the latest one from 2012. The point of analysing strategic plans is that these mirror the vision, mission and values of a university in its current state but, above all, point out the intended road to the future. Although it is well known that strategic plans, more often than not, are not fully implemented, it is still possible to argue that they are important as ways of communicating an intention and will on behalf of an organization. Moreover, strategic plans can be seen as a way for organizations to meet and answer to demands placed on them from various stakeholders.

Forces towards change within the academic field

Forces towards change in the academic field come from various stakeholders, not least from governmental directions. This seems to be a global phenomenon. In the US, criticism has been launched by the National Association of State Universities and Land Grant Colleges, as well as by the Association of Governing Boards of Universities and Colleges, mainly concerning the need for reforming governance systems (Birnbaum, 2004). Similar criticism has been made by the European Commission through its 'modernization agenda' (European Commission, 2011). Inviting member states to develop and implement reforms that are in accordance with national and regional needs and that tackle country-specific challenges mirrors a general trend: that universities are becoming more autonomous in relation to the state. In Sweden, an example is the Autonomy Inquiry discussed above. At the same time, the claims for accountability increase (Huisman, 2009; Stensaker, 2011). Overall, this reflects not only a trend in the field of academia but in the public sector as a whole (de Boer *et al.*, 2010).

It could be argued that there are essentially two main perspectives on both how to define the problems in academia and how to tackle them. The first is rooted in academic traditions of collegial decision-making, shared governance and university autonomy linked to professional autonomy (Enders *et al.*, 2013; Sahlin, 2012; Stensaker and Vabø, 2013). The other main perspective is dominated by concepts like management, markets, results, evaluation and customers, and is often concerned with making academia more efficient. In other words, it is the New Public Management (NPM), as first outlined by Osborne and Gabler (1992) and Hood (1991, 1995). Ideals and norms connected to NPM have also affected the Swedish system. Concepts such as 'control', 'autonomy', 'competition' and 'management' are as common in Sweden as elsewhere in French, German or UK universities (Craig *et al.*, 2014). Although, as Paradeise *et al.* (2009) point out, there are differences in interpretations and implementations of NPM in different countries, there are still common patterns on a policy level across countries. Sweden can, thus, be seen as part of a more general trend of globalization (Dunleavy, 1994). Also, internally, universities in Europe have transformed. Organizational structure has become more formalized, the importance of leadership is emphasized, internal governance structures have become more hierarchical and, not least, administrative structures and processes for evaluating performance have increased (Frøhlich *et al.*, 2012). Similar findings were made by Stensaker and Vabø (2013) in an analysis of how a sample of Nordic universities perceives the place and role of governance in their strategic plans. Stensaker found that the dominant model for tackling change and responding to demands by various stakeholders is the entrepreneurial model. This puts much weight on leadership in taking initiatives, networking and forming coalitions for change (Etzkowitz *et al.*, 2000). Analysing the strategic plans for the Nordic universities, this is what Stensaker found. Leadership was seen as crucial in stimulating change, as expressed in an emphasis on leadership development and an urge for new types of academic leadership. These findings are in line with the 'managerial' or NPM perspective. And it is not surprising. Academic leaders are under great pressure to initiate change and to embrace an entrepreneurial mind-set (Bolman and Gallos, 2011; Fullan and Scott, 2009). In conclusion, it can be argued that the force towards change stems mainly from outside pressure, such as regulations from the EU, as well as contemporary norms of how to govern universities in accurate ways. How this is visible in Sweden is the subject of the next section.

The public debate on academic leadership

To illustrate the public debate on academic leadership in Sweden, some of the voices heard follow below. In an ongoing debate on academic leadership at the Riksbankens Jubileumsfond (RJ), which is an independent foundation with the goal of promoting and supporting research in the humanities and social sciences, several stakeholders have presented their views. Ylva Hasselberg, professor at the Department of Economic History, Uppsala University, states that 'It is strange nobody reacts when leadership is portrayed as the solution to most problems' (Hasselberg, 2009). In a reply to this, Elisabet Elgan, former chair of the Institute of Contemporary History at Södertörn University, says:

> I believe that leadership obsession has its origins in some fashion theories about how this makes the public sector more efficient. The Leadership cult is associated with the far-reaching decentralization that has taken place in the public sector.
>
> (Elgan, 2009)

Sverker Sörlin, a well-known participator in the public debate, draw parallels between the upcoming debate on management to that of evaluations and rankings. He says that

> [A]ctually, these evaluations is a symptom of lack of independence, and the lack of a responsible leadership.
>
> (Sörlin, 2009)

The debate has been going on over the last years in various public arenas. It mirrors the tension between collegiality and NPM and is still animated. A recent argument from one of the largest daily newspapers is an example of this.

Professors Mats Alvesson and Bo Rothstein are arguing on behalf of collegial leadership. Alvesson works at the Department of Business Administration, Lund University; Rothstein is a professor in political science at Gothenburg University. They are both critical of the way Swedish universities are managed and led, which is expressed in an opinion piece:

> A particular career path to management positions for administrative dexterous people with very limited research credentials in the trunk has been established.... University management now consists often of weakly distinguished academics.... Scientists themselves have never been near the top international research course, know not how to get others to get there.... What we see are academic leaders who fall prey to all sorts of opportunism and put big money on research of dubious quality. Officiously one introduces different systems and procedures that increase bureaucracy.
>
> (Alvesson and Rothstein, 2014)

In a reply, Erik Arroy, who is chair of the Swedish Students Association, says that Alvesson and Rothstein overlook the main issue: the problem is not limited to research. Instead, it is higher education and the total organization and leadership of universities that need reforming. Arroy states that the criticism from the professors are simplifying the problems that universities face (Arroy, 2014).

So far it can be concluded that Sweden, as other countries, are put under pressure to change the way that academic organizations are managed and led, and that the opinions on how to do this vary according to whom you ask. Also, influences from NPM are clearly visible in the public debate, as shown in the focus on leadership.

An interesting question is if anything has actually happened on a concrete level or if it is more talk than action. Looking at one of the major reforms in Sweden, the autonomy reform mentioned in the introduction, as the term 'autonomy' suggests, there was room for universities to maintain or even widen the collegial leadership and control systems. However, it seems as though few, if any, academic organizations have embraced this possibility, as a survey of five universities and higher education organizations indicates. Instead, this survey shows that the collegial decision-making power

> [H]ave been expanded to include more categories of employees at universities.... [In] some cases, collegial decision-making power has moved over to the technical-administrative staff which cannot be said to belong to the category of professional colleagues. Administrative representatives have gained more power in the selection of peer leaders, in decisions relating to employment matters and in matters relating to quality education at undergraduate, graduate and doctoral levels. There is also a tendency that collegial decision-making has been centralized, in the sense that units above faculty have been established, and given decision-making power.
>
> The survey shows that academic freedom has been curtailed with the increased institutional autonomy that was provided through the autonomy reform. Teachers' and researchers' collective right to govern themselves, which is a part of academic freedom, is no longer a self-evident principle neither in law nor in practice.
>
> (Sundberg, 2013)

It is interesting that a reform that was intended to give academic organizations more freedom in the meaning of, among other things, collegiality seems to have had the reverse impact. I will get back to this in later sections. First, I will turn to the viewpoint within universities and see how a Swedish 'Ivy League' university, Lund University, has tackled the demands for change. I will do this by analysing the strategic plans since these are main tools for communicating how organizations look at the future and the demands put on them.

Strategic planning at Lund University

Lund University, LU, was founded in 1666. In its present form it has around 47,000 students and a position of excellence in international teaching and research. LU is consistently ranked as one of the top 100 universities in the world (www.lu.se).

In 1995, the first LU strategic plan, labelled a 'Plan for the Future', was approved by the university board. In its foreword, the vice chancellor states that:

> It has been a unique and educative experience for the university to, for the first time in its nearly 330 year long history, discuss and formulate its own vision for the future
>
> (Lund University, 1995)

It should be noted that producing strategic plans was not an initiative of the universities; instead it was a requirement from the government (Sörlin, 2009).

The strategic plan covers areas such as research policy, education, international cooperation, environmental policy, HR policy, information and IT and gender issues. The formulated goals and strategies state that these have their point of departure in the 'classical university ideals' (Lund University, 1995, p. 5). It is notable that the potential tension between classical ideals and demands from various stakeholders outside the university is recognized by the senior management of Lund University, as is expressed in the plan:

> The university can and should itself control its own development based on their own values and thus also affect the world around her. Free knowledge, free research, education for critical thinking as well as the task of being a carrier of culture and an arena for free debate – all this is included in the statement of the beliefs of a university idea and is thus an expression of attitudes and attitudes can not be 'adapted' to changes in the outside world.
>
> One can describe it as a tension between the demands and expectations of society at the university and the university's basic ideas. It does not imply that there must be expressed contradictions between these – but the university must be developed so that the adjustment that naturally must be made to needs and demands from outside, not simultaneously disrupt the fundamental prerequisites for the University to be a university. This tension between safeguarding the University's fundamental values and on the other hand to adjust its operations in line with demands and needs related to societal changes is an essential starting point for the discussion of the University's goals and strategies.
>
> (Lund University, 1995, p. 8)

The strategic plan thereafter covers the period of 2002–2006. This is a thinner product compared to the 1995 version. The first plan covered strategic issues over 38 pages, while the plan of 2002 does the same over 11 pages. There's also a shift in the point of departure, as this plan starts, in its first sentence, with the law on higher education, stating what universities are obliged to do. After that it is said:

The objectives and strategies as the university itself phrases is thus essential so that the University is able both to meet the obligations that is formulated by the government and to simultaneously develop their full potential.

(Lund University, 2002, p. 4)

This plan also covers 'obligatory' areas for strategic plans, such as vision, values, goals and strategies. It's worth noticing that the formulations concerning academic values are less distinct. The plan is also more general in its formulations, although there are prioritized strategic areas mentioned. Among these are recruitment, leadership development, concentrating on multidisciplinary research areas and collaboration with the society and system for quality control. It is stated in the plan that the responsibility for implementation lies mostly with faculties and departments and that the plan should be seen as general guidelines. However, it does state that one of the most important strategic issues is a strong reputation:

A strong reputation as a University is perhaps the most important value for Lund University as a whole.

(Lund University, 2002, p. 4)

In the following plan, for the years 2007–2011, it seems that Lund University has found its form for strategic plans. At least, when it comes to the number of pages, this plan is also 11 pages long. Also, the plan takes its point of departure from the assignment that is given to universities from the government. However, although this plan is fairly short compared to the first, from 1995, and also moderately general in its formulations, it is possible to spot some differences compared to the previous plan from 2002. In the latter plan, it is more clearly expressed that Lund University cherishes traditional academic values:

Lund University shall, as a leading, creative and cross-border University, stand for basic human and academic values. Academic integrity is absolute. Research and teaching must be morally and intellectually independent of various influencing factors.

(Lund University, 2007, p. 4)

The present strategic plan covers the years 2012–2016. In it, it is stated that:

Lund University has an important role to play internationally, nationally and regionally. This at a time when major global challenges – such as health, environment, human rights and sustainable development – place increased demands on being able to understand and explain the world in order to improve it.

The strategic plan for the period 2012–2016 represents both continuity and renewal. It completes the previous strategic plan 2007–2011 in the areas where this is still relevant, namely in terms of focus on cross-border interoperability, quality, internationalization and leadership. The present strategic plan adds new dimensions in terms of the challenges that the University faces in the 2010s. The University's core values remain unchanged.

(Lund University, 2011, p. 1)

Also, in this plan it is emphasized that the plan is general in its nature and that implementation is primarily the responsibility of the faculties and departments. A slight alteration towards putting education more in the foreground can be seen:

At Lund University, new generations of students learn to explore and understand themselves and their world. Here they develop their ability to cooperate with others to address challenging problems. They lay the foundation for lifelong development of knowledge, creativity and democratic values as guiding principles. Lund University educates future knowledge developers, problem solvers and leaders.

(Lund University, 2011, p. 2)

In the vision and overall goal for the university, there is an alteration in the sense that a 'new' concept – innovation – has appeared. The goal is stated as:

Excellence in teaching, research, innovation and collaboration with the community.
    The goal will be achieved through the following strategies:

- Cross-border cooperation
- Internationalization
- Quality
- Leadership, teachership, employeeship

(Lund University, 2011, p. 2)

A more extrovert than introvert approach from the university seems to continue in the present plan, as the emphasis on collaboration and openness to society continues. Notably, the same goes for the highlighting of leadership, now accompanied with a stress on the importance of teaching and employees. The status and importance of innovation resumes, which is most probably connected to the EU and 'Horizon 2020', EU's biggest research and innovation programme, extending from 2014 to 2020 (European Commission, 2015). Regarding leadership, there is now a more specific emphasis on 'communicative leadership':

The requirements for a well-developed leadership and management are increasing at the university ... there's a pronounced need for a communicative leadership – rooted in the universities' core values and vision – which guides the way in times of change.

(Lund University, 2011, p. 12)

The tension between traditional collegial values and modern managerial values moves in a kind of wavelike motion back and forth when following a chronological journey of strategic plans. From being firmly grounded in traditional values comes a wave of managerialism, where a response to governmental guidelines is put forward, and then a return to values of academic integrity. In the recent plans, however, it seems as though managerial values have gained ground. This is visible in the way that the concept of leadership is put at the forefront as a key success factor for the university. I will elaborate further on the logics of leadership and management after some concluding remarks on strategic plans. These can be perceived as responses to demands from the environment and in that sense serves as illustrations of the transformation process in the field.

Strategic plans as mirrors of norms in the environment

First of all, it is worth keeping in mind that the initiative to produce strategic plans does not come from within universities. It is a requirement from the government. That being said, it is also worth mentioning that the first plan, even if it had not been voluntarily made, was still thorough and is actually the most detailed of the plans. After this, the subsequent plans are less extensive and more general in their character. They were also produced with greater pace, the time between the plans being shortened. Focus shifted from internal to external in the sense that more emphasis was put on collaboration with society, on education and on reputation and 'brand'. The stress on leadership as being of strategic importance is also apparent and in line with Stensaker's (2013) study of Scandinavian universities. It is also possible to view the plans as containing more and more of the NPM vocabulary, although this is said with caution. But, as Bolden *et al.* (2009) make clear, the response to an expanding array of demands has mainly been to shift from collegial models towards managerial models of decision-making. Strategic plans serve as a legitimation device; they can be placed in the 'shop window' to show stakeholders that the university is responding to their demands. In this latter sense, strategic plans serve as a means to legitimize an organization (Karlsson, 1991).

A concluding observation is that the plans seem to mirror the tensions between traditional academic values, i.e. collegiality, and modern managerial values. An illustration of this is when the plans from 1995–2007 put weight on academic values and in a sense brought the values back into the overall strategy. But, after 2007 in the following plans, this stress on academic values is more mixed up with other key words belonging to the NPM context. A cautious conclusion can be that the strategic plans, being more and more general in their rhetoric, are in this sense becoming more like plans for any formal organization. It raises the question whether universities are gradually losing their specific identity. With this question in mind, let us look at how a new vice chancellor at Lund University tackled the logics of leadership and management.

Leadership and management at Lund University

Strategic plans are, ideally, to be implemented by the leaders in an organization. More often than not, the new leader inherits the old leader's strategy. This was the case in Lund. In 2015 the university welcomed a new vice chancellor, Torbjörn von Schantz. Revising and rewriting the strategy was on the 'to do-list' for the new vice chancellor. In his installation speech he gave some hints as to what his intentions were:

> I believe in a future with a developed collegial leadership. Collegially nominated department heads, deans and vice chancellors give legitimacy to the leadership, and give us decision-makers who know what the issues are about, and what an academy is. But the collegial leadership has also – rightly, been criticized as slow, to avoid uncomfortable decisions, and being unable to make priorities.
>
> A collegial leadership requires colleagues who take responsibility – colleagues who develop a collective approach, i.e. an ability to both take responsibility for their own unit, while also taking a broader responsibility for the overall organization.
>
> (Lund University, 2015a)

A similar argument was put forward in answering a Commission of Inquiry, where the Swedish government wanted an analysis of how management and governance within universities could be developed in order to meet future challenges (SOU 2015:92). Lund University, with the vice chancellor in the forefront, stressed the importance of collegial leadership. It is of vital substance in maintaining the academic profession; we need more academic leadership rather than less, the university stated (LUM 2016).

The new vice chancellor has started out as being a firm proponent for collegial leadership. However, in a seminar with some 50 managers from Lund University, and also expressed in his blog (Lund University, 2015b), when emphasizing the need for a collegial leadership he calls attention to the need for more clarity in the 'chain of command'. Accountability on behalf of all managers in the university was stressed, while also highlighting the need for all leaders to take responsibility not only for their own functions but for the whole university. Hence, the new vice chancellor gives voice to a more modern collegial leadership, translating collegiality with reference to NPM.

As has been discussed before, there is an increasing focus on leadership appearing in the strategic plans. However, this does not seem to be connected to a decreasing focus on management. The same observations hold true when listening to the new vice chancellor's opinions. His way of using 'academic leadership' seems to comprise traditional academic values, with a strong grounding in collegiality at the same time as pointing to the need for accountability and responsibility. The sharp distinction between the concept of leadership as based in academic values and management as based in managerial values, observed by Bolden *et al.* (2012) in studies of higher education in the UK, is thus not so visible in Sweden. Instead, it is more fruitful to talk about an interplay between the two logics.

The interplay between collegiality and managerialism

Based on the empirical illustrations presented before, it seems that traditional collegial values are challenged by a modern logic of managerialism, in a way that is similar to other public organizations. Following this, it is possible that academic organizations are on their way towards losing their specific identity and becoming more and more 'company-like'. The logic of managerialism, with its emphasis on planning, measurement and performance indicators, has even caused some researchers to talk about a 'perverse audit culture' in universities (Craig *et al.*, 2014, p. 1). However, what seems to happen when the logic of managerialism gets a stronger foothold in the academic field is that the logic of collegiality also appears more visible. It becomes a subject in the public debate and is 'guarded' by its proponents. Collegiality has no distinct definition, as has been obvious in the illustrations from the public debate, where differing opinions show. However, when collegiality is on the public agenda and not embedded in the culture and taken for granted within the academic field, it becomes possible to clarify what we mean. In doing this elucidation, it opens up an opportunity for analysis, reflection and formulation of grounding values and norms as well as governance and steering principles in and of academic organizations. The logics of managerialism and collegiality are in many respect in opposition, which is clearly reflected in the public debate. However, at Lund University the concrete expressions of the two logics has resulted in more of an interplay than of a struggle between two competing forces.

Earlier research on public organizations has come to similar conclusions. The public sector field is characterized by paradoxes and has to reflect, accept and try to implement opposing values and norms in society. Public organizations have to handle conflicting demands made on them (Czarniawska-Joerges, 1992; Jönsson, 1988). Maybe this holds true for academic organizations as well. A cautious conclusion about the state of the field is that it is characterized by ambiguity, referring to the possibility of multiple interpretations (March and Olsen, 1976). This points to the non-uniform character of the field. In this ambiguous context, leadership is to be carried out.

The way forward

From the analysis above, some aspects of leadership in the present as well as in the future are worth elaborating on. First, it can be noted that the notion of leadership seems to take up more and more space on the public agenda, on local, national and European levels. It is not likely that this is going to stop. On the contrary, it looks like leadership is perceived to be one of the key solutions to a variety of problems. It is possible to view leadership as part of an ongoing logic of managerialism that is gaining a stronger foothold in the academic field.

Second, if leadership is seen as a social process of constructing change and making sense, then it is probably becoming more and more requested. Derived from the discussion above, conflicting demands, paradoxes and ambiguity capture some important aspects of academic settings. In this setting, leadership as a social influence process becomes a matter of handling the paradoxes as well as making sense of the different logics. Leadership can be seen as handling the interplay of various logics prevalent in the everyday reality. This indicates that, intentionally or not, decoupling can turn out to be of minor importance as a tactic (Sahlin, 2012). Instead, leadership becomes more of managing the interplay of different logics and to manage inconsistencies and paradoxes. These paradoxes can entail meeting demands of being 'modern', as the European Commission defines it, at the same time as being traditional and rooted in collegial values, as defined by the majority of the research society. Or responding to demands of efficiency at the same time as guarding democratic values. This matches Bolden *et al.*'s (2009) findings from studying leadership in 12 UK universities, where the interviewed leaders experienced tensions 'between the need for collegiality and managerialism, individual autonomy and collective engagement, leadership of the discipline and the institution, academic versus administrative authority, informality and formality, inclusivity and professionalization, and stability and change' (Bolden *et al.*, 2009, p. 364).

Finding a third way seems to be the Swedish method. The construction of coordination and change and the way to make sense can be viewed in terms of constructing a middle road. Rather than interpreting the transformation in the field as a process whereby academic organizations gradually lose their identity, it could very well be described as a third way in-between collegiality and managerialism. The approach from the vice chancellor can be interpreted as an expression of this middle road. The new vice chancellor's installation speech in 2015 can be understood as a typical Swedish way of approaching things. Finding a third way, to compromise and negotiate, can be seen as key characteristics of the Swedish culture (Hofstede *et al.*, 2010). In Sweden, then, it is less fruitful to talk of an outright struggle between managerialism and collegiality. It is more fruitful to look at the practical expressions of the logics if we want to understand the transformation in the field. At a closer look, the struggle between collegiality and managerialism, which is so clearly visible in the public debate, transforms into a more pragmatic stance in a typically Swedish way. As for leadership, this becomes a process of muddling through, coping with paradoxes, tensions and logics, still making a way forward.

Note

1 I use the concept of 'field' in the same sense that DiMaggio (1983, pp. 148–149):

> By organizational field, I refer to sets of organizations that together accomplish some task in which a researcher is interested.... The term 'field' is more frequently used in the non-profit sector.... A field is always an analytical construct, and how one defines it depends upon the phenomena of which one is interested. A field consists not only of organizations that produce 'outputs', but also of organizations that supply resources, effect constraints or pose contingencies. The extent to which a field constitutes a network of interactions is always an empirical question.

References

Alvesson, M. and B. Rothstein (2014) 'Universiteten hotar bli sveriges nästa pisa-haveri', *Dagens Nyheter* (2 May 2014).

Arroy, E. (2014) 'Grovt förenklad kritik mot högskolan', *Dagens Nyheter* (5 May 2014).

Birnbaum, R. (2004) 'The end of shared governance: looking ahead or looking back'. *New Directions for Higher Education*, Vol. 127, pp. 5–22.

Björck, H. (2013) *Om kollegialitet* [About collegiality]. SULF:s skriftserie/Report from The Swedish Union for Academic Teachers.

Bolden, R., J. Gosling, A. O'Brien, K. Peters, M. Ryan and A. Haslam (2012) 'Academic leadership: changing conceptions, identities and experiences in UK higher education' (Exeter: Leadership Foundation for Higher Education, University of Exeter, No. 4.1).

Bolden, R., G. Petrov, J. Gosling and A. Bryman (2009) 'Leadership in higher education: facts, fictions and futures – introduction to the special issue'. *Leadership*, Vol. 5, No. 3, pp. 291–298.

Bolman, L. G. and J. V. Gallos (2011) *Reframing Academic Leadership* (San Francisco, CA: Jossey-Bass, John Wiley and Sons).

Craig, R., J. Amernic and D. Tourish (2014) 'Perverse audit culture and accountability of modern public university'. *Financial Accountability & Management*, Vol. 30, No. 1, pp. 1–24.

Czarniawska-Joerges, B. (1992) *Styrningens paradoxer: Scener ur den offentliga verksamheten* (Stockholm: Norstedts).

de Boer, H., B. Jongbloed, J. Enders and J. File (2010) Progress in Higher Education Reform across Europe, in *Governance Reform, vol. 2. Report* (Twente: University of Twente).

DiMaggio, P. J. (1983) State Expansion and Organizational Fields, in R. H. Hall and R. E. Quinn (eds), *Organizational Theory and Public Policy* (London: SAGE).

Dunleavy, P. (1994) 'The globalization of public services production: can government be "best in world"?'. *Public Policy and Administration*, Vol. 9, No. 2, pp. 36–64.

Elgan, E. (2009) *Flosklema eller makten* (Stockholm: Riksbankens Jubileumsfond, RJ, 20090609).

Enders, J., H. de Boer and E. Weyer (2013) 'Regulatory autonomy and performance: the reform of higher education re-visited'. *Higher Education*, Vol. 65, No. 1, pp. 5–23.

Etzkowitz, H., A. Webster, C. Gebhart and B. R. Terra (2000) 'The future of the university and the university of the future: evolution of ivory tower to entrepreneurial paradigm'. *Research Policy*, Vol. 29, No. 3, pp. 313–330.

European Commission (2011) *Com 567. Communication from the Commission to the European Parliament, the Council, the European Economic and Social Committee and the Committee of the Regions. Supporting Growth and Jobs – an Agenda for the Modernisation of Europe's Higher Education Systems*. Available online at http://ec.europa.eu/taxation_customs/resources/documents/taxation/other_taxes/financial_sector/com (2011) 594_en.pdf.

European Commission (2015) *What is Horizon 2020?* Available online at http://ec.europa.eu/programmes/horizon2020/en/what-horizon-2020 (accessed 25 February 2015).

Frøhlich, N., J. Huisman, S. Slipersäter, B. Stensaker and P. C. P. Bótas (2012) 'A reinterpretation of institutional transformations in European higher education: Strategising pluralistic organisations in multiplex environments'. *Higher Education*, Vol. 65, No. 1, pp. 79–93.

Fullan, M. and G. Scott (2009) *Turnaround Leadership for Higher Education* (San Francisco, CA: Jossey-Bass).

Hasselberg, Y. (2009) *Alma mater, Dr. Jekyll och Mr Hyde* (Stockholm: Riksbankens Jubileumsfond, RJ). Available online at http://debatt.rj.se/?p=44.

Hofstede, G., G. J. Hofstede and M. Minkov (2010) *Cultures and Organizations: Software of the Mind*, 3rd edition. (New York: McGraw-Hill).

Hood, C. (1991) 'A public management for all seasons?'. *Public Administration*, Vol. 6, No. 3, pp. 3–19.

Hood, C. (1995) 'The "new public management" in the 1980s: variations on a theme'. *Accounting, Organizations and Society*, Vol. 20, No. 2–3, pp. 93–110.

Huisman, J. (ed.) (2009) *International Perspectives on the Governance of Higher Education. Alternative Frameworks for Coordination* (London: Routledge).

Jönsson, S. (1988) *Kommunal organisation – från programbudgetering till kommundelsnämnder* (Lund: Studentlitteratur).

Karlsson, A. (1991) *Om strategi och legitimitet: En studie av legitimitetsproblematiken i förbindelse med strategisk förändring i organisationer*. Doctoral thesis, Lund University.

LUM (2016) *Lunds universitets magasin*, No. 2.

Lund University (1995) *Lunds universitet inför framtiden. (strategisk plan/strategic plan)* (Lund: Wahlin & Dalholm).

Lund University (2002) *Strategisk Plan/Strategic Plan 2002–2006* (Lund: Wahlin & Dalholm).

Lund University (2007) *Strategisk Plan/Strategic Plan 2007–2011* (Lund: Holmbergs).

Lund University (2011) *Board of Directors, Strategic Plan/Strategic Plan 2012–2016, dnr ls 2011/162* (Lund: Lund University).

Lund University (2015a) *Installation Speech of Torbjörn von Schantz*. Available online at www.lu.se/sites/www.lu.se/files/tvs_installationstal_2015_mall.pdf.

Lund University (2015b) *Vice-chancellors blogg*. Available online at http://rektor.blogg.lu.se/ (accessed 9 April 2015).

March, J. G. and J. P. Olsen (1976) *Ambiguity and Choices in Organizations* (Bergen: Universitetsförlaget).

Osborne, D. and T. Gabler (1992) *Reinventing Government* (Reading: Addison-Wesley).

Paradeise, C., E. Reale, I. Bleiklie and E. Ferlie (eds) (2009) *University Governance: Western European Comparative Perspectives* (Dordrecht: Springer).

Sahlin, K. (2012) The Interplay of Organizing Models in Higher Education Institutions: What Room is There for Collegiality in Universities Characterized by Bounded Autonomy?, in B. Stensaker, J. Välimaa and C. Sarrico (eds), *Managing Reform in Universities* (Basingstoke: Palgrave Macmillan).

SOU (2008) *'Independent HEI's': The Swedish HEI Autonomy Inquiry*, SOU:104 (Stockholm: Ministry of Education).

SOU 2015:92 (2015) *Utvecklad ledning av universitet och högskolor* (Stockholm: Regeringen).

Stensaker, B. (2011) 'Accreditation of higher education in Europe – moving towards the US model?'. *Journal of Education Policy*, Vol. 26, No. 6, pp. 757–769.

Stensaker, B. and A. Vabø (2013) 'Re-inventing shared governance: implications for organisational culture and institutional leadership'. *Higher Education Quarterly*, Vol. 67, No. 3, pp. 256–274.

Sundberg, E. (2013) *Autonomireformen – vad hände med det kollegiala styret?* (Uppsala: Uppsala University).

Sörlin, S. (2009) *Förvaltare sitter vid rodret*. Available online at http://debatt.rj. se/?p=46.

Part III

Marketization and modernization

> Shift to greater competition in public sector.
>
> (Hood, 1991, p. 5)

There is an increased occurrence and reliance on market solutions in the Swedish public sector. However, there is a structural impediment to the development of internal markets in Scandinavian countries. There is a limited presence of non-profit entities. This makes the Scandinavian quasi-market a straightforward choice between public or private providers. Nevertheless, markets work as facilitators of competitive forces improving the cost/benefit relation in public services, and the four examples in this section indicate a willingness to experiment with these forces. We see several examples of choice-based arrangements, based on deregulation and incentives for private investors to engage in a diverse set of activities in public service provision. As is suggested in one of the chapters, the overall experience is that the consequences of the extension of market solutions have been less profound than has been argued by either proponents or adversaries.

The uneven results of 'quasi-markets' implementation are discussed in this section. In the case of primary care, research studies suggest that general accessibility has improved and costs are controlled: all well and in line with NPM ideas. However, the impact of the reform on the efficiency and effectiveness is uncertain and no consensus on experiences has been reached – any harmonization in any particular market solution is not apparent. This kind of 'trial and error' is recurrent in the examples and may be considered the cost of spearheading the experimentation with market forces. In the last 25 years, the elementary school sector in Sweden has undergone radical decentralization and deregulation and is currently (2016) the only school system in the world which allows tax-funded private schools to earn a profit and decide on dividends to owners. NPM and the marketization of elementary schools have challenged the deeply ingrained professional values of school teachers. Simultaneously, but not necessarily as a consequence, Sweden has experienced a radical drop in the so-called PISA ranking, where the school performance of children is measured in a wide range of countries throughout the world. This was the most debated issue during the 2014 election campaign in Sweden, dividing political parties and citizens into opposing standpoints. In a typically Swedish way, both the debate and the investigations of what to do about the declining school results, converge and seek a middle ground where professionalism and market forces could work side by side.

One extraordinary market reform in Sweden is the example of introducing personal assistants for 'functionally impaired' people. This reform replaced collective institutional care with individual choice and the largely unregulated establishment of companies providing personal assistance. Subsequently, the reform has been marked by fraud, public mistrust and cost increases considered more or less rampant. In this section, this is considered an experimental full-scale policy implementation. It is argued that ideas of how to implement market mechanisms in welfare services such as, for example, health care, elderly care or disability care seldom come ready-made: they may be good-hearted but ill-conceived and in need of tender care themselves. Any reversal of the marketization efforts in Sweden are still not yet visible.

Reference

Hood, C. (1991) 'A public management for all seasons?'. *Public Administration*, Vol. 6, No. 3, pp. 3–19.

12 Market solutions

Fredrik Andersson

Summary

The reliance on market solutions by the Swedish public sector has increased significantly in recent decades. The Swedish example is characterized by an openness to market solutions in many public-sector activities and by a mix of procurement arrangements and choice-based arrangements. The overall experience is that the consequences of the extension of market solutions have been less profound than has been argued by either proponents or adversaries. The benefit of an extended reliance on market solutions is hard to evaluate, but in the examples considered in this chapter – elderly care, schooling and health care – a cautious interpretation is that there is evidence of some modest positive effects and little evidence of severely adverse effects.

Introduction

This is a chapter about market solutions, and on my road to concluding I will proceed in three steps. First, I will look briefly at the conceptual notion of markets and market forces, doing so from the perspective of an economist and with a point of departure in standard economic analysis. There is often a misunderstanding about the virtues of market solutions imagined by economists, and I will make an effort to clarify my view on this. I will also articulate the distinction between market governance and the governance of internal organization. Building on this, I will discuss how the driver of market solutions can be either the relevant public body in procurement and contracting or the users in choice-based arrangements. Second, I will look at the reliance on markets and market solutions by the Swedish public sector, providing some basic numbers and trying to clarify how different market forces are brought to bear by branches of the public sector in Sweden. Finally, I will dig into questions relating to the appropriate use of market forces and how it depends on the context and the structural preconditions.

Before entering the core of the chapter, however, let me say a few things as a general note. The Swedish public sector has gone quite far by international standards in adopting market-based approaches to providing and allocating publicly financed services.[1] A distinguishing feature of the Swedish approach to the reliance on market forces is that it combines procurement of specified goods and services in some sectors with extensive reliance on consumer choice-based approaches in other sectors. Examples where market solutions have been adopted are the Swedish school system up to and including high school, care for the elderly and parts of health care, primary care in particular. The choice of examples is motivated by the fact that these three activities are quantitatively significant, both as parts of the public sector and as areas where market solutions are relied upon and have been relied upon for some time. In addition, all three examples are relevant in being areas where the Swedish welfare state faces significant challenges – in terms of financing, quality and innovation – in coming years.

Markets, market solutions and their virtues

Critical views on economics often start with the observation that the notion of a perfectly competitive market and the implications of such a market for economic efficiency are simplistic. It is hard to argue against this criticism, but, contrary to a common presumption of critics, a richer view does not necessarily mean a view that is more critical in terms of the virtues of markets, rather, to the contrary, a more positive one. In principle, market competition unleashes two forces:

- An incentive to save costs and perform any activity as efficiently as possible in terms of resources used.
- An incentive to fulfil the desires of the customers or, more generally, the desires of those who make consumption decisions and pay.

Importantly, these forces are at play however imperfect the market in question and its context may be. There is, for example, no presumption whatsoever about the nature of competition or about goods being homogeneous and directly interchangeable with goods from other producers. These are strong claims and a significant presumption that is necessary for the claims to be valid is a reasonable degree of freedom from corruption; in a corrupt economy, where resource use, production and customer contacts are governed by tit-for-tat exchanges of favours, the claims no longer hold to a meaningful extent.[2]

Both of these forces are virtuous under favourable circumstances but may be undercut by distortions. The incentive to use resources efficiently may be distorted, for example if prices facing a producer do not reflect social costs, a salient specific example being environmental externalities that are not reflected in the prices of goods and services.

The incentive to fulfil the desires of customers may similarly be misguiding the producer if those desires are influenced by trade-offs not reflecting social costs and benefits. A salient example is that of a unit price being imposed on a heterogeneous set of services in a customer choice arrangement. Specifically, for instance, the remuneration in a voucher-based school choice system cannot, at least in practice, reflect the true cost of providing a given pupil with the education that is expected, creating incentives for providers of schooling to attract pupils who are easy or cheap to serve. This, moreover, is a feature that pretty much comes with such arrangements by construction.

In sum, therefore, markets create powerful incentives for efficiency and consumer satisfaction, but there is no guarantee that these incentives ultimately produce socially desirable outcomes.

In the context of making conceptual remarks on markets, it is also worth dwelling a little bit on the distinction between market exchange and internal organization as alternative ways of organizing activities.[3] In principle, an activity – such as running a day-care centre – can either be organized by the body being responsible for it directly or acquired on a market by some arrangement. The choice between these basic ways of doing something is a general one and it is often termed the 'make-or-buy decision'. The trade-offs pertaining to the make-or-buy decision have been analysed in an extensive body of research literature.[4] The conclusions from this literature have been less clear cut than one might expect and we will make our own application of the literature when we get on to discussing the appropriate reliance on market solutions below. At this stage, however, it is important to recognize the distinction between the modes of governance:

- Internal governance with rules and discretionary command as the key instruments for control and incentives.
- Market governance with prices and contracts as the key instrument for control and incentives.

The introduction and extension of market solutions thus means that the latter mode of governance gains ground relative to the former one.

The final conceptual distinction concerns different arrangements within the realm of market governance, but it is nevertheless in a way the most fundamental one for our purposes. It concerns the dichotomy between

- procurement-based models, and
- customer choice-based models.

This distinction is important indeed for the Swedish context, where there are significant examples of both, with procurement being significant in parts of health care and parts of elderly care and with choice-based arrangements being significant in schooling and other parts of the health care and elderly care sectors.

Procurement-based models are characterized by the public body that is responsible for an activity, for example running a nursing home, specifying this activity in terms of requirements and contractual obligations and procuring it in accordance with the relevant regulation for public procurement. With reference to the previous discussion, this model is conducive to price competition. The main disadvantage of this model is the difficulty in specifying the desired qualities of a service well enough to be the basis for a strong contractual commitment; empirical evidence is quite firm in corroborating the presumption that contractually specified qualities are well taken care of, whereas qualities that are not specified are compromised (Andersson and Jordahl, 2013).[5]

Customer choice-based models are characterized by users of a service being allowed to choose among a set of providers – for example, all schools in a district or a municipality – and the remuneration (which may come in part out of pocket) following the user. The set of eligible providers must be controlled to some extent by regulation, but for some services – such as home-delivered assistance for the elderly – structural preconditions may allow close to free entry. The main virtue of customer choice arrangements is the fact that they are conducive to creating appropriate incentives for quality by users voting with their feet and with no need for contractually specifying them. The main risk with this kind of arrangement is the incentive created for providers to try to select the most attractive customers – such as pupils with good backgrounds – while deterring customers that are more costly to serve; this risk can, in principle, be dealt with by appropriately differentiating remuneration, but this is hard in practice.

Importantly, the risks pointed out in both cases below – quality shading in procurement and selective practices by providers in choice-based arrangements – arguably have their roots in the strong economic incentives emanating from the profit motive. From the point of view of economic theory, there is an argument for a weaker profit motive to ameliorate such forces, an argument made by, for example, Glaeser and Shleifer (2001). Empirically, the picture is mixed and it is an interesting fact that the non-profit sector is small in Sweden, but it is beyond the scope of this chapter to go deeper in this respect. It is within the scope of the chapter, however, to note that there is, at the time of writing, an animated public discussion in Sweden about profits in the welfare sector generally and strong political currents trying to outlaw such profits. The main argument against such profits in this discussion, however, is the (putting it politely) simplistic notion that taxpayers' money should not ultimately end up as profit.

Markets, market solutions and the Swedish public sector

Before discussing specific activities and branches of the Swedish public sector, we will provide some aggregate numbers, closely following the general account provided in Swedish by Jordahl and Öhrvall (2013). The total cost for welfare services and medical care by municipalities and county councils in 2013 was approximately 600 billion Swedish Krona (BSEK), and this corresponds to between 15 and 16 per cent of GDP.

When looking at the extent of private involvement, the proportion of services purchased from the private sector is between 10 and 15 per cent for a large range of welfare services (Jordahl and Öhrvall, 2013, p. 40). For day-care services, the proportion is a bit higher, but this is, on the other hand, the only category for which non-profits and cooperatives play a significant role (they play a non-negligible role in schooling as well). It is questionable, of course, to what extent these aggregate numbers measure the true intensity of market competition, but it is a natural benchmark. From this benchmark we are now going to look at three services in more detail: elderly care, schooling and health care.

The first service to consider in more detail is care for the elderly. First, there is an important delimitation to make in relation to health care for the elderly, which is handled by the county councils according to the same principles as health care for the general population. Second, elderly care should be divided into two distinct categories: care organized in centres where persons live on the one hand and home-delivered assistance and care on the other.

In terms of quantities, with numbers from 2013 provided by Bergman and Jordahl (2014), there are about 87,000 seniors (aged over 65 years) living in centres, while there are about 164,000 seniors receiving home-delivered assistance and care with subsidies approved by the municipalities (Bergman and Jordahl, 2014, p. 24). In terms of costs, the total cost for this type of care was about 90 BSEK in 2011, with two-thirds being costs for centres and one-third the cost of home-delivered assistance (Bergman and Jordahl, 2014, p. 24).

Private actors and market mechanisms have been applied in elderly care since the late 1980s, with a major breakthrough in the 1990s. During this period, both home-delivered assistance and centres were provided by private providers according to the procurement-based model. In the following period, the 2000s up to 2009, there was an expansion of customer choice arrangements, and in 2009 there was national regulation with the 'Law about consumer choice systems'.[6] This law provides a framework that makes clear the delimitation of choice-based arrangements. The proportion of residents in privately run centres increased from 10 to 20 per cent between 1997 and 2012, while the proportion of hours assistance delivered at home increased from 5 to 23 per cent between 1999 and 2012.

While there has been substantial public and political discussion about the quality of elderly care in general and the role of private providers in particular, systematic investigations have not, in general, found significant differences between the services provided by private providers compared with those of the municipal providers; this is confirmed, for example, in a recent report by the National Board of Health and Welfare (The National Board of Health and Welfare, 2014).

The next service that we will consider in more detail is schooling, from elementary school to high school. Policy development in Sweden is quite easy to explain, and again much is based on Jordahl and Öhrvall (2013). The centre-right government that was in power in Sweden between 1991 and 1994 implemented a quite far-reaching set of school choice reforms. An important element of the reforms was essentially free entry subject to the approval or accreditation of the national authorities, with limited power for a municipality to stop the establishment of an independent school in its juris-diction.[7] The last part of the existing set of regulations – i.e. the lack of a municipal veto against entry – is a contentious one, with a strong desire among the left-of-centre parties to introduce such a municipal veto; such a veto has not yet been introduced, however.

In terms of numbers, the proportion of elementary school pupils in inde-pendent schools has increased from less than 2 per cent in 1992 to almost 15 per cent in 2012; for high school pupils, the increase has been even larger, with the proportion exceeding 25 per cent in 2012 (Jordahl and Öhrvall, 2013, p. 57). On an additional note, in 2012, 74 per cent of elementary school pupils and 90 per cent of high school pupils in independent schools attended for-profit schools, this proportion having increased substantially over the previous 10 years (Jordahl and Öhrvall, 2013, pp. 57–58).

The record of the school choice model introduced over the last two decades has been much debated, and among the more substantive claims are the following:

- *Competition imposes a discipline that improves all schools.* This claim was made early on by Sandström and Bergström (2005) and has been much disputed.
- *The selection incentives lead to segregation.* As mentioned, the basic consumer choice model of market allocation of public services introduces incen-tives for providers to seek attractive pupils and to discourage pupils with predictable difficulties from applying.
- *The lack of firm regulation of output measures leads to grade inflation.* This has been argued and corroborated in a number of accounts.

The accumulation of empirical evidence has continued and two recent con-tributions by Edmark *et al.* (2014, 2015) nicely summarize the state of the art. We will return to their conclusions in the subsequent section.

When it comes to health care, public provision has dominated Swedish health care for a long period of time. In sketching recent developments, we will follow Andersson *et al.* (2014, ch. 2). Health care has been financed and provided by the county councils, the regional level of government between the national state and the municipalities. In contrast to many other Western countries, primary care has been organized predominantly within this system for a long time (Andersson *et al.*, 2014, ch. 2). Since the 1980s there has been a number of reforms that have opened up and paved the way for private pro-viders; in the 1980s there was some room for private entry into some elective treatments, and in the early 1990s there were initiatives taken to allow private entry into primary care. Although some of the reforms were later retracted, they made room for a sector of private actors. In the 2000s there has been a significant increase in the proportion of health care provided by private actors, with private provision of primary care increasing from just over 15 per cent to more than 30 per cent, and specialized care from just over 10 per cent to 15 per cent (Andersson *et al.*, 2014, p. 55).

One important reason for the increase in private involvement in primary care is the introduction of national regulation of consumer choice in primary care, effective as of 2010; this national regulation followed choice reforms in some regions in the years before and built on the 'Law about consumer choice systems' (Swedish: LOV) mentioned above. The national regulation mandates that county councils must accredit potential providers impartially and that all accredited providers must be treated and remunerated on an equal basis. The councils have considerable autonomy, however, in designing the specifics of regulation and remuneration.

In Andersson *et al.* (2014), there is a thorough discussion of the trade-offs involved in choosing among the various arrangements – in-house production, procurement and consumer choice arrangements. This discussion does not, however, conclude with a general assessment of the appropriate modes of organization in any particular context; rather, the discussion adheres to the conclusion in Hartman (2011) that the current state of knowledge rarely produces a basis for clear normative conclusions. Nevertheless, Andersson *et al.* (2014) do reach the conclusion that the sequence of reforms in primary care, resulting in the current regime with consumer choice and a high degree of freedom of entry, has produced identifiable benefits while not leaving evidence of adverse side effects.

Appropriate use of market solutions and the Swedish experience

Since this is a review rather than a detailed normative assessment, I will start by making a very general point, namely that there is by necessity a boundary between public bodies and the market in a mixed economy. One would not expect hospitals to manufacture their own hospital beds, and one would not expect schools to be chalk producers; on the other hand, one would not expect public bodies to outsource, for example, ultimate decision-making in important matters. This is a simple point but an important one, since it disqualifies lazy references, often made by ideologues, to market solutions as infringements on the integrity of the state, or to public bureaucracy as the ulterior manifestation of inefficiency.

The next step is to make a very sketchy assessment of the appropriateness of current arrangements. This assessment will be based on evidence and guided by the review of both theory and evidence in Andersson and Jordahl (2013); the key message from this review is that contractibility in a wide sense is paramount in determining whether a specific activity is suitable for a market solution and contracting.

Contractibility, clearly, is a key notion here and it is worth articulating its constituent parts from the perspective of an economist. In order for an activity to be contractible:

- it needs to be measurable;
- the measures need to be codifiable in a contract;
- the contract needs to be enforceable by a court or a comparable institution; and
- there need to be competent actors on both the buying side and the selling side to run the apparatus of making appropriate use of these properties.

This definition is kept deliberately loose, but each part can be formulated more stringently, and, formulated as such, can be part of a strict definition.

Going through the cases considered, we start by care for the elderly. As already noted, and as supported by the recent report by the National Board of Health and Welfare (2014), there is no evidence of significant quality differences between privately run and publicly run establishments in elderly care. On a more anecdotal note, there have been some cases, receiving large media attention, of malpractice tied to private establishments, while similar incidents have happened in publicly run establishments, often without an explicit reference to this fact in media coverage; there is to my knowledge no systematic evidence in this regard.

In contractibility terms, the rough analysis is quite straightforward. There is a potential problem with non-contractible quality in contracting based on procurement, while such considerations are, in principle, well taken care of by consumer choice arrangements, dominating home-delivered assistance. Bergman and Jordahl (2014) make an assessment along these lines and conclude that there is no general evidence of quality being compromised in procurement-based arrangements. They also conclude, however, that there is a potential problem with entry barriers being rather too low in consumer choice arrangements for home-delivered assistance. The latter point is in line with a notion that is often visible in popular discussion that the freedom of choice – often involving a large number of providers – is too much to handle for some elderly persons, not least those who are older or otherwise inhibited in their abilities to make decisions.[8] Bergman and Jordahl (2014) propose, among other things, two-stage arrangements, with procurement of a number of eligible providers (rather than pure accreditation) in the first stage as a way of improving the functioning of the market, and then free choice among the eligible producers in the subsequent stage. They also conclude, however, that customer choice arrangements in home-delivered assistance work well in those places where they have been in use for a long time. The observation is in line with the notion that the functioning of a market is critically dependent on institutional features, including tacit knowledge of the workings of the market acquired over time by market participants.

Turning, next, to schooling, there has – as was made reference to above – been an extensive discussion about the benefits and hazards coming with school choice. When approaching schooling it is worth stressing that private schools make up a significant and growing proportion of schools and that private schools are predominantly for-profit entities operating under voucher arrangements with limited means for municipalities to limit entry for schools satisfying basic qualifications.

The fundamental question is whether school choice is a 'tide that lifts all boats' or if it mainly serves to sustain and generate inequality. We will confine ourselves to reporting the conclusions of two recent studies by Edmark *et al.* (2014, 2015). The main conclusion in Edmark *et al.* (2015) – which goes to the heart of the inequality issue – is that school choice is neither a miraculous cure, nor a detrimental threat; rather, effects on relevant outcome variables are small and rarely statistically significant. Edmark *et al.* (2015) look at a number of outcome variables: final grades from elementary school; results in the enlistment test for military service; having been sentenced for a crime by age 22; and having a university or university college degree by age 25. The dominant conclusion from a thorough difference-in-difference statistical analysis is that effects are small and rarely statistically significant, but on the whole lean towards the positive rather than on the negative side – i.e. school choice improves matters, albeit quite marginally and uncertainly.

Approaching school choice from a theoretical perspective, some additional points arise. First, with schooling comes the authority to give degrees and grades, and school choice will unavoidably create an element of an incentive to inflate grades as a means of competing for pupils. I will not go into the evidence of this, but there is quite clearly a need for regulation that supports integrity in this regard in the face of the incentives that are created. Second, there is a concern about the rationality of choices and the ability of parents and pupils – in particular, parents and pupils who are in some sense disadvantaged – to make informed choices; while the kind of evidence just cited gives some comfort in the aggregate, this is a deeply ideological concern.

The health care area is more heterogeneous than elderly care and schooling. There are distinctions to be made based on the nature or treatment and the special role played by primary care. At present, Swedish primary care is characterized by consumer choice and freedom of entry subject to basic accreditation (in this, quite similar to schooling); this significant reliance on market solutions has been quite recent and in Andersson *et al.* (2014) we conclude that there is some evidence of positive effects and little evidence of adverse effects in terms of quality or equity, as is sometimes feared. These conclusions are not uncontroversial and have been challenged, for example by the Swedish National Audit Office (Swedish National Audit Office, 2014). The main claims of the National Audit Office report are that a number of inequalities have been exacerbated by freedom of choice in primary care; while there is every reason to pay attention to this, Anell and Rehnberg (2014) have argued forcefully that the measures used – and the use of the measures – are questionable in a number of regards.

When it comes to planned treatments and emergency care, the overall picture of private involvement and the reliance on market solutions is quite mixed; there are examples of fully outsourced hospitals and there are an increasing number of examples of choice-based arrangements for some planned treatments. While it is beyond the scope of this chapter to go into the details of this matter, Andersson *et al.* (2014) conclude that there is some evidence that the market mechanism is being relied upon where it is most appropriate. This means, roughly, that the application of consumer choice is made where consumers have the preconditions for making sensible choices and where private providers are involved in circumstances where contractibility conditions, as defined above, are overall favourable.

The way forward

My basic point of departure is that market solutions in the context of activities financed by the Swedish public sector are here to stay. This point of departure does reflect a conviction that is not independent of ideological bent, but it also reflects the existing body of experience and evidence that we have made reference to above. This does not mean that current market-based arrangements are to be defended – there may well be reason to reverse the reliance on markets in many cases – but it means that market-based arrangements will in general be part of the set of alternatives to be considered.

After these general remarks, I will make two related points. First, one of the key challenges for market solutions is to define the appropriate unit of contracting. We have already made reference to episodes in health care being defined by the whole chain including investigation, treatment, follow-up and responsibility for dealing with appropriate treatment subsequent to primary treatment. This is an excellent example of the development of a more appropriate unit of contracting.

Second, the first point is in a way a special case of the general point that there is a broad need for encouraging innovation in public-sector activities – as in the economy generally – and that procurement contracting in particular is not inherently well suited for this, a point made by Hart *et al.* (1997). Clearly, however, existing ways of dealing with this are exemplified by extending episodes of care as mentioned. The suggestion of two-stage arrangements, where a procurement-type contest among providers is followed by consumer choice among eligible providers, is another good example. As is argued in Bergman and Jordahl (2014), in procurement it is also paramount to account for quality in practice, not only in theory.

This has been a rather terse review of the employment of market solutions in Swedish public-sector arrangements. To phrase the conclusions differently compared to the chapter so far, an important message is that the extension of market solutions to involve more services, and to be more prevalent in those services where they have been established, is less dramatic than has been argued by either proponents or adversaries. The nitty-gritty work of maintaining the services of various branches of the public sector is in many ways quite similar if one relies on market solutions, where care for details in daily operations is critical for the quality of service. The devotion and motivation of the people doing the work plays a key role.

This observation naturally brings up an omission, albeit it a deliberate one. I have not touched on the question of interactions between intrinsic motivation, incentives and the implications for private versus public provision of services. Such a discussion would have led too far, but my own reading of the literature in this regard is that the existing body of evidence makes clear that motivation is important and that there is an association between occupational choices, the choice between working for a public or a private employer, and motivational traits. Nevertheless, it seems clear that the motivational challenges are quite similar on the ground.

On a final note, I would like to add that the discussion of evidence that is brought to bear on evaluation and the general tendency of such evidence point towards uncertain and small but nevertheless modestly positive effects. This evidence is relevant for incremental changes; it does not address the question whether it would be beneficial to scale back market solutions more generally. It is beyond the scope of the analysis, but such backtracking – to the extent that it is even conceivable – would quite clearly devitalize the mixed economy.

Notes

1 There is a vagueness to 'public-sector activities' since public involvement can be extensive by means of various kinds of regulation even if there is partial or full private financing. For our purposes, the activities considered are publicly financed to high enough an extent for 'publicly financed services' not to be misleading, and this terminology has large advantages in terms of convenience.
2 Arguably, a pure monopoly in a context with limited room for substitution would take us halfway into the realm of corruption. Most existing monopoly powers in market economies are, arguably, not of such malign character, however, but directly or indirectly challenged by existing or potential possibilities for substitution.
3 A more thorough discussion can be found in e.g. Andersson and Jordahl (2013).
4 Important contributions in this tradition include Coase (1937), Williamson (1975, 1985) and Holmström and Milgrom (1991).
5 However, there is also evidence that quality adjustment is pushed less strongly in practice in the ultimate evaluation of tenders than is indicated on paper in the invitation of tenders (Bergman and Jordahl, 2014).
6 Swedish: Lagen om valfrihetssystem (LOV).
7 There have been a number of modifications of the rules, for example in terms of the guiding principles for the remuneration of independent schools. There has also been a change of the national body responsible; it is currently the Swedish Schools Inspectorate.
8 For example, Szebehely (2011) in Hartman *et al.* (2011).

References

Andersson, F., N. Janlöv and C. Rehnberg (2014) *Konkurrens, kontrakt och kvalitet – hälso- och sjukvård i privat regi*. Rapport till expertgruppen för studier i offentlig ekonomi (ESO). 2014:5 (Lund).

Andersson, F. and H. Jordahl (2013) *Outsourcing Public Services: Ownership, Competition, Quality and Contracting* (Lund: Lund University School of Economics and Management and the Research Institute of Industrial Economics).

Anell, A. and C. Rehnberg (2014) Riksrevisionens granskning alltför selektiv, *Dagens Medicin* (26 November 2014).

Bergman, M. and H. Jordahl (2014) *Goda år på ålderns höst? En eso-rapport om konkurrens i äldreomsorgen*. Rapport till expertgruppen för studier i offentlig ekonomi (ESO). 2014:1. (Lund).

Coase, R. (1937) 'The nature of the firm'. *Economica*, Vol. 4, No. 16, pp. 386–405.

Edmark, K., M. Frölich and V. Wondratschek (2014) *Sweden's School Choice Reform and Equality of Opportunity*, Working Paper 1030. The Research Institute of Industrial Economics.

Edmark, K., M. Frölich and V. Wondratschek (2015) 'Det fria skolvalet – varken mirakelmedicin eller undergångsrecept'. *Ekonomisk Debatt*, Vol. 43.

Glaeser, E. L. and A. Shleifer (2001) 'Not-for-profit entrepreneurs'. *Journal of Public Economics*, Vol. 81, pp. 99–115.

Hart, O., A. Shleifer and R. W. Vishny (1997) 'The proper scope of government: theory and an application to prisons'. *Quarterly Journal of Economics*, Vol. 112, No. 4, pp. 1127–1161.

Hartman, L. (ed.) (2011) *Konkurrensens konsekvenser: Vad händer med svensk välfärd* (Stockholm: SNS Förlag).

Holmström, B. and P. Milgrom (1991) 'Multitask principal-agent analyses: incentive contracts, asset ownership, and job design'. *Journal of Law Economics and Organization*, Vol. 7, pp. 24–52.

Jordahl, H. and R. Öhrvall (2013) Nationella reformer och lokala initiativ, in H. Jordahl (ed.), *Välfärdstjänster i privat regi – framväxt och drivkrafter* (Stockholm: SNS).

Sandström, F. M. and F. Bergström (2005) 'School vouchers in practice: competition will not hurt you'. *Journal of Public Economics*, Vol. 89, pp. 351–380.

Swedish National Audit Office (2014) *Primärvårdens styrning – efter behov eller efterfrågan?* (RiR 2014:22).

Szebehely, M. (2011) Insatser för äldre och funktionshindrade i privat regi, in L. Hartman (ed.), *Konkurrensens konsekvenser: Vad händer med svensk välfärd* (Stockholm: SNS Förlag).

The National Board of Health and Welfare (2014) *Kommun- och enhetsundersökningen, vård och omsorg om äldre* (2014: Nationella resultat, metod och indikatorer).

Williamson, O. E. (1975) *Markets and Hierarchies: Analysis and Anti-trust Implications: A Study in the Economics of Internal Organization* (New York: Free Press).

Williamson, O. E. (1985) *The Economic Institutions of Capitalism* (New York: Free Press).

13 Introducing quasi-markets in primary care

The Swedish experience

Anna Häger Glenngård and Anders Anell

Summary

The Swedish experience of introducing quasi-markets in primary care is discussed with respect to the identified objectives of primary care. Empirical studies suggest that objectives related to general accessibility have been met. There is more limited knowledge about the distribution of services between various groups in the population. Problems with coordination and continuity, mainly due to a shortage of general physicians, persist. Costs are controlled but the impact of the reform on the efficiency and effectiveness is uncertain. To maintain and develop governance models, to achieve traditional objectives and to support informed choices among citizens remain important challenges for the 21 county councils. The way forward is likely for county councils to draw on experiences from each other and to harmonize models for governance and support to providers.

Introduction and background

Strengthening primary care is generally seen as central to enhancing equity and efficiency in health care (Saltman, 2006; Starfield, 1998; Starfield *et al.*, 2005; World Health Organization, 2008). Primary care is often defined in terms of its relation to the rest of the health care system. Barbara Starfield (1998, pp. 8–9) defines primary care as:

> that level of a health system that provides entry into the system for all needs and problems, provides person-focused (not disease-oriented) care over time, provides care for all but very uncommon or unusual conditions, and coordinates or integrates care provided elsewhere by others.

Although it is difficult to define the content of primary care, there are some overall objectives that primary care should achieve (Lamarche *et al.*, 2003, p. 6): effectiveness, efficiency (including cost control), equity, accessibility, continuity, responsiveness and quality.

There is no simple solution on how to best organize health care services to better meet some objectives without adverse consequences for others (Bevan et al., 2010). In most other OECD countries, primary care is usually provided by private GPs working in small groups with the limited involvement of other health care staff. In contrast, Swedish primary care is traditionally organized as large, publicly run practices with a mix of staff categories and comprehensive responsibility for patients based on geographical catchment areas (Anell et al., 2012a). Fixed payment to providers based on the size of the catchment population has usually been practised. This model theoretically performs well with respect to efficiency, continuity, equity and quality of care but may display problems with accessibility and responsiveness (Lamarche et al., 2003). Problems with accessibility and responsiveness towards patients' preferences and expectations, and with continuity in contacts with patients have also been prevailing in Swedish primary care (Vårdanalys, 2014a).

In response to perceived problems with efficiency and responsiveness, several reforms have been introduced since the early 1990s. Reforms first focused on the purchaser–provider split, the decentralization of decision-making to providers, activity-based payment and privatization through contracting out. In the 2000s, explicit measures of performance have been introduced and reforms have focused on patient choice and client orientation (Anell, 2011). Since responsibility for financing and provision of health care in Sweden lies with the 21 county councils, reforms are usually implemented at that government level and diffused gradually throughout the country. This was also the case for the choice reform introduced in 2007–2010, whereby choice of primary care provider for the population was combined with privatization and competition among providers. The choice reform constitutes a major change in how primary care services are organized and resources are allocated. The new governance models can best be described as quasi-markets.

In this chapter, the Swedish experience of introducing quasi-markets in primary care is discussed with respect to the fulfilment of identified objectives. Based on findings from empirical studies, implications for future governance are discussed.

Introducing quasi-markets in Swedish primary care

The first steps towards increased choice for patients in Swedish primary care in the early 1990s did not combine choice for patients with privatization and freedom of establishment for private providers. Payment generally did not follow patients' choices. Consequently, there were limited alternatives for the population to choose from and limited incentives for providers to respond (Anell, 2011). The recent choice reform has combined choice for citizens with competition among providers. Freedom of choice of primary care provider for the population and freedom of establishment for providers has been mandatory since 1 January 2010, following a change in the Health Care Act.

Payment to providers must follow individuals' choices. The choice reform was implemented in Halland County Council in 2007, and it was then gradually followed by other county councils over the 2008–2010 period.

Choice models originate from Hirschman's (1970) reasoning about exit, voice and loyalty. Members of any organization who are not satisfied may exit (withdraw from the relationship) or they may voice (repair/improve the relationship through communication/complaints). The intended outcomes of expanded citizen choice and provider competition are improved efficiency, quality of services and responsiveness of providers in relation to citizens' expectations through market mechanisms (Le Grand, 2007, 2009). Markets can be defined as a place (physical or non-physical) where actors engage in transactions, normally services or goods in exchange for money. Quasi-markets differ from conventional markets: on the demand side, consumers do not express their purchasing power in monetary terms but with an earmarked budget (Le Grand and Bartlett, 1993). Providers cannot compete on price but they can by means of the quality of services provided. Economic theory suggests that competition should have a positive impact on the quality of services provided in markets with regulated prices (Propper, 2012). On the supply side, although independent public and private providers compete with one another to carry out the provision of services, they are not necessarily profit-maximizing or privately owned. For choice models to work in practice, without negative consequences for other objectives, at least five preconditions need to be fulfilled (Le Grand, 1991, 2007):

- The market should be competitive or contestable. For a quasi-market to work in terms of providing the necessary incentives for greater quality, efficiency and responsiveness, actual and/or potential competitors are essential.
- Individuals must be interested in choice and have access to information on which to base their choice of provider upon.
- Transaction costs should be low.
- The motivation for providers should be at least partly financial. Providers should be motivated to be responsive.
- Opportunities for adverse selection, i.e. cream-skimming and skimping, should be limited. Cream-skimming refers to providers avoiding or choosing patients for some characteristic(s) other than their need of care, for the purpose of improving their profitability or reputation. Skimping refers to providing inadequate or low-quality services in order for a provider to reduce costs and maximize profit.

Objectives behind the choice reform in Swedish primary care varied depending on priorities in each county council. Some (e.g. Halland) had the ambition of restructuring health care services in favour of primary care. Others (e.g. Stockholm) primarily aimed at improved access for patients within the existing structure. Overall, important political objectives behind the choice reform were to tackle 'new' problems related to accessibility and responsiveness towards patients' preferences and expectations and to improve continuity in contacts with patients. Ideally this should be accomplished without negative consequences for traditional objectives related to equity (Anell, 2011; Glenngård, 2013a).

Studies of Swedish primary care since the introduction of the choice reform

As the responsibility for financing and organization in Swedish health care lies with 21 county councils, somewhat different primary care models have been implemented following the choice reform. By law it is stipulated that citizens may register with any public or private provider accredited by the local county council and that payment to providers must follow individuals' choices. Accredited providers are not allowed to prevent an individual from registering at their practice. The requirements for accreditation primarily focus on minimum levels of clinical competencies and services available at the practice. The same requirements apply to both private and public providers.

With one exception (Stockholm), the implemented primary care models are heavily inspired by the traditional Swedish primary care model. In most county councils, fixed payment per registered individual (capitation) is combined with a small proportion of fee-for-service and pay-for-performance schemes. Comprehensive financial responsibility is practised. Besides visits, providers have financial responsibility for diagnostic tests and the prescription medicines used by registered patients (Anell *et al.*, 2012b).

Studies of the impact of the reform have predominately been carried out in separate county councils rather than on a national level. One reason for this is that comparative data is limited at the national level as there are differences across the country regarding what information about providers is monitored. Early studies mainly focused on two important preconditions for quasi-markets to fulfil in order to meet their objectives without negative consequences for equity:

- individuals must be interested and informed to make a choice of provider, and
- the market must be competitive/contestable.

Some of the early studies were carried out as experiments or surveys of preferences even before the choice reform was implemented. A few years after the introduction of the choice reform, as the effects have become visible, a number of reports and articles related to important objectives in Swedish primary care have also been published.

Interest in choice

Several studies indicate that individuals are interested in making a choice of provider in primary care. In a population survey, with 1,449 respondents in the county councils of Halland, Skåne and Västra Götaland, 84 per cent of all respondents agreed to 'It is important to have the possibility to make a choice of primary care provider' (Glenngård *et al.*, 2011). This finding is in line with a report by Vårdanalys (2013a) that concluded that 76 per cent of 3,355 respondents to a national Internet survey were interested in making a choice of provider. Similar results have been reported by the Swedish Competition Authority (2012), based on a national population survey of 1,700 respondents. Moreover, previous research based on surveys and stated preference techniques have demonstrated that individuals are generally interested in choice and participation in Swedish primary care (Hjelmgren and Anell, 2007; Vårdanalys, 2013a).

Information about the extent to which individuals actually make a choice of provider is more limited. On average, 62 per cent in the study by Glenngård *et al.* (2011) stated that they had made a choice of provider in connection with or after the choice reform. This figure varied between 47 and 74 per cent in the nine municipalities included in the study. The proportion of citizens who had shifted provider is smaller, however. In three of the municipalities included in the survey, this figure varied between 11 and 27 per cent, compared to between 56 and 62 per cent for respondents who answered yes to the question in the survey. Hence, individuals regard both shifting provider and staying with their current provider as making a choice. In a more recent study by the Swedish Agency for Health and Care Services Analysis, 24 per cent of the respondents stated that they had shifted provider since the introduction of the choice reform (Vårdanalys, 2013b).

Previous research suggests that individuals who actually shift provider tend to do so in connection with the introduction of choice of provider (Anell and Paulsson, 2010). Once having made an initial choice to shift provider, few individuals in general shift provider again. This is even more prominent among individuals with a strong preference for continuity of care.

It is not a problem in itself that individuals choose to stay with their current provider as long as the services provided are in line with their expectations. Several studies have shown that the population's trust in primary care providers is generally high in Sweden (see e.g. Glenngård *et al.*, 2011). The report by Vårdanalys (2013b) also specifically pointed to the fact that individuals who had not changed provider were satisfied with their current provider. Continuity is also a relevant parameter for the quality of primary care and is an often-cited objective in this context. However, it is a problem if individuals for different reasons cannot shift provider despite wanting to. Such reasons may be the limited availability of alternative providers or a lack of information about how to shift provider.

Availability and use of information

As choice for individuals has been expanded, the gathering and compilation of comparative information about primary care providers have been improved and made publicly available. The National Patient Survey is a recurrent patient survey administered to all primary care providers since 2009, coordinated by the Swedish Association of Local Authorities and Regions (SALAR). The results are summarized into eight broad categories on patients' views of the quality of providers when presented to the public: overall impression; respectful and considerate attendance; participation in decisions; information about medical conditions; accessibility; confidence; need being adequately taken care of; and whether the patient would recommend the provider to others. There is also information about location, opening hours and the categories of staff working at various clinics available on practices' own websites and on regional and national websites.

Comparative information about the quality of providers, besides what is collected through the National Patient Survey, is limited. Generally, information about clinical quality and the ability to coordinate care for patients among different caregivers is lacking. Such aspects may be important for individuals. For example, 90 per cent of respondents in the study by Glenngård *et al.* (2011) stated that an important factor when making a choice of provider was the provider´s ability to coordinate their needs with other caregivers. The studies by Vårdanalys (2013b, 2014b) also show that individuals are interested in information about coordination and the continuity of care. This kind of information is likely to be of more importance to certain groups of individuals, e.g. older individuals with multiple diagnoses. Among younger individuals, who are rarely in contact with their provider, accessibility is likely to be a more important factor.

The interest in information about clinical quality may also vary between different groups. Compared to perceptions about quality, such information is more difficult to measure and report, and for individuals in general to interpret. Individuals with chronic diseases, e.g. diabetes, may be better equipped to absorb information about clinical quality concerning their disease and find it useful in their choice of provider compared with individuals in general. Making information about clinical quality publicly available would then enable certain groups of individuals with frequent contact with primary care to make an informed choice of provider. It might also be more important for such individuals to strike a careful balance when choosing a provider since they will make frequent visits.

Individuals rarely use comparative information about providers when they choose a provider. Individuals think that they have enough information to make a choice of provider but seem rather passive; they rarely change providers and are not active in searching for information on alternatives (Glenngård *et al.*, 2011; Vårdanalys, 2013b). The most common source of information to base choices of provider upon tends to be the chosen provider and friends or relatives.

Availability of alternative providers

There has been an increase in providers by almost 20 per cent throughout the country since the introduction of the choice reform. In autumn 2012, a total of 267 new practices, of which 258 were private, had been established and 77 practices, of which 60 were private, had stopped. Throughout the country, some 80 per cent of the citizens had less than a five-minute drive to an alternative provider from their home. In most cases individuals can chose between public and private providers. A majority of the new providers have established in densely populated areas. The Swedish Competition Authority (2012) conclude that in rural areas it is important to establish relatively more practices in order to maintain a high level of service. This means that in sparsely populated areas the number of practices needs to be greater than their population share. It may be difficult to motivate health care providers to establish in rural areas. An alternative is for already-established providers to open branches in these areas. In 2011 there were 56 branches in Sweden, of which 12 had been established after the choice reform. This to some extent improves the situation in rural areas with respect to accessibility.

Accessibility

Objectives related to accessibility have largely been achieved. Both the number of individuals who visit primary care and the number of visits per individual have on average increased following the choice reform. As the establishment of new providers is closely tied to density in population, the accessibility varies across the country. About 32,000 citizens (mainly in the northern part of the country) have more than a 40-minute drive to an alternative provider. The increase in the number of primary care providers has not been accompanied by a corresponding increase in the number of physicians in primary care, however. There is a shortage of physicians of about 30 per cent according to a report by the Swedish Medical Association (2014).

There is little variation in characteristics between providers. In most cases individuals can choose between public and private providers. The proportion of private providers has increased by 69 per cent since the introduction of the choice reform, from 288 to 486 units. Private practices are on average smaller than public ones. Besides the public/private dimension, size and opening hours, there is little variation. With very few exceptions, providers have not chosen to specialize their practice in any direction. Overall, the range of services is similar across primary care providers.

Quality

Several studies suggest that choice of provider is positively correlated with individuals' perceptions about the quality of services. According to a Swedish literature review, there is a value in itself related to choice of provider

(Winblad *et al.*, 2012). Swedish and international research show that individuals having made a choice of provider are more satisfied with services compared to individuals not having made a choice, irrespective of the actual content of the services.

Knowledge of the consequences of individual choices for the quality of medical care is limited (Anell, 2013; Glenngård, 2015; Winblad *et al.*, 2012). This is partly due to limited comparative information on performance and outcomes among primary care providers. One recurring conclusion is that information describing what providers do and what values their activities lead to among patients is largely lacking. This makes analysis of the impact on the quality of medical care difficult.

Responsiveness

On an overall county council level there are no notable differences in the level of patient satisfaction between five years after and the year before the choice reform was introduced (Glenngård, 2015). However, responsiveness towards patients' expectations varies significantly with respect to both characteristics of patients and location of providers. Glenngård (2012) and Glenngård and Anell (2012b) found that in a sample of 400+ primary care providers located in the county councils of Skåne, Västra Götaland and Halland the most common factor associated with a lower satisfaction was high overall social deprivation among registered individuals. The opposite was found for the overall level of illness of individuals, as measured by mix of diagnoses.

Continuity and coordination of services

Problems with continuity in contacts with patients, and of coordination with other caregivers, seem to persist in Swedish primary care. According to a recent study (Vårdanalys, 2014c), less than half of patients think that their primary care provider is able to help coordinate their need for care with other caregivers if needed. This is much lower than in other comparable countries. There have been no notable improvements with respect to the coordination of care since the choice reform was introduced. Findings regarding the impact on continuity do not allow drawing any certain conclusions.

Effectiveness and efficiency

Based on empirical studies so far, it is not possible to draw any conclusions about the impact of the reform on the effectiveness of primary care. Winblad *et al.* (2012) conclude that costs have been under control when implementing the reform but further evaluations of the impact on effectiveness and efficiency are needed. On a national level, the resources allocated to primary care as a proportion of total health care expenditures have not increased following the reform. In some county councils, which introduced reform on a voluntary basis, rather than after changes in the national Health Care Act in 2010, the proportion allocated to primary care has increased slightly.

The Swedish Medical Association (2014) also notes that, in Sweden as a whole, primary care's share of total health care expenditure has not changed in the last decade. It has been fairly stable at around 18 per cent. The proportion varies considerably across the country, from 15 per cent (Gotland) to 22 per cent (Norrbotten), however. Several of the county councils that have a relatively large share of health care expenditure in primary care are found in sparsely populated areas of the country, but the pattern is not consistent. While the share of health care expenditures has remained constant, primary care percentage of doctor visits has increased. This suggests that the gap between primary care's resources and its mission has rather increased.

There are several studies of productivity in primary care based on data from individual county councils using data envelopment analysis (DEA) (Glenngård, 2013b; Glenngård and Anell, 2012a; Janlöv and Rehnberg, 2011; Vårdanalys, 2014a). In these studies, the number of health care contacts is related to costs in primary care. The ability of a primary care provider to produce a maximum amount of output (e.g. visits or percentage of satisfied patients) given a certain amount of input or resources (e.g. money) is calculated. Results indicate that the productivity of providers varied between county councils both before and after the introduction of the choice reform. It is difficult to link changes and/ or differences between county councils to differences in the principles for payment or the financial responsibility of providers. The fact that it is mainly studies of technical efficiency that have been conducted is associated with the availability of data. Data describing what providers actually do and how well they perform is lacking. To a large extent, one is limited to measuring the number of health care contacts in relation to costs.

Equity

Knowledge about objectives related to equity in the distribution of services across different groups of the population is limited, although some research has been done (Beckman and Anell, 2013a, 2013b; Ekström *et al.*, 2013; Fredriksson, 2012; Janlöv and Rehnberg, 2011; Rehnberg, 2014). Studies are limited by the availability of data, primarily the lack of information about the content and distribution of visits (Anell, 2013; Glenngård, 2013a; Vårdanalys, 2014a). This makes analysis of how resources are allocated to different groups a challenge, particularly for analyses on a national level. In individual county councils, it is often easier to make more in-depth analysis based on information gathered in local or regional registers.

Findings based on data from the county councils of Stockholm, Skåne and Östergötland show that the increased volume of visits has benefited all groups in the population at large. In a study of the same county councils by Vårdanalys (2013b), the authors could not find that an increase in primary care consumption in certain groups was at the expense of a reduction in health care consumption in other groups. In Skåne, the increase in the volume of visits is more prominent in the general population than in groups with great needs. Such conclusive results are not found for Stockholm. One possible explanation is related to differences in provider payment systems. In Skåne, where providers are paid a fixed amount per registered individual, patients with greater needs might receive longer rather than more visits. In Stockholm, where providers are paid according to the number of visits, the opposite might be the case. Another possible explanation is that individuals with greater needs had better access to services compared to the general population in Skåne before the choice reform and that the main impact of the reform has been improved accessibility for the general population.

The Swedish experience: preconditions for quasi-markets and objectives in primary care

The implementation of health care reforms is generally difficult as it involves introducing a new balance between potentially conflicting objectives and the redistribution of benefits across actors. Important political objectives at the national level behind the choice reform in Swedish primary care were to tackle problems with accessibility and responsiveness towards patients' preferences and expectations and with continuity in contacts with patients. Following the usual Swedish pattern in health care reforms, individual county councils introduced the choice reform gradually. The county councils also had slightly different ambitions with the choice reform and different starting points, whereby the importance of different reform objectives differed. This has led to variation across the country with respect to the choice of primary care model implemented, e.g. principles for paying providers and models for monitoring providers. Despite these differences, some overall conclusions regarding the preconditions for quasi-markets and the fulfilment of objectives in primary care can be made.

Preconditions for quasi-markets

On an overall level, important preconditions for quasi-markets to fulfil in order to meet the aims of increased efficiency, quality and responsiveness, without negative consequences for equity, are largely met. The Swedish primary care markets are competitive or at least contestable. Providers have first of all entered and to a limited degree exited the market since the introduction of the reform. Most citizens have alternative public and private provider(s) to choose from within a reasonable geographical distance. The availability of alternative providers varies with population density, leading to better accessibility in more densely populated areas.

Individuals consider themselves to be both interested and informed enough to make a choice of provider, although they are rather passive in their search for information. Moreover, comparative information about providers besides opening hours, locations and patients' perceptions of the quality of care is largely missing. This indicates that individuals base their choice on parameters that they can observe themselves, which is in line with economic theory about the behaviour of individuals in health care (Sheaff *et al.*, 2002). It is also in line with previous empirical research in the area (Kastberg, 2014). Empirical beliefs, as opposed to facts or comparative information, guide individuals' choices of provider (Glenngård, 2016).

As payment to providers follows individuals' choices, motivation for providers in Swedish primary care is at least partly financial, which is a third important precondition. As patients can change provider if they are not satisfied with their current provider, they can cause a loss of income for providers. Hence, providers have incentives to respond to articulated preferences of both registered and potential new patients.

In principle, opportunities for cream–skimming and skimping are also limited. Both national legislation and the county councils' models for governance, including principles for paying providers, limit possibilities for adverse selection and skimping on quality. Providers cannot deny any individual the right to register with their practice. More or less sophisticated systems for risk–adjusting the fixed payment to providers in order to avoid adverse selection have been introduced in connection with or after the choice reform. In a great majority of the 21 county councils, primary care providers are allocated extra resources to compensate for greater health care needs, based on information about age, diagnoses and socio–economic conditions among registered individuals. In all county councils, variable and performance-based payment for visits and certain services is used to complement the fixed capitation for registered individuals to incentivize a high level of quality and an appropriate volume of important services. Variable payment gives providers incentives to increase the amount of services while performance-based payment is intended to incentivize a high level of quality (Barnum *et al.*, 1995). In most county councils, performance-based payment targets aspects of quality related to prescription of antibiotics and other drugs, accessibility, patient views on quality and participation in national quality registers (Anell *et al.*, 2012b).

In practice, it is difficult to prevent skimping on clinical quality and the under-provision of services when using a capitated payment. Options to follow up on activities based on information in registers are limited. Traditional measures of productivity are not sufficient to assess if resources allocated on the basis of needs are used as intended (Glenngård, 2013a, 2013b; Janlöv and Rehnberg, 2011). For such purposes, information about the length, content and distribution of visits and ideally outcomes is needed. Hence, other complementary governance mechanisms are needed to prevent skimping on quality and the under-provision of services, besides design of payment systems and monitoring of services based on information in registers.

Fulfilment of objectives in primary care

Empirical studies presented so far do not permit any firm conclusion regarding the extent to which overall objectives in Swedish primary care are fulfilled. They are to a large extent limited by what information is available at the regional and local levels. Objectives related to accessibility have been met since the introduction of the choice reform but the distribution between various groups in the population is uncertain. Problems with continuity persist, as this is more related to a limited number of general physicians. Costs seem to be controlled but it is uncertain what impact the reform has had on efficiency and effectiveness. Fulfilment of objectives related to responsiveness towards individuals' expectations seem to vary with respect to socio-economic differences and differences in overall illness among patients, similar to findings from studies in other countries (Campbell *et al.*, 2001a, 2001b; Kontopantelis *et al.*, 2010).

Choice of provider seems to constitute a value in itself for individuals and is positively associated with perceptions of quality. Choice of provider may also have a positive impact on clinical quality. Adherence to the treatment agreed upon may increase if patients feel that they are more involved due to the fact that they have chosen rather than been assigned a provider. A better adherence may in turn affect medical outcomes positively. Evidence from the UK suggests that choice of provider for the population in combination with fixed prices for providers is associated with improved quality of care in terms of mortality, without negative consequences for equity (Propper, 2012). Knowledge about consequences for clinical quality and how primary care works for groups of individuals with different conditions in practice is limited in Swedish primary care, partly due to limited comparative information on the performance and outcomes among providers.

Implications for governance

As the responsibility for financing and the provision of health care is decentralized in Sweden, different models for governance have been developed across the country in connection with the choice reform. On the one hand, this diversity creates opportunities for country councils to learn from each other and for researchers to evaluate and compare different solutions to problems. On the other hand, the decentralized responsibility leads to difficulties in terms of monitoring of processes, outcomes and results among providers at the national level.

Based on findings from empirical studies, county councils need to continue to monitor, evaluate and hold providers accountable for objectives where mechanisms related to choice are not enough. Individuals' assessment of providers is based on individual expectations and preferences rather than overall objectives with services. Individuals do not possess information about allocated resources or the distribution of services in the population. Individuals, through their choices, therefore cannot be expected to hold providers accountable for objectives related to equity, efficiency or effectiveness. However, personal experiences, reputation and recommendations from friends and relatives might be good enough or even better than comparative information about providers to guide choices with respect to responsiveness, continuity and accessibility.

County councils also need to continue to hold providers accountable for objectives related to the quality of primary care. Individuals may assess quality as perceived by them as patients. It is usually not possible for individuals to assess technical quality, including compliance with guidelines and the appropriateness of services providers, in their contacts with providers. County councils need to monitor and assess this from a population perspective. What is perceived as high quality from the individual perspective might be the opposite from a population perspective. For example, the prescription of antibiotics for uncomplicated infections may seem rational from an individual perspective. From a population perspective, it is important to be restrictive since a generous prescription of antibiotics might lead to antibiotic resistance.

Also, from a theoretical point of view it is important to maintain and develop accountability relationships between governments and providers of public services when introducing quasi-markets. In a similar fashion to the mechanisms for corrective action between citizens and providers, exit might also give power to voice for governments. As providers know that they might be forced to exit the market if they do not comply with requirements imposed on them by governments, they will have incentives to act upon complaints raised through voice from governments as well. Hence, voice can be a powerful mechanism for corrective action between providers and governments. Mechanisms related to voice (dialogue between providers and county councils) can be assumed to be more informative for both providers and county councils compared to mechanisms related to exit.

The way forward

The new structure of governance, involving several mechanisms for corrective action, seems to be appropriate for achievement in relation to a mix of traditional and new objectives. New accountability relationships between providers and citizens are appropriate for holding providers accountable for new objectives related to accessibility and the responsiveness of services towards individuals. These objectives are visible to individuals at their point of contact with the provider. Such accountability relationships are not enough to achieve all overall objectives, however. To maintain and develop their governance models in order to achieve traditional objectives and to support processes for individuals to make informed choices of providers remain important challenges for county councils.

For county councils to be able to follow up on providers' activities, there is a need to develop information in registers to include content and distribution of services and, ideally, outcomes. There is also a need to use other mechanisms alongside the monitoring of performance indicators to hold providers accountable for their activities. The way forward is likely for county councils to draw on experiences from each other and to harmonize their models for governance and support to providers. In 2016, a national platform for gathering information on processes and outcomes in primary care was launched. This is an important step towards developing registers where information on content of visits and outcomes of inputs is collected. The purpose of this platform is for providers, researchers and policymakers to be able to take part of the results, to compare performance across providers and over time and ultimately to improve the quality of primary care services. County councils have also gradually adjusted their models for payment to providers, leading to less variation across the country. In 2016, all providers are using a formula with a heavy reliance on fixed capitation. Most county councils risk-adjust the fixed payment for socio-economic conditions and overall illness among registered individuals. County councils are also sharing experiences on models for governance and support in projects coordinated by SALAR. Models where indicators are used alongside dialogue to monitor and hold providers accountable are increasingly being introduced and used across the country.

References

Anell, A. (2011) 'Choice and privatisation in Swedish primary care'. *Health Economics, Policy and Law*, Vol. 6, pp. 549–569.

Anell, A. (2013) *Vilken betydelse har vårdval och ersättningsprinciper i primärvården?*, Paper presented at Gothenburg Public Management Seminar Gothenburg, 2013.

Anell, A. and G. Paulsson (2010) Valfrihet och konkurrens i primärvården, in A. Anell and U.-G. Gerdtham (eds), *Vårdens utmaningar* (Stockholm: SNS Förlag).

Anell, A., A. H. Glenngård and S. Merkur (2012a) 'Sweden: health system review'. *Health Systems in Transition*, Vol. 14, No. 5, pp. 1–159.

Anell, A., P. Nylinder and A. H. Glenngård (2012b) *Vårdval i primärvården. Jämförelse av uppdrag, ersättningsprinciper och kostnadsansvar* (Stockholm: Sveriges kommuner och landsting).

Barnum, H., J. Kutzin and H. Saxenian (1995) 'Incentives and provider payment methods'. *International Journal of Health Planning and Management*, Vol. 10, pp. 23–45.

Beckman, A. and A. Anell (2013a) 'Changes in health care utilisation following a reform involving choice and privatisation in Swedish primary care: a five-year follow-up of GP-visits'. *BMC Health Services Research*, Vol. 13, No. 452.

Beckman, A. and A. Anell (2013b) 'Hur har individers konsumtion av läkarbesök förändrats efter införande av hälsoval skåne?'. *Läkartidningen*, Vol. 110, No. 12, pp. 622–623.

Bevan, G., J.-K. Helderman and D. Wilsford (2010) 'Changing choices in health care: implications for equity, efficiency and cost'. *Health Economics Policy and Law*, Vol. 5, pp. 251–267.

Campbell, J. L., J. Ramsay and J. Green (2001a) 'Age, gender, socioeconomic, and ethnic differences in patients' assessments of primary health care'. *Qualitative Health Care*, Vol. 10, No. 2, pp. 90–105.

Campbell, J. L., J. Ramsay and J. Green (2001b) 'Practice size: impact on consultation length, workload, and patient assessment of care'. *British Journal of General Practice*, Vol. 51, No. 469, pp. 644–650.

Ekström, H., S. Holmberg and A. Karlsson (2013) *Vårdval kronoberg. Kartläggning av primärvården i kronobergs län före och efter vårdval – en jämförande studie* (FoU Kronoberg. FoU-rapport 2013:2).

Fredriksson, M. (2012) *Vårdval i uppsala län. Extern granskning av tillgänglighet, valfrihet, resurser och kvalitet* (Uppsala: Institutionen för folkhälso–och vårdvetenskap, Uppsala University).

Glenngård, A. H. (2012) 'Is patient satisfaction in primary care dependent on structural and organizational characteristics among providers? Findings based on data from the national patient survey in Sweden'. *Health Economics Policy and Law*, Vol. 8, pp. 1–16.

Glenngård, A. H. (2013a) *Objectives, Actors and Accountability in Quasi-markets: Studies of Swedish Primary Care*. Dissertation, Lund University.

Glenngård, A. H. (2013b) 'Productivity and patient satisfaction in primary care – conflicting or compatible goals?'. *Health Policy*, Vol. 111, No. 2, pp. 157–165.

Glenngård, A. H. (2015) *Primärvården efter vårdvalsreformen: Valfrihet, effektivitet och produktivitet* (Stockholm: SNS Förlag).

Glenngård, A. H. (2016) 'Experiences of introducing a quasi-market in Swedish primary care: fulfilment of overall objectives and assessment of provider activities'. *Scandinavian Journal of Public Administration*, Vol. 20, No. 1, pp. 72–86.

Glenngård, A. H. and A. Anell (2012a) *Produktivitet och patientnöjdhet i primärvården – en studie av region halland, region skåne och västra götalandsregionen* (Lund: KEFU).

Glenngård, A. H. and A. Anell (2012b) *Vad påverkar patientupplevd kvalitet i primärvården?* Myndigheten för vårdanalys, 2012b (Rapport 2012:1) (Stockholm).

Glenngård, A. H., A. Anell and A. Beckman (2011) 'Choice of primary care provider: results from a population survey in three Swedish counties'. *Health Policy*, Vol. 103, No. 1, pp. 31–37.

Hirschman, A. O. (1970) *Exit, Voice, and Loyalty: Responses to Decline in Firms, Organizations, and States* (Cambridge, MA: Harvard University Press).

Hjelmgren, J. and A. Anell (2007) 'Population preferences and choice of primary care models: a discrete choice experiment in Sweden'. *Health Policy*, Vol. 83, No. 3, pp. 314–322.

Janlöv, N. and C. Rehnberg (2011) *Uppföljning av husläkarsystemet inom vårdval stockholm – år 2012. Rapport nr 2011:15* (Stockholm: Karolinska Institutets Folkhälsoakademi).

Kastberg, G. (2014) *Valfrihet i vård, skola och omsorg* (Stockholm: Sveriges kommuner och landsting).

Kontopantelis, E., M. Roland and D. Reeves (2010) 'Patient experience of access to primary care: identification of predictors in a national patient survey'. *BMC Family Practice*, Vol. 11, No. 61, pp. 1–15.

Lamarche, P. A., B. Marie-Dominique, R. Pineault, A.-P. Contandriopoulos, J.-L. Denis and J. Haggerty (2003) *Choices for Change: The Path for Restructuring Primary Healthcare Services in Canada* (Ottawa: Canadian Health Services Research Foundation, New Brunswick Department of Health and Wellness, Saskatchewan Department of Health, Ministère de la santé et des services sociaux du Québec and Health Canada).

Le Grand, J. (1991) 'Quasi-markets and social policy'. *The Economic Journal*, Vol. 101, No. 408, pp. 1256–1267.

Le Grand, J. (2007) *Delivering Public Services through Choice and Competition – The Other Invisible Hand* (Princeton, NJ: Princeton University Press).

Le Grand, J. (2009) 'Choice and competition in publicly funded health care'. *Health Economics Policy and Law*, Vol. 4, pp. 479–488.

Le Grand, J. and W. Bartlett (1993) *Quasi-markets and Social Policy* (London: Macmillan).

Propper, C. (2012) 'Competition, incentives and the English NHS'. *Health Economics*, Vol. 21, pp. 33–40.

Rehnberg, C. (2014) *Vårdvalets påverkan på tillgänglighet.* I 'Låt den rätte komma in'. Rapport 2014:3. Vårdanalys (Stockholm).

Saltman, R. B. (ed.) (2006) *Primary Care in the Driver's Seat? Organizational Reform in European Primary Care* (Maidenhead: Open University Press).

Sheaff, R., S. Pickard and K. Smith (2002) 'Public service responsiveness to users demands and needs: theory, practice and primary healthcare in England'. *Public Administration*, Vol. 80, No. 2, pp. 435–452.

Starfield, B. (1998) *Primary Care: Balancing Health Needs, Services and Technology* (New York: Oxford University Press).

Starfield, B., L. Shi and J. Macinko (2005) 'Contribution of primary care to health systems and health'. *The Millbank Quarterly*, Vol. 83, No. 3, pp. 457–503.

Swedish Competition Authority (2012) *Val av vårdcentral – förutsättningar för kvalitetskonkurrens i vårdvalssystemen. Konkurrensverket: 2012:2* (Stockholm).

Swedish Medical Association (2014) *Kostnader och produktion i primärvårdens vårdval* (Stockholm: Sveriges läkarförbund).

Vårdanalys (2013a) *Vad vill patienten veta för att välja? Rapport 2013:4* (Stockholm: Myndigheten för vårdanalys).

Vårdanalys (2013b) *Vem har vårdvalet gynnat? En jämförande studie mellan tre landsting före och efter vårdvalets införande i primärvården. Rapport 2013:1* (Stockholm: Myndigheten för vårdanalys).

Vårdanalys (2014a) *Låt den rätte komma in – hur har tillgängligheten påverkats av apoteksomregleringen, vårdvalet samt vårdgarantin och kömiljarden* (Stockholm: Myndigheten för vårdanalys).

Vårdanalys (2014b) *Vem vill veta vad för att välja? Rapport 2014:1* (Stockholm: Myndigheten för vårdanalys).

Vårdanalys (2014c) *Vården ur patienternas perspektiv – jämförelser mellan sverige och 10 andra länder. Resultat från the commonwealth fund 2014 international health policy survey. Rapport 2014:11* (Stockholm: *Myndigheten för Vårdanalys*).

Winblad, U., D. Isaksson and P. Bergman (2012) *Effekter av valfrihet inom hälso- och sjukvård – en kartläggning av kunskapsläget* (Stockholm: Myndigheten för Vårdanalys).

World Health Organization (2008) *The World Health Report 2008: Primary Health Care: Now More Than Ever* (Geneva: World Health Organization).

14 Managing profits and professionalism in the Swedish school system

Robert Wenglén

Summary

During the last 25 years the elementary school sector in Sweden has undergone radical change due to decentralization and deregulation. The logic of professionalism in the organizational structure of the public professional bureaucracy has been challenged, giving way for more of market logic. In tandem, at least from year 2000, the results in the PISA ranking have declined dramatically, leading the OECD to claim that Sweden's school system is in need of urgent change. This combined development was the most debated issue during the 2014 election campaign, dividing political parties and citizens into two rather digital positions – pro or con profits in the sector. Hardly surprising, the analysis of the arguments in the public debate shows that the nonprofit arguments are closely related to the logic of the traditional public professional bureaucracy, whereas the pro-profit arguments are to a large extent related to the logic of the free market. However, the political establishment wants to go a third, pragmatic way, blending the two logics. This puts, it is concluded, demand on the local management of schools to develop a management control competence that simultaneously meets and balances the logic of professionalism expressed in the school law and the demand for attractiveness and financial healthiness that comes with acting on a (quasi-) market. Surprisingly, the effect of political decisions on these local management control matters is absent in the debate.

Introduction

Elementary school in Sweden is mandatory for children from the age of 7 to 16. It is regulated by a school law and national curriculum, free of charge and provided by both public and independent (private) schools. Up to 1991, public professional bureaucracies produced elementary education. Since then the sector has undergone major reforms closely related to the ideology of New Public Management (NPM). Two reforms have had major effects. In 1991 the national parliament decided to increase the municipalities' responsibility for elementary school and all teachers became employed by municipalities. In 1992 the sector was deregulated, allowing private alternatives (SOU 2013:56).

The major aim was decentralization and a shift from rules to result control. The intention was that this would lead to better knowledge results, better cost-efficiency, democratization and professionalization, in terms of strengthening the autonomy of the teachers. The parties to the left were opposed to both of these reforms, decentralization and deregulation, arguing that these would challenge equity (Skolverket, 2009).

Alongside deregulation, the compensation system was changed. All schools, irrespective of who the principal was, got the same compensation. At first private alternatives received a fixed income per pupil financed by the state. Since 2011 the private alternatives have been compensated by a fixed income per pupil by the local municipality, corresponding to the average cost per pupil of the local public alternatives. Every eighth pupil in elementary school and every fourth pupil in secondary school went to a private alternative during 2011/2012. In 2010, half of the independent school companies had an operating margin (EBIT) higher than 4 per cent. Of the almost 400 companies, 7 per cent had an operating margin of 15 to 19 per cent and an equal number of companies had profits above 20 per cent (SOU 2013:56).

The Swedish system, where tax-financed private schools can make profits, is unique. In all other countries only non-profit organizations can run tax-financed schools and profit-seeking private schools are privately financed.

Almost 25 years after the deregulation, the school debate is still intense. Sweden has fallen in the PISA ranking. The PISA result has 'declined dramatically, from near the OECD average in 2000 to significantly below the average in 2012. No other country participating in PISA saw a steeper decline than Sweden over that period' (OECD, 2015, p. 7). Bluntly, OECD claims that the Swedish school system is in need of urgent change, i.e. new reforms. Further, the status of the teaching profession is in decline and Sweden is facing a growing deficit of teachers. Not least, the existence of profits in the school sector has led to much debate. In fact, this was the most debated issue in the Swedish election campaign in 2014.

A majority of the voters are against profits and shareholder dividends in the welfare sector. Simultaneously, there is strong public support for freedom of choice and multiple welfare service providers. Seven out of 10 people want to be able to choose between public and private schools (Ohlsson, 2014a).

This to some degree paradoxical demand of the people, combined with the idea of professionalism, is central to this chapter. As will be illustrated, there are forces that want to prohibit profits and forces that are strongly pro-profits but the political establishment pursues another plan. It wants to keep the school choice and allow profits but increase the regulation. This puts new demand on the local management of the professional school organization.

I will come back to arguments presented in the debate regarding profits in the school system and the implications for the local management of schools, but before that the Swedish school system will be described in more detail, not least how the law regulates a logic of professionalism.

The logic of professionalism in the Swedish school sector

Starting on a more general level, there has been much written about professions (the traits of certain occupational groups), professionalization (the journey to become recognized as a profession) and professionalism (a particular work and management control logic). With this in mind, this chapter leans heavily on the work of Eliot Freidson and the concept of professionalism. He claims that professionalism, in the most elementary sense, is a set of institutions which permit the members of an occupation to make a living while controlling their own work. Another way of putting it is that professionalism is a logic by which professionals maintain and apply a specialized theoretical knowledge, quality assured by exams and sometimes certificates, in a collegial form with the political legitimacy to carry out a particular societal task (Freidson, 1983, 2001).

The logic of professionalism can be differentiated from two other logics. One is the logic of the free market, stemming from the work of Adam Smith, where the customer controls the work by voting with their feet. Another is the logic of the bureaucracy, stemming from the work of Max Weber, where the superior manager controls the work by various bureaucratic management control systems (Freidson, 2001).

There are a number of characteristics of the Swedish school sector that support a practice that follows the logic of professionalism. Somewhat simplified, four key features of the logic of professionalism can be highlighted, primarily based on the reviews of Brante (2014) and Wenglén (2013): (1) state regulations of means and ends; (2) labour market restrictions; (3) application of knowledge and skills grounded in specialized theoretical knowledge; and (4) professional discretion in the pupil/class work.

Even though there are no formal restrictions in regards to education and experience of education for becoming a principal supplier of elementary education, there are formal restrictions (a school law and a national curriculum) regulating what suppliers of elementary education are obliged to do and accomplish. A central part of this regulation is *equity*, i.e. that schools shall compensate for individual, socio-economic etc. preconditions rather than filtering and sifting out. All pupils have the right to get support based on their individual needs. Basically, the state regulation is well in line with Parson's classical characterization of professions, also known as the (naive) *professional values*: affective neutrality, universality and collectivism (Brante, 2009; Nolin, 2008). All pupils should be given equal opportunity (universality), i.e. be treated similarly, unhampered by artificial barriers or prejudices or preferences except when particular distinctions can be explicitly justified (affective neutrality), with the common good in mind (collectivism).

Second, the sector is characterized by *labour market restrictions*. Suppliers of elementary education are restricted in regards to who can be employed to do the job, i.e. people with formal teacher competence/certificates (Skollagen, 2010, ch. 2, §13 and §20). This means that labour consumers are not free to choose with whom to contract. There is a market shelter (Freidson, 1999) – or a social closure and a free trade barrier.

Third, teachers' work is regulated by the school law (Skollagen, 2010, ch. 1, §5), that is, teaching has to rest on scientific grounding and proven experience, fully in line with the idea that professionals base their work on the *application of knowledge and skills grounded in specialized theoretical knowledge* (Abbott, 1988; Brante, 2014; Freidson, 1999). Teachers' work is divided into different subjects and the idea is that teachers are only allowed to teach subjects that they have the proper theoretical and practical knowledge of. It should be noted, though, that this knowledge base is constantly emerging and contested. This implies that it is seldom a matter of applying scientific truths. It is rather a matter of awareness of theoretical schools and application of various 'best thoughts' related to them. Put differently, in a well-functioning profession practice builds on theory in a way so that know-why and know-how are in harmony (Brante *et al.*, 2015). In more concrete terms, professional work embraces the ability to diagnose, to infer and to treat, in varying order, where inference is the purest professional act. It takes, according to Abbott (1988), the information of diagnosis and indicates a range of treatments with their more or less predictable outcomes. We should keep in mind, though, that knowledge work, including professional work, is often understood as ambiguous both in terms of process and outcomes (Alvehus, 2006; Alvesson, 2004; Løwendahl, 2008).

Finally, the control mechanism in schools follows the idea of *discretion based on knowledge asymmetry*. This builds on the belief that the knowledge and skills embedded in the performance of professional work are exogenous to both individual consumers and managers, who lack the knowledge and skill to perform, and to adequately control, the work of those they employ (Freidson, 1999). The right of discretion is thus based on a knowledge asymmetry, where teachers are seen as best suited to act in the interests of both the pupil and the state. It is also based on the idea that professional work, including the work of teachers, cannot be standardized, rationalized and commoditized (Freidson, 2001). This discretion should however be limited to the content and organization of the professional work (Abbott, 1988), i.e. it should not include decision power over e.g. economic prerequisites.

In Sweden, and probably elsewhere, elementary schools have thus a long tradition of discretion. Teachers do much of their core work, i.e. preparing, carrying through and following up lessons, on their own and through collaborations with their peers. The head teacher has the task of leading and organizing the pedagogical development but much of e.g. the lesson-specific planning, as well as the marking and grading, is controlled by the teachers. The discretion is also to some degree regulated in the school law, where it is stated that the head teacher decides on the intrinsic organization of their unit and has the responsibility to allocate resource according to the various needs (Skollagen, 2010, 2 Ch. §10). Further, a certified teacher has the responsibility of the education they carry out (Skollagen, 2010, 2 Ch. §15).

Worth mentioning is that the characteristics of professionalism have been heavily criticized. A significant number of studies of professions claim that professions are an expression of some groups in society having obtained privilege and undue advantages at others' expense (Abbott, 1988; Brante, 2009, 2014). There has also been criticism in relation to whether professionals live up to these characteristics in practice:

> The idea that everything will be fine if you give status and freedom to professionals is naive. Professions are characterized not only by ethics and skills but also by inertia, let go spirit, guild thinking and group selfishness.... A professional group cannot just demand respect, status and autonomy.... Occupational groups must be evaluated in much more qualified ways than is the case today. This often requires external qualified assessments with penalties for poor performance, something that loyal guild representatives can have difficulties with.
>
> (Alvesson and Rothstein, 2014)

Nevertheless, the legislation in Sweden restricts and permeates the overall logic in the school sector. In many other industries the state, through elected politicians, is more or less uninterested in industry-specific interfering, trusting the actors of the market to solve conflicts of interests and come to agreements. Further, the professional values of equity and collectivism are not necessarily strong in many other sectors. In many less-regulated sectors, companies are expected to try to maximize profits. This includes price management, i.e. customers paying different prices for the same service. Likewise, loyal customers get special service and, in general, universality is not necessarily part of a businessperson's moral compass – they often have more faith in ad hoc negotiations. Neither is striving for the common good rather than the self-interest of the company a particularly strong value in many sectors.

With this in mind, not least that it is only the state, through the democratic parliament, who 'has the power to establish and maintain professionalism' (Freidson, 1999, p. 123), we now move over to presenting and analysing arguments in regards to profits in the school sector published on the websites of the political parties in the Swedish parliament as well as debate articles by various stakeholders and political commentators. The selection of the latter has been done without any rigorous scientific method and should be seen as illustrations of commonly raised arguments. The empirical material has been divided into three broad positions: a non-profit position, a free market position and a pragmatic position. The first is primarily expressed by the left (V) but to some extent also in regular journalistic work, the second by liberal commentators, businesspeople and entrepreneurs in the sector, whereas the third, the pragmatic stance, is the common position held by the political establishment in the Swedish parliament, i.e. all parties except (V) and the nationalists (SD), who did not sign the agreement.

Non-profit position

Schools should be committed to humanity and the common good

People should be comfortable about being treated as people in need of education and not seen as profitable or not profitable customers. Elementary education is not an ordinary industry. The purpose of elementary school suppliers should be to serve the citizens – primarily a social and societal commitment. Basically, tax money should exclusively go to serving the citizens and not to profits (The Left Party, 2016).

Privatization and school choice has led to inequity

The reform has led to inequity. One part of this is that the responsibility for the future of our children has landed on the parents:

> Equity in our schools is only a memory. The responsibility of the future of our children has landed on their parents, instead of making sure that society is responsible for schools being equally good.
>
> (The Green Party, 2016)

Another part of the inequity is that the school choice has led to segregation, which for instance has been voiced by the driving force behind the deregulation law, former minister of finance and director of the private school association, Kjell–Olof Feldt:

> The problem (with school choice) is equity.... The good pupils stream to the same schools, leading to half-good schools getting drained from the good pupils, and then becoming a school with problems.... The school choice reform went wrong, at least as it works today. I do not know how we thought.
>
> (SVT, 2014)

Privatization has led to oligopoly and quasi-markets

A small number of private companies stand for most of the turnover in the private school sector. Academedia is the giant, owned by a risk capitalist with a turnover in 2014 of 6.3 billion Swedish Krona (BSEK), more than the seven biggest private competitors together, with more than 50,000 pupils in elementary and secondary schools. Earnings were 450 million Swedish Krona before interest and taxes and 212 MSEK after. The eight biggest school companies showed earnings (EBIT) in total of 640 BSEK. Concurrently, the interest in opening new schools is the lowest in 10 years (Olsson and Delin, 2015).

Private companies have lower staff ratios and inferior working conditions

In general, there is a strong concern about the existence of shareholder dividends that otherwise could have been used to increase the staff ratio. This also has some empirical support. Privately driven schools have a lower staff ratio (teachers per pupil) than public organizations in the same sector, about 8 per cent in primary school and about 19 per cent in secondary school (Olofsson *et al.*, 2014). Lower staff ratios are also said to have increased stress among teachers.

Profits in tax-financed schools are an international anomaly

The Swedish system is extreme in allowing private companies to make limitless profits from tax-financed elementary education:

> [S]ince Chile recently changed its legislation, [Sweden] is the only country in the world allowing limitless profits and dividends from tax-financed schools.
>
> (Gedin *et al.*, 2015)

In summary, the non-profit position has much in common with the logic of professionalism. The school sector should not be seen as an ordinary sector. It is a sensitive sector for society, characterized by labour market restrictions, professional values of universality and collectivism, and professional discretion, or at least a high degree of employee influence. The ideological arguments are supported by empirical arguments that privatization has led to inequity, oligopoly, lower staff ratios in private schools, and the fact that the Swedish system is extreme from an international perspective.

Free market position

Profits are a sign of quality and economic rationality

To survive, grow and be profitable, companies must offer education that people demand. They must be a good employer and attract and maintain skilled and qualified employees so that they in turn make the company attractive for pupils and their parents. Only when these goals are achieved can a company become financially sound (Berglund *et al.*, 2014).

Profits are also a sign of economic rationality: 'Profits not only show which products that are most profitable to produce, but also the most profitable way to produce them' (Ohlsson, 2014b).

Markets facilitate innovation

> It is incomprehensible that so many want to prevent these welfare organizations to grow freely. Think only at export possibilities.... Market forces are needed to open to innovations and new concepts. Who today would think of the idea to start a business with a municipality or a county as a geographic limitation?
>
> (Moberg, 2015)

Inefficiency and losses are equally important to discuss as profits

The debate is dominated by a discussion about profits in the sector – and losses are seldom discussed.

> What happens when private actors show red figures? The owners lose money, which they hopefully can earn back through improving the business in the coming years. When public actors make a loss, it is the taxpayers who will have to take the bill. And the deficit can go on for years.
>
> (Sanandaji, 2015)

To some degree this argument is related to risk and rewards. If the principal, i.e. the municipality, wants to lower its economic risk by handing it over to a private entrepreneur, the principal is expected to accept that the entrepreneur will demand a possibility of making a profit.

Additionally, profits in private alternatives can be equated with inefficiencies in public alternatives:

> As far as I can judge, based on different studies, private companies do not have worse quality than public organizations.... What should be debated is the fact that public organizations are run with too high costs. Public organizations do not pay company tax, do not build reserves, do not create new capital for investments and do not give dividends to stakeholders. Therefore they should in the normal case ... deliver to 6 per cent lower costs.'
>
> (Olofsson, 2014)

Economic surplus is a long-term necessity for all school organizations

As matter of fact, even public organizations need and are obliged to have surpluses in their operations in order to make room for future investments, build reserves for tougher times and inflation etc. According to the so-called balance claim in the municipality law, municipalities are obliged to show a surplus, consolidating their finances after inflation. In practice, this is often understood as budgeting and reaching a surplus of 2 to 3 per cent (Wikstrand, 2015).

In summary, markets are said to be better at facilitating innovation and the efficient use of scares resources. It is noticed that all school organizations need and are obliged to create surplus for long-term financial consolidation. In the long run, markets with functioning competition and low entering barriers are supposed to be the best for society, it is argued. Hence, one could say that the free trade followers want to reduce the logic of professionalism by eliminating trade barriers, even though it is not always explicitly expressed.

The pragmatic position

The political establishment in Sweden, i.e. all (six) parties in the parliament except the left (V) and right (SD) wings, have signed a common treatment (SOU 2013:56). In this, the parties agree that independent schools are here to stay but they want more restrictions for the sector, including: examination of the education provider's suitability regarding conduct and financial orderliness; assessment of owners' suitability and long-term approach; consultation with the municipality before establishing an independent school; protection of sources for employees of independent schools; transparency and public access to information; and stronger sanctions for serious shortcomings (SOU 2013:56).

The six parties, representing two coalitions, are thus all against prohibiting profits, although there are differences in their positions. The Moderate Party (M) claims that quality should be in focus, not forms of ownership or profit levels (The Moderate Party, 2016). The Christian Democrats (KD) claims that choice and diversity means higher quality, increased power for the individual and more employers to choose from for the employee. They are against prohibiting profits, claiming that that would reduce the citizens' possibility of choice (The Christian Democrats, 2016). The Centre Party (C) holds the same position, stressing a focus on people's needs and possibilities to choose (The Centre Party, 2016). The Liberal Party (L) indicates some concerns:

> We should all have the possibility to choose as much as possible when it comes to welfare. We shall put high quality demands on both public and private actors and make sure that there is a long-term owner responsibility. Profits are okay in well-run businesses.
>
> (The Liberal Party, 2016)

The other coalition, in government after the election in 2014, raises stronger concerns. The Green Party claims that the school sector is not an ordinary sector and that profits should stay in the sector, i.e. profits need to be reinvested (The Green Party, 2016). The Social Democratic Party (S) opposes 'profit hunting' and wants to restrict the profits in the welfare sector (The Social Democratic Party, 2016). The red/green coalition's concern regarding profits was manifested in a formal investigation, called the profit investigation, commissioned by the government in 2015. Worth noting is that the Social Democratic Party has a long tradition on looking upon profits as a necessary evil:

> For [S] profits is a necessary evil. This pragmatic socialism has been the Swedish Social democrats' companion. Already Nils Karleby, the parties' frontier thinker, defended the profit interest … in 1926: 'There is no reason to assume that the shoemaker fixes or the shoe shop floor maker does shoes in the interest of the public. His interest aims at the payment he can win … In this sense all paid work is a production for profit'.

Even Kjell-Olof Feldt, the social democrat minister of finance 1982–1990 highlights the significance of profit:

> Its task is not only to be a measurement of efficiency and different ways of using the economic resources. Profit interest is also the only pure watcher of resources being used efficiently…. If the employees take over they get squeezed between their own self-interest in higher wages and secure employment, on the one side, and the company's need of efficiency, on the other side.
>
> (Ohlsson, 2014b)

In sum, the political establishment takes a pragmatic position, wanting to keep school choice and independent schools and allow profits – and to increase the regulation of the market. One might also say that the establishment is in search of a balance, a middle ground – a position that is often seen as typical for the Swedish culture.

Discussion

From the above illustration of the debate, one can identify a few political trade-offs. One is a tension between socialism and liberal economics, and Marx's classical trade-off between work and capital. How do we avoid the risk of too much suboptimal self-interest by shareholders or by employees? A second trade-off is between regulation/collectivism and deregulation/individualism. How far can we stretch the idea of equity without hampering and precluding the school choice, or vice versa, i.e. how far can the idea of school choice be stretched without increasing inequity? A third political trade-off is between making regulations for reducing the risk of excess profits and reducing the risk of inefficiencies.

Of the above trade-offs, the OECD is mostly concerned with equity, as 'the highest performing education systems across OECD countries are those that combine excellence with equity' (OECD, 2015, p. 3). Put simply, striving for equity is important. But so is striving for professionalism. According to the advice of the OECD, Sweden needs to (1) establish conditions that

Table 14.1 Arguments for and against allowing profits in the school sector

Non-profit arguments	Pro-profit arguments
Risk of shareholder self-interest guiding work should be avoided	Risk of employee self-interest guiding the work should be avoided
Regulation is important in order to secure equity	Deregulation is important in order to secure school-choice and that the needs of the individual can be met
Profits in private companies are a problem	Inefficiencies in public organization are a problem

promote quality with equity across schools; (2) build capacity for teaching and learning through a long-term human resource strategy; and (3) strengthen steering of policy and accountability with a focus on improvement (OECD, 2015). Included in the second piece of advice is 'developing professional standards to underpin appraisals and career structure; more selective entry into teacher education programmes; and adequately resourced continuous professional development for educators to support school improvement efforts' (OECD, 2015, p. 9). Included in the third recommendation is the importance of local management control and how it fits with the national goals and regulations. This has also been pointed out as a main problem in the Swedish school system in another investigation:

> This inquiry indicates that many of the problems head teachers experience result from deficiencies in the school system's 'chain of command'.... One problem is that the dialogue conducted between the various levels in the chain of command is often unclear in various respects. Consequently, the dialogue does not result in a common strategy on how to achieve the national goals in the individual school.... Head teachers need to be better at organising and managing schools in the context of the national school assignment, pupils' development and the results of systematic quality enhancement work.'
>
> (SOU 2015:22)

By chain of command the investigator means the sequence consisting of central government–school governing body–governing body's management–head teachers–teachers in public schools, and the corresponding chain in independent schools. Another key result in this study is the need to strengthen the pedagogical leadership of head teachers in schools.

Accordingly, both the OECD report and the above SOU investigation somewhat challenge the dominant idea within the research field of professional bureaucracies, i.e. that management control should be based on the idea that professionals learn the values and tricks of the trade during education, where after it is more or less a matter of informal mutual adjustment among colleagues (Mintzberg, 1980), clan control (Ouchi, 1980) and professional discretion. In more concrete terms, the reports challenge the (indirect) form of management control where management is primarily about hiring, training and keeping the right people (Løwendahl, 2008), combined with managers functioning 'as senior members of a community, rather than representatives of a formal hierarchy' (Alvesson and Kärreman, 2001, p. 1015).

Put differently, it is the local management, i.e. principals but foremost head teachers, that are facing a situation, including a crossroad of conflicting interests, where they need to handle the trade-offs, regulations and various recommendations. In more concrete terms, there is a continuous negotiation between meeting the demands of the professionals (higher salaries, more time and resources for competence development and collegial learning, fewer pupils in the classroom and extra resources for pupils with special needs) and the demands of the principal (adequate study results within budget). Head teachers are also continuously negotiating with teachers about finding tailor-made solutions that meet the needs of the individual pupil or class (which not seldom are experienced differently by parents, teachers and head teachers) without violating the obligation to follow the regulations stipulated in the school law.

The local management is also in a situation where it needs to handle and blend the logic of the free market, the bureaucracy and professionalism (Freidson, 2001). In fact, many of the practical problems in the local management of schools can be seen as deriving from conflicts between these logics. They need to be able to act in line with the free market to attract and maintain both pupils and teachers. They need to be able to create and maintain a well-functioning bureaucracy in order to meet the requests of e.g. the Swedish Schools Inspectorate. They also need to be able to nurture the logic of professionalism to meet the request of the school law and the recommendations from the OECD. Also, at the teachers' level these logics seem to be present. Demand is put on teachers to be customer-oriented, while handling bureaucratic reports and financial constraints and finding time to develop their teaching and teaching abilities. This puts head teachers in a situation where they need to understand the challenges of the school from the perspective of the different logics and continuously weigh them against each other when making decisions (Wenglén, 2016).

Coming back to the political debate, it seems surprising that the consequence of the school choice reform (which includes giving private alternatives a right to make a profit) for professionalism and local management have been more or less absent in the debate. In the field of research on professionalism this was however already mentioned in 1983, when Freidson claimed a global trend from the traditional self-regulation in professional work to new management control methods that better control the cost of service and the quality in performance of professionals (Freidson, 1983).

Conclusions

This chapter has been concerned with profits and professionalism in the Swedish elementary school sector. The analysis of the political debate, before and to some degree after the election in 2014, shows that the theme of profit has totally dominated the debate involving two logics. The non-profit followers prefer the (public) bureaucracy, whereas the pro-profit followers put forward arguments connected to the logic of the free market. The political establishment wants to blend these logics into a regulated market open for both public and private (profit-seeking) principals.

This puts, it is concluded, the local management of schools in a situation where they have to balance the logic of professionalism expressed in the school law and the demand for attractiveness and financial healthiness that comes with acting on a (quasi-)market. Not least, the head teachers need to manage profits and professionalism. This has put new demands on the local management and its management control competence. Before deregulation and decentralization, professional teachers were more or less self-organized and self-controlled, and local management rather administrative. After the reform, both the state and the parents demand an active local management, taking steps to assure high performance. Basically, local management needs to be able to lead a professional organization in a free market. This probably includes industry-specific management skills in quality assessment, result control, normative control (leadership) and strategic human resource management.

The way forward: thoughts about the future of management of professionalism in schools

The demand for knowledge-intensive work and theoretical qualifications will probably continue to increase. At the same time, globalization and democracy will support free trade and customer influence. This might lead to a situation where the profession of teaching will come to be like the profession of engineering. Engineers in most capitalist nations work in private firms concerned with the production of profitable goods. They have no clear jurisdictional boundaries, a fragmented division of work and an incomplete labour market shelter. This implies that 'the degree of professionalism permitted them is almost entirely a function of the executive staff of the private or public firm that employ them' (Freidson, 1999, p. 128). It would then be up to the local management of the elementary school, private or public, to develop and maintain some degree of professionalism. The state might continue to enforce professionalism through legislation, but the actual degree of professionalism in an organization is foremost a matter of management control, where managers manage professionals in a way that nurtures and controls the application of knowledge and skills grounded in specialized theoretical knowledge.

References

Abbott, A. (1988) *Systems of Professions* (Chicago: University of Chicago Press).

Alvehus, J. (2006) *Paragrafer och profit. Om kunskapsarbetets oklarhet.* Doctoral thesis, Lund University.

Alvesson, M. (2004) *Knowledge Work and Knowledge-intensive Firms* (Oxford: Oxford University Press).

Alvesson, M. and D. Kärreman (2001) 'Odd couple: making sense of the curious concept of knowledge management'. *Journal of Management Studies*, Vol. 38, No. 7, pp. 995–1018.

Alvesson, M. and B. Rothstein (2014) 'Universiteten hotar bli sveriges nästa pisa-haveri', *Dagens Nyheter* (2 May 2014)

Berglund, R., L. Elmgren, C.-A. Palm and C. Tavakolinia (2014) 'Jonas sjöstedt, du är en välfärdspopulist!', *Dagens Samhälle* (30 January 2014).

Brante, T. (2009) *Vad är en profession? Teoretiska ansatser och definitioner.* Vetenskap för profession, rapport nr 8 (Borås: University of Borås).

Brante, T. (2014) *Den professionella logiken: Hur vetenskap och praktik förenas i det moderna kunskapssamhället* (Malmö: Liber).

Brante, T., E. Johnsson, G. Olofsson and L. G. Svensson (2015) *Professionerna i kunskapssamhället* (Stockholm: Liber).

Freidson, E. (1983) 'The reorganization of the professions by regulation'. *Law and Human Behavior*, Vol. 7, pp. 279–290.

Freidson, E. (1999) 'Theory of professionalism: method and substance'. *International Review of Sociology*, Vol. 9, No. 1, pp. 117–129.

Freidson, E. (2001) *Professionalism, the Third Logic* (Cambridge: Polity Press).

Gedin, H., H. Thomé and S. Svensson (2015) 'När konkurrens ersätter samarbete blir helheten sämre', *Sydsvenskan* (20 February 2015).

Løwendahl, B. (2008) *Strategic Management of Professional Service Firms* (Copenhagen: Copenhagen Business School Press).

Mintzberg, H. (1980) 'Structure in 5's: a synthesis of research on organizational design'. *Management Science*, Vol. 26, No. 3, pp. 322–341.

Moberg, Å. (2015) 'Robotföretagen slipper bråka om sina vinster', *Dagens Samhälle* (5 May 2015).

Nolin, J. (2008) 'In search of a new theory of profession'. *Science for Professions*, No. 4 (University of Borås).

OECD (2015) *Improving Schools in Sweden: An OECD Perspective.* Available online at www.oecd.org/edu/school/Improving-Schools-in-Sweden.pdf.

Ohlsson, P. T. (2014a) 'Högervinden har mojnat betydligt', *Sydsvenskan* (22 June 2014).

Ohlsson, P. T. (2014b) 'Rakt ut i det blå', *Sydsvenskan* (24 August 2014).

Olofsson, D. (2014) 'Förbättras verksamhet när vinster förbjuds, då borde metoden användas i fler branscher', *Sydsvenskan* (11 May 2014).

Olofsson, E., T. Boucher, N. Sandqvist and C. Wahlgren (2014) 'Osmakliga grepp förstör vinstdebatten', *Dagens Samhälle* (30 January 2014).

Olsson, H. and M. Delin (2015) 'Lönsamt men lågt intresse för nya friskolor', *Dagens Nyheter* (11 February 2015).

Ouchi, W. G. (1980) 'Markets, bureaucracies, and clans'. *Administrative Science Quarterly*, Vol. 25, No. 1, pp. 129–142.

Sanandaji, N. (2015) 'Öppna era ögon för välfärdens förluster', *Dagens Samhälle* (18 June 2015).

Skolverket (2009) 'Vad påverkar resultaten i svensk grundskola? Kunskapsöversikt om betydelsen av olika faktorer', *Kunskapsöversikter* (Stockholm).

SOU 2013:56 (2013) *Friskolorna i samhället – betänkande av friskolekommittén.*

SOU 2015:22 (2015) *Rektorn och styrkedjan – betänkande av utredningen om rektorernas arbetssituation inom skolväsendet.*

SVT (2014) *Kjell-olof feldt: Det var fel att införa fritt skolval.* Available online at www. svt.se/nyheter/sverige/kjell-olof-feldt-det-var-fel-att-infora-fritt-skolval.

The Centre Party (2016) Available online at www.centerpartiet.se (accessed 21 April 2016).

The Christian Democrats (2016) Available online at www.kristdemokraterna.se (accessed 21 April 2016).

The Green Party (2016) Available online at www.mp.se.

The Left Party (2016) Available online at www.vansterpartiet.se (accessed 21 April 2016).

The Liberal Party (2016) Available online at www.liberalerna.se (accessed 21 April 2016).

The Moderate Party (2016) Available online at www.moderat.se (accessed 21 April 2016).

The Social Democratic Party (2016) Available online at www.socialdemokraterna.se (accessed 21 April 2016).

Wenglén, R. (2013) *Professionalism i välfärden: Förutsättningar och tumregler. KEFUs skriftserie 2013:3* (Lund: Institute of Economic Research, Lund University).

Wenglén, R. (2016) Professionellt skolledarskap, in M. Jarl and E. Nihlfors (eds), *Ledarskap, utveckling, lärande – grundbok för rektorer och förskolechefer* (Stockholm: Natur och kultur).

Wikstrand, M. (2015) *Politikernas ekonomibok* (Stockholm: Dagens Samhälle).

15 Welfare choices

A story of market forces and social progress

Hans Knutsson

Summary

The implementation of market solutions has been widely attempted in many different parts of the public sector. This chapter concerns a groundbreaking social reform, which introduced personal assistants for 'functionally impaired' people. It was a far-reaching and liberating reform aimed at making disabled people part of society. It replaced collective institutional care with individual choice, in turn built on a number of market-oriented mechanisms. The reform, though, soon grew costly and has been plagued by fraud and public mistrust. The chapter discusses how ideas of market mechanisms are not equal to ready-made solutions; they may come ill-conceived and before long be in need of revision and negotiation. The chapter provides a case of a major Swedish social reform, which illuminates, first, an experimental full-scale policy implementation and, second, how market ideas easily become confused with and substituted for the idea of individual choice.

Introduction

> Control (or governance) is always for some purpose, even if it is only survival (in living systems). So 'ensuring a level playing field' could be a goal of government, but only towards a higher goal.
>
> (Dunsire, 1990, p. 16)

This is a story about the relentlessness of Swedish social reform. It also concerns the complexities and interconnectedness of implementing reforms within reforms. The discussion revolves around the concept of policy implementation (see e.g. Hill and Hupe, 2014) and the marketization aspect (Brunsson and Hägg, 2010) of the reform. Policy implementation is a classic within the field of public policy, however, closely related to management control and, hence, NPM. The policy in question, the reform serving as a case study, is 'the Act concerning support and service for people with functional impairments', known as LSS (Lagen (1993:387) om stöd och service till visa funktionshindrade). The Act is built upon the individual choice made available to the functionally disabled, which has made it possible for many more to take part in everyday life on their own terms. The case illustrates how the Swedish model of public-sector organization is strained and challenged by one of the most generous but complex reforms made in the history of Swedish social reform.

Sweden has earned a reputation as a progressive country in terms of social reforms (see e.g. Cox, 2004). General elections have been held since 1921, when women were extended voting rights. Between 1936 and 1976, a period which saw large social reforms laying the foundation for the Swedish welfare state, government was led by social democrats. In 1989, the Social Democratic government initiated a parliamentary inquiry, which led to a widely supported law giving disabled persons an unprecedented right to support and services. 'The right to a personal assistant is the most revolutionizing in the care of handicapped people since the 1960s,' said the disability expert Karl Grünewald (1994). From the outset, the main objective of the reform has been to give the disabled the right to lead a life on their own terms. To accomplish that, the organization of the Swedish disability care was changed from collective and large institutions to a deregulated market for providers of small-scale personal services.

The LSS reform covers 10 different kinds of support and service, e.g. counselling, the right to housing, and relief service for families with functionally disabled members. The most dominant and pervasive part of the legislation concerns the right to personal assistance in everyday life. The disabled person got to choose both provider and assistants independently, even to employ assistants privately. The state-level Social Insurance Agency (SIA) was assigned the financial responsibility for the bulk of the reform, which was partly carried by municipalities. The municipalities were designated as principals, carrying the responsibility for the provision of the legislated support and service. However, the reform was designed around personal choice on the market for personal assistance.

Creating the market for personal assistance

Creating a market for personal assistance has required a number of different mechanisms to be introduced. Personal choice, weaker labour rights of personal assistants and low hurdles to establish alternative providers of personal assistance are three core imperatives within the reform.

The LSS Act has been built upon the free choice of the functionally disabled. Such a standpoint necessitates abandoning the municipal monopoly of service provision. The following section presents, first, the disabled person's right to choose their care provider, followed by a note on the special labour law regulating conditions for personal assistants. Thereafter, the far-reaching right to start a personal assistance business is described, continued by the remuneration system and the associated control of the use of the remuneration.

The right to choose an assistance provider is a recognition of the right of the disabled person to live their life as they choose and also a reaction to the observation made in the Handicap Inquiry (SOU, 1991) about the complete absence of influence on the part of the disabled person. The choice can be described in different ways, but one initial and essential choice is between a private or public provider. The public provider is the municipality, which has the basic responsibility for provision; the municipality is the default choice. If the disabled person chooses a private alternative, there are a few principal ones to choose from. There are three main types of private providers of personal assistance – the private company, the private non-profit organization and the disabled person being a private employer of their own assistants.

In Sweden, labour laws regulate terms of employment and rules of termination. If a disabled person is dissatisfied with a personal assistant, there is legal support for immediate termination of the assistance, albeit with two weeks' notice of termination of employment. The general rules state that an employee has the right to one month's notice before the employment is terminated, which increases with the time of employment. Since the disabled person becomes dependent on the personal assistant, the quality of the assistance is firmly associated with the trust and safety built up between the two. No routines or general agreements can compensate for the lack of personal trust. This is a key reason why personal assistants are made an exception to the general labour legislation in Sweden. Without consideration of the length of employment, a personal assistant is entitled to only a fortnight's notice before termination. Thus, there is a real and strong mechanism of personal choice built into the LSS Act. Still, this is oftentimes a right given to the legal guardian of a mentally disabled person. The effect of that is that oftentimes a representative needs to decide on the matter of trust and safety.

Today, anyone who wants to start a business providing personal assistance can do so, so long as, first, the person is not subject to unpaid tax debts or other legal offences and, second, that the company is approved by the NBHW. Previously, no such approval was needed and the spirit of free enterprise soared in the industry of personal assistance. In 2002, almost 70 per cent of those granted personal assistance relied on a municipal provider, a figure which nearly halved in 2014. The development of private alternatives as providers has in the same period moved from 15 per cent to 65 per cent, an increase of well above 300 per cent. In May 2014, the total number of private companies offering personal assistance was 888, spanning from very small (one customer) to very big (1,900 customers). Individual employers numbered about 400 at the same time (Assistanskoll, 2014).

Two different public organizations handle the applications sent in by the disabled person. When the need is less than 20 weekly hours, the municipality in which the disabled person lives handles the application. The SIA handles applications covering 20 or more weekly hours of assistance. Once the decision is made granting the disabled person personal assistance, either by the municipality or by the SIA, the disabled person will be paid the remuneration on a monthly basis. The disabled then reports back the use of the granted hours. Unused hours are subject to repayment on a six-monthly interval. The form used for reporting the use of hours is a simple matter of stating the number of hours used, signed by the disabled or its representative.

The legislation requires that the SIA remunerate the disabled person by a standardized hourly rate set by the government each year. Currently (spring 2016), each hour approved entitles the disabled person to SEK 288. This is mainly intended to cover the wage paid to the assistant but it also goes towards a share of overhead costs. Initially, the money paid to the disabled person and furthered to an assistance company was not accounted for at all. Money that was not spent on direct or indirect costs for personal assistance equalled profit. The only check on the use of the money was made through a form in which the company signed 'in honesty' how many of the hours approved were used. Later, the SIA started to recommend and enforce that no less than 87 per cent of the hourly rate was spent on salaries. No sanctions were associated with the change.

In 2011, the government legislated that private companies offering personal assistance needed to be certified by the NBHW. A private company is certified when it can present, and be approved for, a quality assurance system. It revolves around an implementation plan, where it is documented what activities should be done and why. Furthermore, it contains a wide range of stipulated routines to be documented and is particularly detailed on issues concerning children. Examples of routines are how deviations from the implementation plan are to be reported, how the company meets the standards set by legislation and how the entire documentation around the disabled is stored and secured.

Analysing the implementation from these events, a certain logic in the initial set-up of how to implement the new LSS Act may be observed. Private initiatives were actively stimulated by the ease with which anyone so inclined could start up a personal assistance company. This mechanism acknowledged the free choice of the disabled person, which was the basic premise of the LSS Act. From necessity, weaker labour rights were appended to the reform, which further made it cheaper and more convenient for employers to replace employees who did not fit the disabled person. Gradually, however, the government and incumbent agencies started to regulate and control the spending of the remuneration. This indicated a government frustration over unduly profits and was soon accompanied by an introduction of a certification obligation for private for-profit companies (LLCs). Both of these actions also contradict the initial freedom of choice and the induced variation of private providers. Nevertheless, the past few years have seen instead a rapid decline in the municipal provision of personal assistance. Though efforts have been made to control the private provider, obviously something is done in private companies that is not done in municipalities: the market for personal assistance becomes more private and more consolidated – and it grows.

Consequences of a growing market

In the government bill preceding the LSS Act (Prop. 1992/93:159, 1993), the cost of the reform was estimated to be 1.6 billion Swedish Krona (BSEK) (about 200 million euro). In the first year of the LSS reform, 1994, the actual cost of it was 1.8 BSEK. Four thousand people were granted personal assistance. Eighteen years later, the cost was 25 BSEK and personal assistance was granted to 20,000 people. Even though this is a 'law of rights', it is apparent that the growth of the reform use has had financial implications. In a panel debate in June 2014, one of the government representatives in the Social Committee was heard uttering: 'Now, I don't want to point towards any in particular, [but] there is a Ministry of Finance which is a bit complicated to deal with…' (Andersson, 2014).

The pressing financial situation created by increasing LSS costs has not been limited to the government level. The basic LSS support is approved and financed by the municipalities. The LSS Act, being a 'law of rights', renders the municipalities obliged to provide support to those who meet the stipulated criteria without being weighed against other posts in the municipal budget. This is why the parliament in 2004 issued a dedicated 'equalization' system, in which the costs of LSS in the municipalities are carried collectively: those with low costs share the burden of those with higher costs. This law was modified in 2009, excluding large parts of the LSS costs (SCB, 2009). This in turn led the Swedish Association of Local Authorities and Regions (SALAR) to demand a further revision of the law in 2011, showing how its current form did not meet the expectations of municipalities. In so doing, SALAR also questioned the financial responsibility being located at the municipal level in the first place (SALAR, 2011).

Parallel to this volume growth and municipal financial challenge, the share of personal assistance delivered by private providers outgrew the share of public providers (Assistanskoll, 2016). Today, more than 50 per cent of all those who are approved for personal assistance get it from a private company. Less than 35 per cent get it from municipality providers. The remainder is mainly from private non-profits, predominantly cooperatives.

There has been a close and frequent media attention given to how private firms and users engage in various kinds of abuse of the LSS Act. The examples are as numerous as they are appalling. A suspicion of the business of personal assistance has grown. This has also included streaks of unwarranted xenophobia:

> I would like to say that all types of people are into this. There are types of fraud that only people from foreign countries can pull off, as a native Swede you cannot all of a sudden claim a cerebral palsy diagnosis, but that is possible if you come from another country where we cannot expect access to documentation. In the same way a person from a foreign country can't as easily create a facade of a legitimate assistance company, that's much easier for a native Swede
>
> (Svante Borg, Director of Insurance, SIA, quoted in Assistanskoll, 2012)

The suspicions about the reform being abused worry those who really need the support and service from the LSS Act and some of the following developments may be understood partly in light of the actual abuse of the reform.

Stifling the demand for personal assistance

Market growth is generally a positive thing. In this case, it is problematic and has rendered some counter actions from the central government and the SIA, the main government agency responsible. When the SIA determines the need for personal assistance, there is a general distinction made between basic needs and particular needs. Within the agency, a new regulation was issued in 2007 stating that the basic needs should no longer cover certain parts of the daily lives of users. The example most written about is how anyone who can lift food to their mouth is not granted personal assistance during meals, even if the person is not able to move to and from the table. In effect, the initial ambition of the legislation to make the disabled person independent through the right to choose was seen as being compromised. Still, the Supreme Administrative Court ruled in favour of the SIA in 2009 (SAC, 2009), thereby adjusting the initial intentions of the law downwards. 'The ruling has completely cramped the intentions of the Act. You now have got an entirely different definition of basic needs and integrity-sensitive parts of the assistance. This is not what our party wanted with this assistance legislation', said Maria Lundquist-Brömster (Liberal Party) (Lundquist-Brömster, 2014). The diversion from the intentions of the Act is clear, and that it is driven by an agency decision is underscored by another politician in the Social Committee: 'This is the case ruling that the SIA chose to turn into practice, there are no political decisions behind this at all', said Agneta Luttropp, representing the Green Party (Miljöpartiet) in the Social Committee (Luttropp, 2014). There is an apparent stand-off between policymakers and 'street-level bureaucrats' (Arnold, 2015; Lipsky, 2010 [1980]), which is clearly acknowledged by a senior manager at the SIA when he states:

> [What the Social Committee says] we consider a part of the democratic process, but as an agency we follow the law and judicial practice. Of course, a statement from a committee could be important if it then leads to a change of the legislation, but in this case no change has been made.
>
> (Assistanskoll, 2010)

From the examples above, it seems that a reduction of the total number of hours – the market for personal assistance – has been an objective of the government. However, such an objective has been paired with a profound questioning of the remuneration levels in terms of too high an hourly rate to the providers of personal assistance. In 2012, the government initiated yet another public inquiry, this time about the way that providers of personal assistance are remunerated. The instruction was explicitly pointing towards the profitability levels earned by large private providers, particularly those derived from apparent economies of scale. In 2014, the investigation concluded that private providers (without any distinction in size) earn too high a profit (SOU, 2014). The hourly rate, accordingly, was suggested to be lowered by 8 per cent. Moreover, the private firms' costs of sick leave, which are currently covered in full by the municipalities, were to be covered by the private firms themselves.

Regulating service quality

From the outset in 1994, the provision of personal assistance in Sweden was audited by the County Administrative Boards, i.e. the central government's regional organization. On 1 January 2011, the government issued a small change of the LSS Act, stating that private providers of personal assistance need to be approved and certified by the NBHW, whereas public providers need only to report the operation. Private companies providing personal assistance had to apply by submitting a comprehensive quality assurance programme, explicitly outlining routines, responsibilities and how current legislation is considered throughout operations. Forty per cent of active providers were denied certification and thereby prohibited from providing personal assistance.

At the time of the introduction of the requirement for private providers to be certified, the NBHW initially also took the role of auditor of personal assistance provision. On 1 June 2013, a new inspection agency – the Health and Social Care Inspectorate (IVO, Inspektionen för Vård och Omsorg) – was created by separation from the NBHW. The main reason was to stress the importance of auditing (Assistanskoll, 2013). One of the new agency's responsibilities is to audit certified providers of personal assistance. This is done along the lines of the provider's own quality assurance programme. In particular, an individual 'implementation plan' is created, specifying what is to be done for that particular individual in order for that person to lead a life on their own terms. Considering that there are about 16,000 disabled people who have personal assistance, there is most likely a large variation in the contents of these implementation plans. This makes the auditing cumbersome: one interviewee of the case company described how two ladies came to the office of the company for two full days and went over the documentation in the quality assurance programme – not what the content was, merely checking the existence of orderly documentation. The 'ritualistic' character of auditing (Power, 1999) is striking.

Implementation and marketization of personal assistance

> Markets are assumed to diffuse power well – to all customers and sellers who are assumed to be able to choose what they want to buy and to sell. Power appears to be evened out – all and hence nobody is assumed to

have power in the marketplace. Markets also are assumed to lead to an efficient use of resources. In the public sector, markets have many proponents.

(Brunsson and Hägg, 2010, p. 7)

In 1993, when the parliament decided to go through with the LSS Act, the time was ripe for further development of the social reforms done to date. Also, New Public Management was on its rise. Markets were endemic in the classic Hood (1991) doctrines of disaggregation and competition.

Below, the implementation and marketization of the LSS Act will be discussed in two separate sections. First, the move from political decision to improved conditions for the disabled will be analysed in terms of policy formulation and implementation. This part is a general discussion about the reform. Second, the particular marketization of disabled welfare services will be looked at from what Brunsson and Hägg (2010) frame as the ideas, rules and practice of markets. When it comes to the practice of the market for personal assistance, that will be split into demand and supply and how each has been influenced over time. The upshot is a reflection about how high ambitions may drive complexity and, in turn, how complexity may require goal-orientation and perseverance in the ongoing interplay between policy formulation and implementation.

The implementation of the LSS Act

Two observations of how the implementation of the LSS Act came along can be singled out. To begin with, the reform constituted a systemic shift, a shift of mind-set. Reforms may be described, as Matland (1995) has suggested, in two dimensions: ambiguity and conflict.

With low levels of both ambiguity and conflict, implementation is an administrative matter. When ambiguity and conflict are high, then it is about having it your way; it is a matter of symbolic implementation. The introduction of the reform could be seen as an administrative implementation. The basic actors, rules and routines were outlined and decided on. However, as more and more disabled people applied for personal assistance, the more frequent the difficult cases became. Looking at all the turns that the LSS Act has taken since, in courts and in recurring public inquiries, the implementation became more ambiguous and, thus, more of an experimental implementation. The fact that the SIA got a Supreme Court ruling in direct conflict with the explicit political intentions of the LSS Act could – some say should – have made the parliament clarify the legislation. In that way, the Supreme Court ruling could have been compensated for and upheld. Such a political implementation, however, implies high conflict and low ambiguity. The case shows a unanimous Social Committee commenting on the implications of the court ruling, so the level of conflict was likely to be low. So, as the level of political conflict never increased, the level of ambiguity of the reform

remained high. Following the Matland matrix, it is not far-fetched to catego-
rize the implementation of the LSS Act as experimental.

The LSS Act is characterized by a move away from collective institutional
care to individual independence. It involves customer choice, remuneration
assigned to the individual and competition between providers. Public-sector
competition takes different forms and in Sweden four types have been commonly used: deregulation, competitive tendering, customer choice models
and voucher systems (Jordahl, 2006). All but competitive tendering are apparent components in the description above. Still, competitive tendering has
been used by some municipalities who chose not to take the role as provider
themselves, e.g. the municipality of Lund. Considering the fact that all four
types of competition are represented, the LSS Act could be seen as an 'all-
encompassing reform'.

Implementing such a complex reform is presumably a difficult task. Observations support such a view. First of all, the volume of personal assistance
needed was grossly underestimated. The legislators were also taken aback by
the high growth rate of the personal assistance applied for and granted.
Second, the behaviour of the multiple actors involved does not seem to have
been predicted, as far as all crimes committed, the public inquiries and the
court rulings are concerned. Third, and perhaps most important, there was no
previous experience.

The implementation is problematic and the case illustrates how unrealistic
a top–down ideal of policy implementation is. The top–down approach may
be represented by Mazmanian and Sabatier (1982, p. 20), defining policy
implementation, as 'the carrying out of a basic policy decision, usually incorporated in a statute but which can also take the form of important executive
orders or court decisions'. The bottom–up approach in turn is often defined
following Lipsky (2010 [1980]), who shows how civil servants have discretionary power and are forced to interpret the legislation with inadequate
resources. This drives them to develop routines of their own, not necessarily
in line with the political will expressed in the legislation.

A picture of a reform battle develops. The actual implementation is in line
with the intentions of the initial policy, but it seems that the legislators did
not foresee the extent to which the services of personal assistance would be
utilized. A rebound is noted, which seems to be derived from a generous
implementation based on far-stretched freedom of choice and deregulation,
in turn attracting dubious private providers. Cost increases, along with scandals and public reactions, have driven an upward movement of reformulation
efforts, reinterpretation attempts and cries for cost reductions and transfer of
financial responsibility. It should also be noted that the previous Swedish government made a strong case for its ability to take effective financial action in
the period of economic austerity since 2008 (SvD, 2011), which coincides
with the cost-focus taken in relation to the continuous implementation of the
LSS Act.

The marketization of personal assistance

A far-stretched freedom of choice attracting dubious private providers: is this an appropriate characterization of the Swedish market for personal assistance? In order to analyse markets, Brunsson and Hägg (2010) distinguish between the ideas, rules and practice of markets, empirical examples derived mainly from a Swedish context. This set of concepts serves as a basis for a looking at how the marketization part of the LSS reform has influenced the reformation of disability care in Sweden.

The idea. A common view of a market is a system based on justified selfishness with an opposite moral that makes it wrong to consider other interests than mere self-interest:

> Market actors seek their own utility, are highly rational and strongly independent. The relations between actors are moreover assumed to be only market-oriented: they concern the exchange of goods and are not influenced by other social relations.... The more general idea [is that] the market is a means to an end when striving for growth and efficiency and the means are evaluated in relation to these objectives.
>
> (Brunsson and Hägg, 2010, pp. 16, 18)

It is important to note that self-interest is expected from both buyers and sellers. This is what Adam Smith (1776) held with his 'invisible hand': making good things happen. The basic objective of the LSS Act, in particular the substitution of personal assistance for institutional care, is to make severely disabled people part of society on their own terms. The situation, however, is characterized by dependence: the essence of personal assistance is a social relation, exactly what the fundamental market transaction lacks.

The market for personal assistance is not a case of multiple suppliers of identical services that the disabled may effortlessly shift between. There are quality differences derived from what Grönroos nowadays calls 'the service logic', where co-creation is at the centre of value creation (see e.g. Grönroos and Gummerus, 2014). The quality of personal assistance is developed in the relationship between the disabled and the assistant and their organization. So, instead of having created an efficient market for personal assistance, the Swedish LSS Act is basically built upon the presence of choice. It is the mere fact that there are alternative suppliers that is the most important, creating a 'way out' for the disabled person when the co-creation of value has failed. The idea of the market driving efficiency through swift choice thus does not seem to hold true in the case of personal assistance. Nevertheless, the existence of choice is a crucial condition if the objective is to create a sense of independence and power over your own situation as a disabled person in need of assistance.

The rules. If efficiency, the most basic argument for creating a market, does not hold true in the market for personal assistance, that would imply a strong rule system to compensate for the non-presence of Adam Smith's (1776) 'invisible hand':

> The rule systems could answer a number of questions. Who may sell and buy in a certain market? In many markets some authorization is required. What goods are allowed to trade in a certain market? That is: what is a product in a certain market? What requirements should it fulfil? For a product to be considered a car certain requirements exist, for example, that it has to have more than two wheels.
>
> (Brunsson and Hägg, 2010, p. 12)

It is revealed in this case how the government as well as agencies have gradually formed the rules regulating the supply and demand for personal assistance. The very rapid growth of demand for assistance, i.e. the number of approved hours, took them by surprise. Increasingly, the handling of applications has become stricter and the number of rejections of two-year reassessments has increased. From the supply side, the initial conditions were generous and overly so. Money that was not spent on personal assistants remained in the assistance firm. The SIA, which paid out the remuneration, did not control, at first, how firms spent it.

The ease with which anybody could start a business was gone by 2011. Then the NBHW introduced a certification requirement. The certification was also the first attempt to articulate rules for how to specify the quality of personal assistance in relation to an individual person in need of it. Also, in effect, the number of private suppliers declined overnight. In the same action, it was assumed that a large share of the lesser suppliers was ruled out of business. However, the share of private companies offering personal assistance has increased. In comparison with the rapid demand growth, it has increased slowly yet steadily over the years. Roos (2009) offers a possible explanation for this: private providers offer a higher quality of support and service than municipal providers, potentially related to the fact that private providers on average provided 18 per cent more hours of personal assistance than the municipal providers.

The practice. When Brunsson and Hägg (2010) discuss the practice in a market, they suggest three different patterns of competition. First, there is a pattern of price competition. Second, a pattern of quality competition exists as well. Third, there is a pattern of power struggle to be seen in a market.

The pattern of price competition should not be subject to discussion, but it is. The remuneration rate is set and goes undivided to the organization that the disabled person gives the assignment to. It could be a municipality, a for-profit company or a not-for-profit organization, or it could be the disabled person themselves, paying the assistants directly. Regardless of provider, there is one major cost item to work with: salary. Young people are paid less. The job of personal assistant is also a less qualified job, with few opportunities for formal training. The job is often a first entry into the labour market. Whether the recruitment strategies of different organizations affect the quality of personal assistance has not been subject to criticism or investigation. However, the prime driver of indirect costs for personal assistance is scale, thereby making it tempting to grow the business and employ an increasing number of personal assistants on a given number of overhead staff.

The pattern of quality competition changed as the NBHW initiated the certification requirement in 2011. The system that was introduced is still only an indirect quality control, primarily stopping companies unable to become certified. The formal controls check whether routines are in place, not the extent to which the actual quality of the personal assistance is high, low or changing (cf. Power, 1999).

A pattern of power struggles is apparent. A few corporations have actively acquired smaller companies over the years and thus grown very big. Not only can a large company economize on overhead costs, it can also hire lawyers to fight the SIA and the municipalities both head on and in courts, thereby maintaining or increasing revenues. In one of the recent public inquiries made, the profitability levels of these corporations were criticized. The directions for the inquiry were straightforward. The profit margin of the private companies indicated that the remuneration rate was set too high (ISF, 2012) and thus needed adjustment. The increase of the remuneration to 2014 was 1.8 per cent, to 2015 it was 1.4 per cent. Both increases were lower than nationally negotiated and established wage increases.

The way forward

Designing social systems may seem mechanistic or authoritarian. However, all social systems have been designed. Laws redesign political and economic systems. Such redesigns are experiments using a country as a laboratory. The case of the LSS Act involves two key observations. First, the reform that the parliament legislates and the government subsequently implements is subject to interpretation and negotiation on its way through the public organization of agencies and civil servants. What is said is not automatically done. The formulation and implementation of a reform are inextricably connected and interdependent with each other. This relates to the second key observation. The LSS Act is actually a package of at least three reforms. The first reform is the shift from collective to individual disability care. The second reform concerns the funding of disability care. The third reform introduces market competition between private providers into highly institutionalized, publicly run disability care. Neither the disabled persons nor the providers had any significant experience of a deregulated market of social welfare. With the benefit of hindsight, one could accuse the legislators of having high and naive expectations of market forces. It has taken a long time to improve the control systems and they are not yet in place. The market for personal assistance is gradually regulated, for what seems to be efficiency-oriented reasons. Central government is trying to 'level the playing field'. And, above this playing field, there is a higher goal still aiming for equal human conditions for disabled people who cannot fend for themselves. And taking care of the weak maintains and develops just societal conditions and values.

References

Andersson, A. (2014) *LSS Debate June 3 2014*. Available online at www.youtube.com/watch?v=HxUGegsat1Q (accessed 10 June 2014).

Arnold, G. (2015) 'Street-level policy entrepreneurship'. *Public Management Review*, Vol. 17, No. 3, pp. 307–327.

Assistanskoll (2010) *Endast en lagändring i LSS § 9a kan ändra vår tillämpning av grundläggande behov*. Available online at http://assistanskoll.se/20100618-Forsakringskassan-lagandring-i-LSS-9a-andra-tillampning-av-grundlaggande-behov.html (accessed 20 June 2014).

Assistanskoll (2012) *Det finns ett intresse för assistansersättning bland grovt kriminella*. Available online at http://assistanskoll.se/20121128-Svante-Borg-Forskringskassan-assistansersttning-kriminella.html (accessed 14 June 2014).

Assistanskoll (2013) *De flesta av oss brinner för de här frågorna*. Available online at http://assistanskoll.se/20130813-Kristina-Soderborg-IVO-Brinner-for-de-har-fargorna.html (accessed 8 February 2016).

Assistanskoll (2014) *Parlamentariska utredningar istället för snabba enmansutredningar*. Available online at http://assistanskoll.se/20140626-VAL-VAnsterpartiet-snabba-enmansutredningar.html (accessed 26 June 2014).

Assistanskoll (2016) *Personer som valt olika typer av assistansanordnare i %*. Available online at http://assistanskoll.se/assistans-statistik.php.

Brunsson, N. and I. Hägg (2010) *Marknadens makt* (Stockholm: SNS).

Cox, R. (2004) 'The path-dependency of an idea: why Scandinavian welfare states remain distinct'. *Social Policy & Administration*, Vol. 38, No. 2, pp. 204–219.

Dunsire, A. (1990) 'Holistic governance'. *Public Policy and Administration*, Vol. 5, No. 4, pp. 4–19.

Grünewald, K. (1994) 'Utvecklingsstörd – ett socialt arv', *Dagens Nyheter*.

Grönroos, C. and J. Gummerus (2014) 'The service revolution and its marketing implications: service logic vs service-dominant logic'. *Managing Service Quality*, Vol. 24, No. 3, pp. 206–229.

Hill, M. and P. Hupe (2014) *Implementing public policy. An introduction to the study of operational governance*, 3rd edition. (London: SAGE).

Hood, C. (1991) 'A public management for all seasons?'. *Public Administration*, Vol. 6, No. 3, pp. 3–19.

ISF (2012) *Assistansmarknaden. En analys av timschablonen* (Stockholm: Inspektionen för socialförsäkringen).

Jordahl, H. (2006) *Avregleringar, entreprenadupphandlingar, kundvalsmodeller och vouchersystem* (Stockholm: Ratio).

Lagen (1993:387) *Om stöd och service till vissa funktionshindrade* (Stockholm: Riksdagen).

Lipsky, M. (2010 [1980]) *Street-level Bureaucracy: Dilemmas of the Individual in Public Services* (New York: Russel Sage Foundation).

Lundquist-Brömster, M. (2014) *LSS Debate June 3 2014*. Available online at www.youtube.com/watch?v=HxUGegsat1Q (accessed 10 June 2014).

Luttropp, A. (2014) *LSS-debate June 3 2014.* Available online at www.youtube.com/watch?v=HxUGegsat1Q (accessed 10 June 2014).

Matland, R. E (1995) 'Synthesizing the implementation literature: the ambiguity-conflict model of policy implementation'. *Journal of Public Administration Research and Theory*, Vol. 5, No. 2, pp. 145–174.

Mazmanian, D. and P. Sabatier, A (1982) *Implementation and Public Policy* (Glencoe, IL: Scott Foresman).

Power, M. (1999) *The Audit Society: Rituals of Verification* (Oxford: Oxford University Press).

Prop. 1992/93:159 (1993) *Regeringens proposition, 1992/93:159 om stöd och service till vissa funktionshindrade* (Stockholm: Regeringen).

Roos, J. M. (2009) *Quality of Personal Assistance. Shaped by Governments, Markets and Corporations.* Doctoral thesis, Department of Psychology, University of Gothenburg.

SAC (2009) 'Supreme administrative court, verdict case 5321–07'.

SALAR (2011) *Yttrande om LSS-utjämningen och sol-insatser för funktionshindrade* (Stockholm: SALAR).

SCB (2009) *Utjämning av LSS-kostnader mellan kommuner* (Stockholm: Statistiska Centralbyrån).

Smith, A. (1776) *An Inquiry into the Nature and Causes of the Wealth of Nations*, Eighteenth Century Collections Online edition (Oxford: Oxford University Press).

SOU (1991) *Handikapp, välfärd och rättvisa. SOU 1991:46.* Report for Socialdepartementet (Stockholm).

SOU (2014) *Förändrad assistansersättning – en översyn av ersättningssystemet. Betänkande av assistansersättningsutredningen. SOU 2014:9* (Stockholm: Socialdepartementet).

SvD (2011) *Borg korad till bäste finansminister.* Available online at www.svd.se/naringsliv/borg-korad-till-baste-finansminister_6655396.svd (accessed 3 September 2014).

Part IV
Ending note

16 Modernizing the public sector

The Scandinavian way

Hans Knutsson, Ola Mattisson, Ulf Ramberg and Åge Johnsen

Summary

Looking at the Swedish public sector from a Scandinavian perspective, this chapter argues for a challenged but resilient (although not uniform) Scandinavian public sector. Sweden is a nation with a long tradition of decentralized decision-making, semi-autonomous government agencies and independent local governments. This is considered a receptive context for continuous and incremental modernization. It has fostered a high degree of experimentation in terms of modes of production and distribution, albeit without the risks associated with purely market-driven social reforms based on privatization of both production and financing. The variations on the Swedish modernization theme are many, involving various forms of marketization initiatives, boundary-spanning cooperative efforts and an open attitude and willingness towards trying and sharing experiences. High levels of transparency and trust are two initial traits signifying the Scandinavian public sector, which have been both amplified and challenged by the NPM agenda. The inherent strive of NPM for compartmentalization, quantification and performance measurement challenges some of the institutional glue of the welfare state, which has kept the parts together in a solid unity. Simultaneously, many NPM reforms – with their emphasis on performance measurement and reporting for increasing transparency and improving the outcomes of public polices and services – contribute both to sustained trust and welfare. The chapter concludes that Sweden keeps defending the Scandinavian model and values of universalism, solidarity and market independence, a defence in which developments in society and future public management reforms may prove wanting.

Introduction

When it comes to models of governance, the Scandinavian countries are far more different than is commonly believed.

(Lindvall and Rothstein, 2006, p. 61)

The exposé in this book of different public management reforms in Scandinavia has been centred on Sweden. It is shown how Sweden is changing in terms of public-sector organization and influence over the Swedish population. This chapter reflects on the different examples given in the book, to see what they make of Sweden as a guiding light in an ever-changing public sector.

As a consequence of one of the typical signifiers of Sweden, transparency, we are able to tell what it looks like from the inside. A reform pattern emerges. Here we do not aim at any outright evaluation, though; it would be like 'nailing a pudding on the wall' (Bovaird and Löffler, 2003, p. 316, in Pollitt, 2011). Rather, we consider this reflection an updating contribution to different accounts previously made of Swedish public-sector management and reforms.

The chapter begins with a look at some general views on Sweden and its public sector, meant to form a contrasting background to what we have described in this book. Descriptions are reflected upon in terms of the willingness, ability and approach to change, which the Swedish public-sector institutions have fostered. These traits have created a wide variety of new ways to manage the public sector, whether at the central or local level. In conclusion, Cox's (2004) description of what constitutes the Scandinavian welfare model – universality, solidarity and market independence – will be re-examined as we try to interpret where modern public management may take us.

Is Sweden particularly receptive to reform?

When looking at what others say about Sweden and its public sector, words like left-wing and high-NPM (Hood, 1995), humanistic, democratic and participative (Ferlie et al., 1996), optimistic and incremental (Pollitt and Summa, 1997) and 'one of the world's most extensive and redistributive welfare states' (Pierson, 1996) are used. Although overall pleasant to read, these descriptions were written more than 20 years ago. Are these accounts still valid?

A basic and important condition for the Swedish progressive reforms seems to be how Swedes trust the government. We could see in Alexander Paulsson's text (Chapter 6) how Swedes have for a long time comfortably complied with registration, first done by the church and later by the state. Legislators eventually had to restrict themselves by forming a particular law not to have too much information about citizens. But is this openness, the attaching of a universal 'personal number' to each individual citizen, reflecting something typically Swedish? If not typically Swedish, registration at least seems like something not deserving of any drama. During the first half of the twentieth century, Sweden saw its own version of the US prohibition era. In Sweden, people were not denied alcohol, but instead had to succumb to registration of purchases of alcohol, which they did.

Trust in the government could be indicated from the above examples and may look like a gullible national spirit. However, there may be more to the story. Could trust be related to the Swedish constitution and organization of the public sector? The Swedish parliament decided on dualism in 1720 and made a clear distinction between political and administrative responsibilities. Administrative organs are independent of ministries and the constitution prohibits ministerial rule (Andersson, 2004). Moreover, in 1862 the first municipal reform was introduced, separating the administration of public concerns from the church, a secularization completed in 2000. Central and local government have both offered distinctions in the governing of the nation. Separation of roles, responsibilities and powers is a key paragraph in constitutional law, the Instrument of Government, and people have grown used to having influence. Sentiment, however, may be related to constitution only vaguely, but it is definitely related to economic conditions.

The current Swedish welfare state is a result of on an economic development booming in the 1950s, when there was financial means for reforming the social welfare. The reform climate was also attuned to conflict resolution. Lindvall and Rothstein (2006) have described the Swedish way of organizing the reform efforts as done, initially, in large 'reform bureaucracies' responsible for implementing the social welfare programmes. Municipalities were consolidated, from almost 2,300 to 282 in less than 20 years. They were also given more responsibility for policy implementation. Local government autonomy is still an important factor in social welfare development. An elaborate equalization system, with a significant portion of central government grants, transfers money from richer municipalities and counties to poorer ones, in order to create similar economic conditions for all local governments throughout the country.

There is an institutional foundation and tradition in place: policymaking, implementation and management are set in a context of participative deliberation on several levels. The last 35 years of progressive modernization may be considered in line with that tradition, as citizens have been given a voice as consumers of welfare services. So, as the demography may develop in a problematic way, Sweden has institutional, physical and financial, as well as social, capital to leverage when the country deals with current and future challenges.

The challenges ahead are met in different ways in different parts of the country. This is not only a function of different political inclinations in the different local governments but also a consequence of very different structural conditions in terms of geography, demography and economy. Political accountability in local governments drives initiative and experimentation, both on an operative level and an institutional level. In Sweden, there have been recurrent investigations about how to reorganize counties and municipalities, geographically and operationally. Unlike Denmark and Finland, which both consolidated their local government structures into fewer units in 2007, and Norway, which will do the same in 2018, Sweden has so far not yet come to any decision in that matter.

Modernization and Swedish experimentation

The sentiment of the Swedes in combination with a permeating decentralization and autonomy of the public sector, have likely produced a fertile ground
for trying to solve problems in different ways. This may on the one hand be
considered inefficient. On the other hand, widely distributed problem-solving
incentives may generate, in the long run, more experience to learn from. The
system may be seen as an expression of trust in human capacity and belief in
the strength that comes from distributed powers.

Marketization has taken different forms in Sweden, and Fredrik Andersson
(Chapter 12) discusses procurement-based and customer choice-based ways of
engaging market forces in the delivery of public goods and services. In this transformation, Sweden has kept privatization limited to the production and distribution of welfare services, not the financing of them. Welfare is not abandoned, but
the traditional delivery of it has been altered, relying increasingly on NPM ideas.

In his classic article, (Hood, 1995) suggested that NPM is more than an
'English disease'. Tom Karlsson (Chapter 3) shows how Swedish officials have
been curious about private-sector methods long before the standard NPM era
of the late 1970s and early 1980s, in which the UK and the USA took these
private-sector management ideals to heart. This is right in line with Hood's
remark about the disputable novelty of NPM:

> The term 'new' does not imply that NPM doctrines appeared for the first
> time in the [1980s]. Many NPM doctrines repackage ideas which have
> been in public administration since its earliest beginnings.
>
> (Hood, 1995, p. 94)

The Swedish market-based reforms started in the early 1990s, and are often
attributed to the conservative government that came into power in 1991.
However, as noted in Chapter 2, Social Democrats initiated performance
management in central government in the mid-1980s. Both social democratic
and liberal-conservative governments have been involved in the development
towards deregulation, competition and marketization. All of this happened in
a time burdened by a financial crisis, austerity and increasingly inefficient
central planning. What is forgotten in standard descriptions of this time is also
that local governments were eager to reform the welfare system. This trig-
gered different initiatives to increase the use of markets and allowed for competition in public services. Since then, there has been a relentless
experimentation in how central and local governments approach their public
tasks. This follows a pattern observed by Pollitt and Summa 20 years ago:

> What is characteristic of the Swedish approach is that reform is an
> ongoing process. At any time, dozens of reforms are under way, many of
> which are dealing with administrative organization.
>
> (Pollitt and Summa, 1997, p. 13)

In this way, Sweden may have circumvented some of the more prevalent top–down implementation problems noted by many (see Pressman and Wildavsky, 1984 for a well-known example). It can be noted that the NPM reforms have been a crucial component in driving change in the public organizations, in their structures and their ways of operating. Prior to these reforms, politicians and leading officials signalled frustration and difficulties in steering and governing public organizations. Over a long period of time, public organizations had been involved in developing the different provisions and, therefore, the necessary structures. Over the years, many of these structures became inert, making it more difficult to change and adapt. Both in central and local government organizations, politicians gave testimonials about budget sessions, taking the existing capacity as a starting point. It was important to make use of the resources at hand. All attempts to change structures or directions faced major opposition. Driving change was burdensome and many public organizations were criticized for the inefficiency of activities and lack of relevance in offerings.

Seen in retrospect, two observations can be made from these efforts. The first observation is about how many of these reforms were introduced. In general, the reforms were focused on one or a few aspects at a time. When introducing market solutions, there has been a focus on creating market conditions and competitive terms. The marketization part of this book shows how competition has been considered a positive force. Referring to the NPM tools, the advantages sought were big enough to motivate radical changes and the effects were vague and long–term enough to make it difficult to change path once the decision was made. NPM tools became a prime mover in questioning and changing the present systems, and the prospects were strong enough to overcome opposition.

The second observation concerns how these reforms were followed up and evaluated. In the book, we see a number of studies on the effects of competition in different sectors and services. The outcomes of the reforms are measured by how well competition works within the particular service. Conclusions are drawn on how to improve competitive conditions. This has resulted in a situation where each sector regulates and re–regulates. After some two decades it can be seen that the different sectors have taken different paths for development. The efficiency and performance of each of these sectors are evaluated on their own terms, one by one. The consequence of the NPM reforms is a fragmented overall picture for the public bodies to deal with. The more specific the different activities become, the more difficult it gets to coordinate and organize the public welfare provision as a whole. We make improvements for efficiency for each service, isolated from others. The result is improved efficiency in details but, perhaps, lower overall public-sector effectiveness.

The chapters have indicated a resilient Swedish public sector, prone to adopt and adapt different management ideas in order to maintain and improve the public service system. Sweden has a long tradition of decentralized decision-making, semi-autonomous government agencies and independent local governments in county councils and municipalities. However, Louise Bringselius (Chapter 7) indicates an ongoing re-centralization of decision-making to the government from its agencies: central government takes more control over agencies and the implementation of legislation. Central government also influences the roles and responsibilities of local government, on the one hand through legislation and on the other through state grants. The tendency of re-centralization is also observed at the Swedish local government level (Hellström and Ramberg, 2016).

Even though the opportunity for NPM implementation may be viewed beneficial, the zeal with which the Swedish public sector has embraced the different NPM ideas may be best understood as a Swedish version of checks and balances: central government legislation and agency and local government autonomy and accountability. The balance between top-down, legislation-driven reforms and the bottom-up, decentralized mandate of implementing major parts of the welfare system may be considered conducive to continuous and incremental modernization of the welfare state, but that balance is currently shifting.

Despite different degrees of experienced success for modernization from the reforms, a reflection from the examples in this book is how Sweden is designed for experimentation, both in mind and matter. The variations in application of different NPM tools drive change.

Variations in application and results

The built-in tension between central and local government is key. The legislature determines the majority of tasks undertaken by local governments, so decentralization and autonomy need to be explicated here. Municipalities and counties are autonomous in the execution of tasks and impose an income tax as the most important source of finance for the services provided. Ola Mattisson (Chapter 9) presents multiple aspects of this tension, where many local governments seek cooperation in order to, mainly, make ends meet. In some instances, cooperative efforts are made to approach long-term, strategic issues together, like investment in transportation infrastructure. The main reason for cooperation, though, is current problems of maintaining the welfare provision.

This book offers other examples of how an experimentation attitude in Swedish local authorities leads to variation. Anna Glenngård and Anders Anell (Chapter 13) give a detailed account of what has happened when counties were given the opportunity to introduce consumer choice models in primary care. County councils have decided on different models and various experiences are gained from that fact. The effects of population density on availability are clear, and availability has increased overall. However, there are indications that groups with moderate and infrequent needs of care are well served, whereas heavy, i.e. unprofitable, patients are less tended to. What is also shown, though, is a tendency towards local evaluations, where each county has made its own assessment of the effects. The lack of a coordinated national learning strategy suggests that the 'innovation-inducing' decentralization may not be used to its full extent. Hans Knutsson gives a similar indication on the LSS disability reform (Chapter 15), a reform which by design has brought forward a wide range of private providers of personal assistance to choose from. The most eye-catching consequence of this freedom of choice seems to be fraud, embezzlement and that unserious providers have taken advantage of the disabled and the open and trust-based system. Audit and coordinated quality evaluations are mainly absent.

Although Sweden has been willing to try out different NPM-related devices, we see few signs of relinquishing the public welfare responsibility. Rather, there has been an inventiveness and readiness for adopting market-oriented solutions motivated by freedom of choice and, to a lesser extent, efficiency aspirations. It could be seen as a typically Swedish trait to seek the middle ground when enticing individual driving forces but maintaining the public financial responsibility for the public services now being subject to competitive market forces. The risks associated with purely market-driven social reforms based on the privatization of both production and financing have been largely mitigated.

The system for person numbers, as used in the Scandinavian countries, tracks the status of each citizen and helps in organizing and planning welfare production. It also helps keeping track of costs in the system. Universal rights of citizens can be fended for when there is a reliable system of information, without any corruption or special channels or solutions for some but not for others. Self-reporting legislation, some relate it to whistle-blowing, has been in place, for example, in health care in Sweden since it was discovered in 1936 that patients had been injected with disinfectants by mistake. In social care, similar legislation was not introduced until 1999. A general protection for whistle-blowers is found in the constitution, which gives civil servants the right to inform media and prohibits their employer to investigate the origins of the information. The Scandinavian countries are often associated with ideas of equality, fairness and transparency. The Scandinavian countries regularly score highly on the ranking of non-corrupt countries, but still there are disconcerting signs of change in Sweden (Linde and Erlingsson, 2013), as well as in other Scandinavian countries. Anna Thomasson (Chapter 10) exemplifies one of those signs: beyond the general elections, the political party decision-making mechanisms become opaque when appointing different positions on the boards of public councils and municipal or county companies. The importance of relationships beyond strict merits is also apparent in Bring-selius's description (Chapter 7) of how different directors-general in the Social Insurance Agency have each had quite different relations to government officials and the various departments. Although this observation does not suggest corruption in any way, the fact remains that, even if there is a strong institutional groundwork, the quality of individual relations appears important when public policy is to be implemented. In a recent report, the Swedish National

Audit Office (Riksrevisionen, 2013) has also identified a tendency in the government agencies towards underestimating the risk of corruption in their own organization.

The rather comprehensive application of markets and subsequent reports on companies making excessive profits have provoked the debate about whether deregulation and market reliance have gone too far. In primary and secondary schools and in disability care, the side effects of deregulation and marketization have reached a point where the reforms are questioned by some. In particular, school sector reform has proved itself unique as the only national reform in the world allowing private school companies to earn a profit from tax-funded operations.

The Scandinavian countries have been active reformers for making the public sector transparent and efficient, and have often used performance measurement, benchmarking, performance audit and evaluation for these purposes. Åge Johnsen, Kristin Reichborn-Kjennerud, Thomas Carrington and Kim Klarskov Jeppesen discuss how performance audits have different impacts in the Scandinavian countries, partly reflecting different institutional setups (see Chapter 2) and partly reflecting different strategic choices in the national Supreme Audit Institutions (Chapter 8). Robert Wenglén (Chapter 14) gives an initiated view of how the political establishment tries to come to grips with the deteriorating scores on the OECD's regular international comparative survey of student performance in a wide range of countries (PISA), lately also taking Sweden by surprise. The observation is typical. In the struggle between centralized management control and decentralized professional control, the majority of political parties again seek middle ground. Private schools serve the purpose of providing alternatives and professional teachers should be in charge of finding out how to take Sweden back to the top of the PISA ranking. Varying experiences from decentralization may be good to have, since measurement is insufficient when deciding what to do:

> PISA measures are attractive and useful, though with some significant pitfalls concerning what the tests do and don't mean, and with a considerable gap between the results and the drawing of policy conclusions.
>
> (Pollitt, 2011, p. 453)

Central planning and the management of professionals appear to be problematic. The same conclusion is supported by Christine Blomqvist (Chapter 11) in her text on how Lund University struggles to strike a balance between management control and professional autonomy. New Public Management is strongly associated with quantification and measurement as well as decentralization and empowerment (Hood, 1991). Management control and professional autonomy are often regarded a problem as measurement and self-control is, paradoxically, often seen as being at odds with professional autonomy. The public sector is labour-intensive and a significant portion of total costs and services depends on the capabilities and resources of employees. There is a natural wish from managers to have a solid knowledge base about the workforce. How do they perform, what are they doing and when and how are they doing it? Gert Paulsson's (Chapter 5) review of two health care organizations exemplifies how NPM includes a process orientation in management control and, with that, an increasing attention to non-financial aspects of welfare provision. What the outcome should be is mainly a political issue, but the configuration and quality of the output are concerns for both politicians and civil servants. In labour-intensive operations, most of the output is service-related. A service is consumed as it is produced and the quality of it is a more or less intangible experience. Hence, the efforts to capture quality in performance indicators have been laborious and evasive. One issue is about what quality is. This is connected to who should be the definer of quality. Quality directly articulated by the one who is experiencing it is different from quality as an index from survey responses. Pollitt (2011) talks about the 'synoptic legibility' of such indexes, and how value in them decreases as they are filled with different, ever more general and weighed factors.

Performance indicators are at the core of New Public Management, yet they are inherently problematic. Some expect performance indicators to inform people what to do next, in particular that decision makers could learn and improve from the measurements. However, this 'cybernetic' view on action and feedback requires stability both in the surrounding environment and in the measurement methods. If this is not the case, experienced feedback will be ambiguous and difficult to act upon (March, 2010). There are problems related to a simplistic cybernetic view. First, maybe the Scandinavian political 'consensus' tradition, marked by negotiations and compromises, does not lend itself easily to fixing political objectives, translated into specific performance indicators (Johnsen and Vakkuri, 2006; Ramberg, 1997). Johnsen and Vakkuri (2006, p. 304) suggest that 'the Nordic perspective may favour a homeostatic model more than a cybernetic model', by which 'homeostatic' is meant a system of multiple factors, all adapting to each other so to maintain an equilibrium.

Second, performance indicators are used for more than merely measuring what is provided for the citizens, at what cost and with what quality. In the Swedish election campaign in 2014, for example, one of the more important debates concerned unemployment and job creation. It was clear to see how important performance indicators (PIs) really are when a policy is offered and argued for by politicians. Here, one side had successfully created more jobs but the opposition only had eyes and ears for the increased unemployment rate. Johnsen (2005) has identified performance indicators as a political battlefield of its own, discussing how

> PIs may effectively produce 'creative destruction' of the present political or managerial status quo. Thus, PIs in political competition may be as important as prices in market competition.
>
> (Johnsen, 2005, p. 9)

Variations in performance as a result from wide-ranging experimentation are one thing; the interpretation of indicators is another. Pollitt (2011) calls for 'moderation in all things'. The Swedish National Audit Office is deeply concerned with the lack of follow-up routines presented by many agencies (Riksrevisionen, 2010) and is equally bothered by the lack of coordination in the collecting of statistics (Riksrevisionen, 2015). What should be noted is how the Swedish National Audit Office focuses on follow-up routines and statistics, not application, understandability and relevance in decision-making by the electorate, political bodies or by civil servants. The Swedish deregulations have rendered Swedes with an abundant number of choices to be made and in need of information. There has long been a basic trust in the government and the public sector, far higher than other developed countries outside Scandinavia. Although there is a general decline in trust in politicians, and declining participation in political parties, there is an equally significant increase in social media participation. Social media is characterized by smaller groups with particular opinions and interests. The 'market square', where people met to discuss and try differences in opinion against each other, has been replaced by bubbles of self-referencing groups convincing one another. In that process, matters are black or white. How do you deal with a biased and sometimes uninformed public when it comes to choosing between different providers of public welfare? One good example is how the Swedish pension reform in 1994, which was made more publicly known in the Thaler and Sunstein book *Nudge* (Thaler and Sunstein, 2008), was designed so that the default alternative was the best option set by a government agency. This did not reduce the freedom of choice; there are still a large number of alternative options for citizens wanting to actively choose by themselves.

The historical development of the Swedish public systems is disciplined and structured. Central directives have been implemented in an organized and consistent way. Structures and procedures have been characterized as homogenous both in central and in local government organizations. However, the situation is changing. There is a striking consensus about being in a difficult situation. Due to demographic changes it will be more demanding to preserve the present level of supply of public welfare services with fewer available resources in terms of competent personnel and financial means. At the same time, as a result of prolonged and varied public management reform, there has never been a greater variety in systems and structures for the supply of public services, at both the central and local levels. On an aggregated level, a crucial question is if all these different initiatives, concepts and tools are integrated enough to bring a consistent supply of public services. The public sector may be seen as a house, in which NPM has helped us in getting the rooms cleaned up, refurbished and nicely furnished. In essence, quantification and comparison require discrete entities to be evaluated. Competition renders efficient entities. There is an inherent tendency to measure the effects in terms of performance and discuss the functionality of the individual rooms. Are we modernizing details to the detriment of the whole?

The centralization, joined-up government and governance reforms after 2000 in many countries point in that direction, as these reforms typically aim at improving the coordination and performance of the whole. An interesting issue is, therefore, whether there will still be a distinct Scandinavian model in the future, or whether that model was an ideal model of the past.

The way forward

Efficiency is obtained by specialization. The speciality of Sweden has been an effective social inclusion, where the strong has helped the weak. Is it so that the quest for efficiency has drawn attention from historically important goal functions including peace, safety, solidarity, equality and equity of treatment? Many developed countries face similar challenges, and recent years have added to the list factors like international unrest, huge migration, people looking for refuge, nationalism, xenophobia and a labour market split between insiders and outsiders. The way forward would be hard to predict under whatever normal circumstances we might have had, so prediction is futile. As Kahneman wrote in 2011,

> We reach the point of diminishing marginal predictive returns for knowledge disconcertingly quickly.
>
> (Kahneman, 2011)

The classic(al) Swedish model revolved around the alliance between a strong state and competitive exporting corporations, creating jobs and taxable wages. Corporatism was the grease in the machinery, where large interest groups were represented in government committees – central planning of policies, but jointly so. Early on, Childs (1936) introduced the term 'the middle way', an image that sticks in many descriptions of Sweden, sometimes called consensual, sometimes moderate, or, to use the Swedish word, *lagom*. It is the land of *lagom*, a country of moderation.

Sweden still may seem radical – also in a Scandinavian context – in its deregulation efforts of the last 25 years, but the pattern of moderation is recognized in the way that the public sector remains in control over major part of the funding of many deregulated public social services. Political adversaries agree on the general direction of public-sector development. In 1991, 37 per cent of employed people worked for a public sector employer; in 2015 it was down to 29 per cent (SCB, 2016). Twenty per cent in 24 years is hardly a revolution, but more likely a modernization by way of a gradual decentralization of decision-making to markets.

The general trend of reorganizing both central and local government may strain the traditional Scandinavian values of universalism, solidarity and market independence (Cox, 2004). Universalism shows in the way social reform is directed towards every citizen regardless of personal wealth. Major parts of the social insurance system in Sweden are designed in that way, sick leave, parental benefits and functional impairments to name but a few. Solidarity denotes mainly a progressive tax system, where higher incomes are taxed progressively higher – rich help the poor through a public–sector redistribution system. The third sign of the Scandinavian welfare model, 'market independence', deserves special attention when we think of how NPM has left distinctive marks of privatization and downsizing of public sectors in many countries.

First, universalism in Sweden is recognized in e.g. social welfare legislation, stating what people are entitled to if you stay or live in Sweden. In 1994, means–tested social protection expenses were 7 per cent of the total; in 2013, it was down by more than half to 3 per cent (ESSPROS, 2016). Universalism is pursued.

As for solidarity, the Swedish redistributive tax system gave rise to a number of absurd consequences noted in the 1970s and 1980s. A reformation of the tax system was necessary and the first one was completed in 1991, where marginal taxes of some 80 per cent were lowered down to a maximum of 50 per cent. There has been a shift in the redistributive tax system, though. The former centre–right government, in power 2006–2014, made cutbacks in the social insurance systems. Mandatory unemployment insurance was removed. At the same time, substantial decreases in labour tax levels were implemented in five steps over seven years. The central government now compensates those employed for part of the taxes paid to municipals and counties. The logic behind the changes is straightforward: make it worthwhile finding employment. Solidarity is under pressure.

When it comes to market independence, majorities in the Swedish Riksdag have changed four times since 1991, but the marketization advances have not been dramatically reversed by any new government. The market forces, though, are in some way kept in tight rein by the fact that it is still taxes that finance much of the privately provided welfare services. Sweden relies on markets, but has not made itself dependent on them for the proliferation of the welfare state.

In the book *The Art of the State*, Hood (1998) uses cultural theory to characterize variations on the NPM theme. The top–down hierarchist, the competing individualist, the bottom–up egalitarian and the 'come–what–may' fatalist all represent different ways of organizing a public sector. Sweden, for a long time a hierarchist, has in the last 25 years taken on the individualist approach. However, as we have seen signs of in several chapters in this book, Sweden faces a revival of the idea of professions on the one hand, and of regaining central control on the other. This picture, according to Hood (1998), is to be expected. No single approach will survive forever and each carries within itself unintended consequences, which sooner or later will have to be acknowledged and approached. There is no straight line towards success:

> What moves people around the cultural configurations is surprise and disillusion at the behaviour of each institutionalized 'way of life' in the face of challenges from its environment. Because each way of life has its

built-in blind spots and weaknesses, along with its corresponding strengths, such surprise and disappointment is inevitable and perpetual.

(Hood, 1998, p. 190)

Sometimes these movements, motioned by surprise and disillusion, are described in terms of a pendulum swing. Expectations serve as a reference point for evaluating how well public management solutions provide for the citizens. What is swinging, then? One key thing that has moved is the locus of decision-making power. Much momentum is now embedded in the choice of consumers and the investment decisions of private entrepreneurs. We have seen little support for re-regulating welfare services, removing decision-making power from citizens and companies. The loudest voices calling for a roll-back want to forbid profit-making in the private, tax-funded welfare sectors such as schools, elderly care and disability care. Very few voices call for less influence. So, the pendulum may swing back, but not along the original trajectory. The axis has most likely shifted its location since the Swedish population has, by and large, seen the virtues of choice and thus formed new expectations of personal influence.

Simon (2000) reminds us that markets need predictability in order to function well. In that respect, Sweden has followed the textbook in that private firms have had clear rules of the game to play by. Keeping financial responsibility close to the body and inviting firms to participate on clear and stable terms, predictability has been secured and so paved the way for private providers of core Swedish welfare services. The question, then, is to what extent such predictability will prevail.

Predictions about the future of the Scandinavian welfare states circle around demography in two ways. First, there is the general trend of an increasing average age, putting strain on the relation between taxpayers and tax beneficiaries. Second, and less talked about in the public debate, is the fact that it is increasingly problematic to maintain the principle of equal rights in all parts of a country. For example, urbanization leaves the small northern municipalities wanting when it comes to service levels equal to those in the southern parts of the country. New Public Management and its focus on quantification and results may have helped to run parts of the public sector more efficiently than before, but it is yet to be seen how the reform toolbox works in upholding effectively the redistributions that for more than 60 years have been the hallmark of the welfare policies in the Scandinavian countries.

References

Andersson, C. (2004) *Tudelad trots allt – dualismens överlevnad i den svenska staten 1718–1987*. Doctoral thesis, Stockholm University.

Bovaird, T. and E. Löffler (2003) 'Evaluating the quality of public governance: indicators, models and methodologies'. *International Review of Administrative Sciences*, Vol. 69, No. 3, pp. 313–328.

Childs, M. (1936) *Sweden: The Middle Way* (New Haven, CT: Yale University Press).

Cox, R. (2004) 'The path-dependency of an idea: why Scandinavian welfare states remain distinct'. *Social Policy & Administration*, Vol. 38, No. 2, pp. 204–219.

ESSPROS (2016) *European Data Center for Work and Welfare*. Available online at www.edac.eu.

Ferlie, E., L. Ashburner, L. Fitzgerald and A. Pettigrew (1996) *The New Public Management in Action* (Oxford: Oxford University Press).

Hellström, M. and U. Ramberg (2016) *Styrning för att möta kommunala utmaningar*. Natkom rapport nr 31 (Göteborg: Kfi).

Hood, C. (1991) 'A public management for all seasons?'. *Public Administration*, Vol. 6, No. 3, pp. 3–19.

Hood, C. (1995) 'The "new public management" in the 1980s: variations on a theme'. *Accounting, Organizations and Society*, Vol. 20, No. 2–3, pp. 93–109.

Hood, C. (1998) *The Art of the State. Culture, Rhetoric, and Public Management* (Oxford: Oxford University Press).

Johnsen, Å. (2005) 'What does 25 years of experience tell us about the state of performance measurement in public policy and management?'. *Public Policy & Management*, Vol. 25, No. 1, pp. 9–17.

Johnsen, Å. and J. Vakkuri (2006) 'Is there a Nordic perspective on public sector performance measurement?'. *Financial Accountability and Management*, Vol. 22, No. 3, pp. 291–308.

Kahneman, D. (2011) *Thinking, Fast and Slow* (London: Penguin).

Linde, J. and G. Ó. Erlingsson (2013) 'The eroding effect of corruption on system support in Sweden'. *Governance: An International Journal of Policy, Administration, and Institutions*, Vol. 26, No. 4, pp. 585–603.

Lindvall, J. and B. Rothstein (2006) 'The fall of the strong state'. *Scandinavian Political Studies*, Vol. 29, No. 1, pp. 47–63.

March, J. G. (2010) *Ambiguities of Experience* (Ithaca, NY: Cornell University Press).

Pierson, P. (1996) 'The new politics of the welfare state'. *World Politics*, Vol. 48, No. 2, pp. 143–179.

Pollitt, C. (2011) '"Moderation in all things": international comparisons of governance quality'. *Financial Accountability and Management*, Vol. 27, No. 4, pp. 437–457.

Pollitt, C. and H. Summa (1997) 'Trajectories of reform: public management change in four countries'. *Public Money & Management*, Vol. 17, No. 1, pp. 7–18.

Pressman, J. L. and A. B. Wildavsky (1984) *Implementation: How Great Expectations in Washington are Dashed in Oakland* (Berkeley, CA: University of California Press).

Ramberg, U. (1997) *Utformning och användning av verksamhetsmått* (Lund: Lund University Press).

Riksrevisionen, S. (2010) *Från många till en: Sammanslagningar av myndigheter* (Stockholm: Riksrevisionen).

Riksrevisionen (2013) *Statliga myndigheters skydd mot korruption*. RIR 2013:2 (Stockholm: The National Audit Office).

Riksrevisionen (2015) *Den officiella statistiken – en rättvisande bild av samhällsutvecklingen?* RIR 2015:3 (Stockholm: The National Audit Office).

SCB (2016) *Statistiska centralbyrån* [Statistics Sweden]. Available online at www.scb.se.

Simon, H. A. (2000) 'Public administration in today's world of organizations and markets'. *Political Science and Politics*, Vol. 33, No. 4, pp. 749–756.

Thaler, R. and C. R. Sunstein (2008) *Nudge: Improving Decisions about Health, Wealth and Happiness* (London: Penguin).

Index

Page numbers in *italics* denote tables, those in **bold** denote figures.